THE CULTURE AND POLITICS OF CONTEMPORARY STREET GANG MEMOIRS

UNIVERSITY PRESS OF MISSISSIPPI / JACKSON

THE CULTURE
AND POLITICS OF
CONTEMPORARY
STREET GANG
MEMOIRS

Josephine Metcalf

www.upress.state.ms.us

The University Press of Mississippi is a member
of the Association of American University Presses.

Copyright © 2012 by University Press of Mississippi
All rights reserved
Manufactured in the United States of America

First printing 2012

∞

Library of Congress Cataloging-in-Publication Data

Metcalf, Josephine, 1975–
  The culture and politics of contemporary street gang
memoirs / Josephine Metcalf.
      p. cm.
  Includes bibliographical references and index.
  ISBN 978-1-61703-281-3 (cloth : alk. paper) — ISBN
978-1-61703-282-0 (ebook) 1. Gangs—United States.
2. Gangs in literature. I. Title.
  HV6439.U5M48 2012
  364.106′60973—dc23   2011045390

British Library Cataloging-in-Publication Data available

For My Father

CONTENTS

ACKNOWLEDGMENTS

Thank you to Brian Ward and Ian Scott for invaluable feedback and scholarly direction and above all to Eithne Quinn for tirelessly and patiently reading and rereading while inspiring me with her way of thinking; her incredible ideas and imagination underpin this book. Deep appreciation also to Jonathan Munby and Peter Knight, whose indispensable comments have helped ensure a smooth transition from a rigid thesis to a more mature book manuscript. I must also express deep gratitude to mentor Jenel Virden and all those students I have taught over the past few years from whom I have learned so much.

To everyone I met on my fieldtrips who were so enthusiastic about this project, particularly Pati Juaregui, Luis Rodriguez, and many students, teachers and librarians who are part of the LAUSD: your insightful remarks never ceased to enthuse and motivate me. Heartfelt credit is due to all those whom I interviewed and whose comments enrich this book, including Barbara Becnel, Wes McBride, Malcolm Klein, Alex Alonso, Mary Ridgway, Father Greg Boyle, Jesse Katz, and Angela Davis, among others. Thanks to Kayse Gehret for ferrying me around and listening to my tales, and to BAAS, EAAS, and FfWG for funding toward these trips.

I am forever indebted to the brilliant team of Barbara, Luis, and Joanne Berlin, who kindly donated their valuable time to visit the UK and enlighten so many. I would also like to recognize Sanyika Shakur's remarkable flair for writing.

I am grateful to the *European Journal of American Studies*, the *Journal of American Culture*, and *Crime, Media, Culture* for permission to reprint in this book amended versions of articles. I offer extended appreciation to Walter Biggins, Anne Stascavage, and Will Rigby at UPM for making this an enjoyable and exciting process and Auli Ek for her comments on the manuscript. And I must thank Professor Ek again, along with David Brumble, and the handful of other scholars whose intellectual attention to these relatively under-researched texts has inspired and informed my own research.

For John, Eileen, and my brothers, I could not have completed this without you. And while there are many others who have offered me endless emotional support, intelligent conversation, and much-needed dinners throughout the course of the past few years, I must particularly mention Victoria Hughes, Hannah Lowe, Claire Wardle, and Ben Crouch. Also all those friends who have continuously encouraged and focused me—you know who you are! And last not least, this is for Alex, who is my constant sustenance; I feel truly honored that he has been alongside me throughout all of this.

THE CULTURE AND POLITICS OF CONTEMPORARY STREET GANG MEMOIRS

BOOKS MAKING A KILLING
An Introduction

The publication of *Monster: The Autobiography of an LA Gang Member* by Sanyika Shakur in the summer of 1993 generated a huge amount of excitement in literary circles.[1] Michiko Kakutani, who has a fierce reputation as a book reviewer for the *New York Times*, deemed it a "startling and galvanic book," highlighting Shakur's "ear for street language that's as perfectly pitched as Richard Price's, a feeling for character and status potentially as rich as Tom Wolfe's."[2] With the publication of *Monster*, a new trend of gang memoirs emerged in the United States. Their content centered on contemporary street gang life in the ghettos and barrios, offering graphic tales of violent confrontation and territorial belonging. They were written by former gang members, both African American and Latino. The majority were set in Los Angeles (LA), the city that would be dubbed "the gang capital of America."[3] These memoirs formed part of a literary production trend that included journalistic and biographical accounts of gang culture as well as anthologies and memoirs by actual former gang members.[4] Novel-length memoirs were the most lucrative dimension of the trend, with numerous memoirs published in the 1990s alone.[5]

Three of the most successful and influential of these gang memoirs form the subject of this book. Shakur's *Monster* is an account of gangbanging with one of the infamous African American "Crips" gangs in South Central LA during the 1980s. The memoir tells the story of how Shakur earned the nickname "Monster" for his brutal behavior before undergoing a political and personal transformation. By 1999, *Monster* had sold 100,000 hardback and 150,000 paperback copies; to date there are more than 400,000 copies of *Monster* in print in the United States alone.[6] Several months after the publication of *Monster*, Luis J. Rodriguez released *Always Running: La Vida Loca—Gang Days in LA*. Rodriguez reflects on his involvement with Mexican American gangs in East LA during the 1960s and 1970s. Like *Monster*, the narrative balances tales of gang conflict with a politicized conversion narrative, informed by the Chicano movement of the 1960s and 1970s. *Always Running* has sold over 400,000 copies with more than twenty reprints and translation into twenty-seven languages.[7] A publishing representative for the memoir deemed it "one of our strongest backlist titles" and "a much beloved classic" that "continues to sell every year."[8] *Monster* and *Always Running* acted as literary prototypes for this production trend in contemporary gang memoirs, setting thematic and narrative conventions and proving their considerable commercial potential.

In 2004, with more than twenty-five gang memoirs published since *Monster* was first released, Stanley "Tookie" Williams published *Blue Rage, Black Redemption: A Memoir*.[9] Written by one of the co-founders of the Crips gang established in South Central LA in 1971, it offers a longer history of gang culture and conflict. Even between 1993 and the publication of *Blue Rage* in 2004, LA street gangs continued to thrive.[10] Given a death penalty sentence in 1981, Williams converted from notorious former gang member to outspoken peace activist in the early 1990s. In 1996 he authored a series of anti-gang children's books that resulted, quite extraordinarily, in several nominations for the Nobel Prize (in both Literature and Peace categories).[11] In the year following the publication of *Blue Rage*, Williams's struggle for a stay of execution and his eventual execution in December 2005 garnered a great deal of media attention. Because of this controversy *Blue Rage*, which was reissued posthumously, stands as a particularly topical and revealing addition to this production trend. As its title suggests—rage and redemption—this memoir, like the other two, offers a powerful narrative of conversion as well as of conflict and crime. *Blue Rage* proved extremely popular, especially following Williams's execution, when sales of the memoir surged.[12]

The crux of this research is to examine the conflict between the competing forces of violence and pedagogy, as illustrated by the execution of Williams. The controversial execution crystallizes the polarized debates about contemporary gang memoirs, which have been variously demonized as violent and sensationalist or, by contrast, praised as offering a pedagogic and preventative anti-gang stance. Such contradictory responses are reflected in the memoirs themselves. Their narrative arc rests on conversion: the journey from violent young gangbanger, through punishment, on to political enlightenment and the renunciation of violence. The books emphasize both the frisson of violent gang exploits and the sober, salutary reflection of politicized and educated hindsight. This introduction will outline such frames of reference, explain the rationale for the project, and detail the existing scholarly literature on the three memoirs. The main body of the book will offer further information explaining the rise of such memoirs (chapter 1), as well as an examination of the existing scholarship informing the study of gang memoirs (chapter 2). As the chapters unfold, the reader will witness how the book repeatedly returns to the central analytical frames of violence and pedagogy.

In addition to their wide readership, these memoirs constitute a significant topic for study because of their social significance, their engagement with debates about the cultural politics of race and youth (including issues of commerce), and their formal and aesthetic dimensions.

Above all, the memoirs reveal a great deal about social relations, especially pertaining to race, gender, class, and generational issues in an urban context at a particular historical moment. Though far from empirical, the narratives provide a window into the urban environment of LA where contemporary street gangs grew rapidly, particularly from the 1970s onwards. The narratives offer inside accounts of the extreme lifestyles and beliefs of impoverished young people and how they make meaning of their lives through the organization of the street gang. The memoirs illustrate the social problems associated with gangs and the costs to urban communities of high levels of violence. At the same time, the memoirs open up profound insights into and critiques of the social-structural determinants of gangs. They draw out revealing connections between the proliferation of street gangs and both deindustrialization since the 1970s and the erosion of welfare support. Thus these narratives, as representations of everyday gang practices, carry important social commentary. All three memoirs engage with issues of youth unemployment, substandard education, rising poverty levels and racial conflict, though they focus on separate moments of the post-1965 period of crisis and transition.

The production trend of contemporary street gang memoirs formed one key component of a wider body of gangsta culture that commenced in the late 1980s with gangsta rap. Rap was praised by cultural scholars for engaging with the destructive social forces that impinged deeply on the ghetto as material for the music.[13] Artists such as Kid Frost and Ice Cube regularly rapped about the struggle to survive for Mexican and African

Americans in postindustrial urban California. Gangsta rap "emerged from and voiced the experiences and desires of an oppressed community in a period of economic transformation," in the words of cultural scholar Eithne Quinn.[14] Rap artist Chuck D memorably claimed that gangsta rap was "the Black CNN" for the way in which it projected what was happening in the ghettos, while Ice Cube explained, "we call ourselves underground street reporters."[15] Parallel arguments have been made concerning the social significance of gangsta films.[16] Rap and these films demonstrated the importance of taking popular forms seriously. The memoirs merit scholarly attention similar to that paid their popular musical and filmic counterparts because they can be read as social transcripts.

Gangsta rap was extremely popular among both white and minority audiences. Its commercial success by the early 1990s ensured black and Latino young men were thrust into the pop-cultural spotlight. Marginalized youth were becoming central to the commercial cultural landscape as consumers and firmly establishing themselves as artists and producers of this successful musical genre. Even though many were ultimately connected to a white-dominated music industry, they established a clear autonomous space within it. Performers such as Dr. Dre, Snoop Dogg, and Tony G were responsible in both roles for marketing and commodifying tough black and Mexican masculine images for an eager public audience. Marginalized young men could themselves take control in this production process, which was a significant step for Mexican American and African American popular culture. It is critical to explore how gang memoirists have contributed to this cultural terrain.

While playing a role in discussions of contemporary black and Latino popular culture, the memoirs also entered into serious debates in society through their critical reception. These texts prompted extensive media attention at the time of their release and beyond their initial publication. They have developed an extensive life through the media, becoming a site for channeling charged discussions about youth, crime, and violence, including the demonization of black and Latino men. Part of the importance of these texts stems from the various ways they have been engaged discursively by the media. In similar but separate discussions of consumption and reception, the ongoing use of these books in high school classrooms and libraries suggests they may also hold great significance for young people, especially marginalized youth. As one LA high school librarian stated, "all these books are very, very popular."[17] Despite their calculated, commercialized formula, they remain on some level grounded in a local, "real life" context. These memoirs justify scholarly attention because of their cultural reach among young adults in the United States and beyond.

As well as demonstrating social, historical, political and cultural relevance, the memoirs warrant scholarly examination on account of their aesthetic significance. The authors appropriate and adapt life writing and prison narrative conventions pioneered in the 1960s and 1970s by authors such as Malcolm X, George Jackson, and James Carr.[18] They participate in longstanding expressive traditions of oppressed groups, focusing on issues of language and learning that stem from marginalization. Since its inception as a slave narrative, African American autobiography has been used as a means of asserting individual identity and addressing sociopolitical realities of the black experience. Such practices can be witnessed in the African American prison narratives that thrived in the 1960s and 1970s and that serve as an important precedent to gang memoirs. While African Americans were prohibited from learning to read and write in slavery, language was a very charged issue for Mexican immigrants historically because of language barriers. Mexican American life writing likewise has a lengthy history, functioning as representative of both individual and group experiences on both sides of the border. Contemporary gang memoirs tap into and rework such longstanding literary traditions.

Given the success of this literary production trend and the multivalent significance of the memoirs, the texts have been surprisingly underresearched. The scholarly writing that has emerged can be organized into five broad categories: historical, sociological, educational, literary, and cultural. *Monster* has received the most scholarly attention and *Blue Rage* the least, partly due to the more recent publication date of the latter. Such existing scholarship has helped stimulate this study, but has hardly exhausted the avenues for analysis.

Discussions of contemporary gang memoirs can be found in texts on contemporary Californian and Latino history. *Monster* and *Always Running* are mentioned in Kevin Starr's *Coast of Dreams: A History of Contemporary California*, while *Always Running* is discussed in David Wyatt's *Five Fires: Race, Catastrophe and the Shaping of California* and Victor Valle and Rodolfo Torres's *Latino Metropolis*, among others.[19] Such studies present the memoirs as serious evidence of life as a Mexican American or African American young man in post-industrial urban California. Starr predicts that when a comprehensive history of LA gangs is finally published, the two memoirs will "undoubtedly constitute classic sources."[20]

Wyatt describes *Always Running* as "one of the most powerful testimonies to adaptation and resistance" of immigrants trying to survive in contemporary California.[21] Starr in particular views the memoirs as a manifestation of street gang culture, incorporating his discussion of the memoirs in two chapters dedicated to gangs.[22] The inclusion of such accounts into historical studies suggests that contemporary street gangs offer an important contribution to the makeup of contemporary California and specifically LA. The memoirs are also useful sources for those wishing to understand the structure and significance of these gangs.

Like the historians, sociologists deem the memoirs truthful and constructive sources.[23] Numerous references to *Monster* can be found in sociological monographs and articles discussing urban poverty, race relations, youth violence, and crime.[24] Short references to *Always Running* can also be found in social science and criminology journals, though fewer than for *Monster*.[25] There has been extensive work by sociologists into the nature of modern-day urban gangs, but these gang scholars tend to downplay the cultural dimensions, and there is little research into gang memoirs in their field. Lewis Yablonsky remains the only gang scholar to draw on such memoirs in depth as firsthand insight into gangs.[26] In his referencing of *Monster*, Yablonsky does not justify his use of autobiography; he merely cites the narrative as evidence of the nature of contemporary street gangs. Gang scholar James Diego Vigil momentarily quotes *Monster*, but Vigil and fellow gang researcher Malcolm Klein make scant references to *Always Running*.[27] Klein generally condemns the use of such "bullshit accounts" as relevant evidence.[28] Klein objects that the books (particularly *Monster*) are hyperbolic shams far removed from the behavior of "regular" gang members, and he worries that such accounts carry the potential to excite vulnerable young people. With the exception of Klein, the brief socio-historical accounts that exist tend to construct gang memoirs as useful evidence of and rich insight into gang life.

The focus on gangs as a sociological entity has sparked educational scholarship on the subject. Claudia Durst Johnson dedicates two chapters of her book *Youth Gangs in Literature* to *Monster* and *Always Running*.[29] The book forms part of a series exploring social issues through literature, designed as a resource for teachers and librarians tackling subjects that have consequences for high school students. This particular volume on gangs is designed for educators looking for new ways to present social issues, but also is written with students in mind. The book aims to generate informed discussions on gangs and incorporates both contemporary and canonical literature dating back to Mark Twain's *The Adventures of Huckleberry Finn*. *Monster* and *Always Running* also feature in another article exploring the subject of youth violence in the classroom.[30] *Always Running* is cited more regularly, though still only fleetingly, in pedagogical and teaching journals, often specific to Latino life.[31]

In contrast to the sociological scholarly work on gang memoirs, which is concerned with the subject of gangs themselves, or educational work, preoccupied with issues of language and pedagogy, literature scholars tend to focus on narrative conventions, aesthetic interests, and select figurative themes. A fascinating essay on *Monster* by literature scholar David Brumble, engages with literary figures like Beowulf and Achilles to examine the memoir.[32] His rationale is that some urban youth subcultures have reinvented classic tribalism and warrior cultures in which issues of identity are prevalent. He conducts a close textual reading of *Monster*, paying particular attention to language and literary devices. Recently Brumble produced an essay categorizing "gangbanger autobiography" according to tribal warrior traits, whereby "human beings retain the right to use force in severalty."[33] In this second piece, Brumble subdivides gangbanger autobiography into different types that reveal themselves in the structure of their narratives, offering *Blue Rage* as a primary example for analysis. For the most part, however, there are very few literary readings of either *Monster* or *Blue Rage*. Chapters 3 and 4 stand as correctives to this.

Always Running has prompted more literary scholarship, often framed by racial and ethnic premises. For example, Tim Libretti makes use of Rodriguez's text among other works of Chicana/o literature. He attempts to reconstruct a proletarian literary tradition that recognizes cultural diversity, rather than situating such works within a narrowly defined ethnic/racial category that overshadows their working-class constituents.[34] In another essay, Paula Moya explores notions of "Nation and Belonging" in three newly released critical studies of Latino/a literature.[35] She opens her piece with a poignant anecdote from *Always Running*, in which the young narrator quickly learns about the politics of identity in the United States. Moya contends that the memoir works on several levels, all of which link back to the idea of being an "outsider." Moya notes that "Rodriguez's preoccupations are resonant with Latina/o literature as a whole," as demonstrated in all three of the scholarly books (though only one of these makes brief reference to *Always Running*).[36] Lastly, Vincent Perez and Amaia Ibarraran Bigalondo both select *Always Running* as one of two contemporary Chicano urban narratives for analysis in their respective essays.[37]

Perez's literary reading of his two texts focuses on themes of nihilism and cultural memory; Bigalondo's on inclusion and power, as well as addressing male/female portrayals of gang activity.

The fourth category of existing scholarship on gang memoirs—cultural studies—incorporates some literary discussions while also exploring racial and ethnic representational politics within popular culture. Black cultural scholars Todd Boyd, Auli Ek, and Kali Tal all highlight the cultural politics that are at work in *Monster*.[38] Boyd's text, *Am I Black Enough for You? Popular Culture from the 'hood and Beyond*, offers one of the most revealing explorations of the memoir. Boyd contends African American autobiography is a strategy that makes gangsta into a serious cultural movement. He argues that just as gangsta rap and films warrant serious attention, *Monster* links contemporary concerns to the historical by "using a form that embodies relevant tradition for the overall understanding of African American culture."[39] By using a highly respected form that commenced years ago with the slave narrative, Boyd believes that *Monster* forces us to take seriously those oppressed gangsta voices that operate on the margins of society. Just as Boyd is concerned with black stereotyping, Ek's *Race and Masculinity in Contemporary American Prison Narratives* engages with both film and fiction to explore the dangerous implications of the black criminal stereotype and racial "otherness."

The time period covered by the three memoirs is one of extraordinary change, as illustrated by both Boyd and Tal. The narratives document important historical events such as the civil rights movement of the 1950s and 1960s and the Chicano movement of the late 1960s and early 1970s, as well as the LA riots of 1992 (though Boyd has a longer trajectory stretching back further). The early part of this era witnessed the intensification of identity politics within African American and Mexican American groups, celebrating cultural and racial identities. This definitive upsurge in race and ethnic consciousness is captured in the life narratives of these young men coming of age. The memoirs provide insight into this rise of identity politics within a period of political mobilization and activism. The texts then further explore those racial identities within a subsequent period of declining political consciousness, as demonstrated by Tal and Boyd. The critical work of these two cultural scholars reminds us that these gang memoirs are, among other things, narratives of political transition.

There is one other cultural and political study of *Monster* that is worth mentioning, though it is not specifically concerned with racial politics like Tal and Boyd. Deepak Narang Sawhney reads *Monster* relative to the work

of Gilles Deleuze, the French philosopher renowned for exploring the relationship between identity and difference.[40] Sawhney deems the memoir
to be an excellent illustration of Deleuze's theories of "minor literature"
in relation to "major language." Deleuze claims that minor literature was
not written in a "minor" language nor in a formerly colonized language;
instead, that literature is written in a "major" language or the language
of the colonizers. As Sawhney explains, Deleuze was concerned with the
"deterritorializations" of a major language—in other words, a minor literature written in the major language but from a marginalized or "minori-
tarian" position. Linguistic deterritorialization, for example, may rupture
traditional forms of major languages, as I will reveal later in this book with
Always Running's use of "Spanglish" as a reworked form of English. Such
minor literature was characterized by Deleuze according to its political
nature, something Sawhney attempts to reveal in *Monster.* Sawhney considers how institutionalized power structures such as prison may affect
and influence Shakur's minor literature. His article serves to illustrate the
diverse scholarship that has engaged with contemporary street gang memoirs, itself an indication of their cultural significance.

This book is informed by an interdisciplinary approach, inspired by cultural studies tenets. The cultural studies approaches of Boyd, Tal, and Ek
carefully consider both text and context concurrently. I will argue that the
textual readings of the books are just as important as their historical context. Black culture scholar Tricia Rose justifies the need for this approach:
"Without historical contextualization, aesthetics are naturalized, and certain cultural practices are made to appear essential to a given group of
people . . . without aesthetic considerations, black cultural practices are
reduced to extensions of socio-historical circumstances."[41] Gang scholar
Yablonsky and the Californian historians limit their readings of the memoirs to contextual slants. By contrast, other than a brief paragraph on LA's
historical development, Brumble's aesthetic analysis removes the memoirs from their contemporary social situation, rendering them ahistorical.
While the existing scholarship acts as an important platform from which
to embark on this research, there are clear limitations in such work. I
believe in the importance of positioning cultural texts in their political,
historical, and economic contexts (particularly in terms of LA), drawing
out the intersections and interdependencies between textual and contextual processes.

Due to the multifaceted significance of the memoirs, there is a need
to address the social alongside the cultural, and the aesthetic alongside

the commercial. Accounts of violence must be understood as an opportunist pop-cultural strategy to sell a product, as well as a serious portal into understanding marginalized young people struggling to survive in an extreme social environment. The journey to become politically conscious memoirist from "ignorant" gangbanger must be interpreted as a passage into maturity and political awareness (as a boy becomes a man in a hostile setting), but also the conventional formula for both prison narratives and the life writing of the marginalized. The memoirist is making a living to escape the gang, while simultaneously acting as spokesperson for the ghetto. It is extremely difficult to extricate the cultural from the social and the commercial from the aesthetic; such forces often work interdependently. Such imbrications lead to narrative tensions within the memoirs with authors negotiating these tensions in different ways. They deploy diverse literary strategies, dissecting their life experience with varying levels and kinds of political commitment, coming of age at different moments in the last forty-five years and from different but related racial and ethnic identity positions.

This kind of scholarly work is already being conducted in the fields of black and Latino cultural studies, focusing on identity politics grounded in lived experience, emphasizing both text and context, and raising questions about commercial impetuses. There is a growing body of work exploring gangsta culture in such frames, particularly music and film. Cultural studies scholars such as Robin Kelley, Quinn, and Rose have scrutinized gangsta rap, while Boyd and S. Craig Watkins have considered gangsta's filmic counterparts.[42] As already stated, such scholarly studies (Boyd excluded) have not incorporated contemporary street gang memoirs.

At the same time gangsta culture was gaining momentum in the late 1980s, there was a distinct anthropological turn in the discipline of American Studies, reflecting schools of thought that were already established in British cultural studies. In the early 1970s, British cultural studies began to move away from strict textual readings, to incorporate interest in audiences and the audience's response to texts. In Britain, audience cultural studies were almost exclusively of television audiences. In the United States the pioneering work of Janice Radway in the early 1990s led the way in encouraging studies of literary audiences. Radway wanted to address the "complex social processes" at work in literary production and consumption.[43] She explains that her decision "to move beyond the various concepts of the inscribed, ideal or model reader" and instead "to work with actual subjects in history" was a product of "the difficult questions that had been put to me by colleagues trained in the social sciences tradition and in cultural theory."[44] This has remained a popular approach among American Studies scholars, with recent years producing audience studies of hip hop music and gangsta films.[45] Though this research is by no means a comprehensive reception analysis, my decision to interview teachers and readers (including schoolchildren and former gang members) of these memoirs is driven by the recent intellectual focus on testimony.[46] The project will explore how memoirs are used and interpreted in everyday situations, rather than relying solely on textual analysis or socio-economic contextualization.

This research has three primary objectives. First, to comprehend the production trend of contemporary gang memoirs: why and how did they suddenly emerge? Interviews with Rodriguez and Barbara Becnel (Williams's editor) and written correspondence with Shakur help to understand the complex story of emergence and circulation of the books (though I was fully aware of the limitations of bias and reliability before these interviews were undertaken).[47] For example, they detail the reasoning behind their choice of publisher. Second, this book will analyze the three texts' narrative conventions, using language and violence as exploratory themes to compare how the memoirists narrativize their identities and lived experiences. The third objective is to explore the consumption of the memoirs. The controversial nature of such texts encourages this research to consider how they have been received in various public spheres. Such responses are crucial to understanding the sustained popularity of the texts and their cultural influence and reach. This final objective incorporates press reception and reader response studies conducted at high schools in LA. These two methods are linked by issues of consumption; yet, as this book will reveal, the methods also work on separate levels to reveal how individual readers understand the texts.

Following this introduction, the book opens with a chapter—"From Rage to Rap and Prison to Print"—that addresses the social, cultural, and commercial contexts of emergence of these memoirs. This will include an examination of American society during the early 1990s and the existing trends in black and Latino popular culture at that time. The chapter will delineate the lucrative dimensions of gangsta culture and address the literary origins of contemporary street gang memoirs. While this research is not concerned with actual street gangs, the chapter will reference their sociological coverage in order to comprehend the sensational content of these texts. Chapter 2—"Homeboys Between Hard Covers"—will then outline the critical debates and scholarly approaches that surround and inform the study of gang memoirs, building on theories stemming from British cultural studies, autobiography criticism (specifically ethnic memoirs and prison narratives), and studies of black/Latino representational politics and audiences. This chapter engages predominantly with black-specific criticism in my approach, but I remain conscious of not applying generalizations to two minority groups that have diverse histories and cultural differences.

Chapter 3—"Killer Books"—seeks to analyze and contextualize the representations of violence in the texts. How do the narrators present violent acts? How are the narratives informed by changing socio-political trends, genre conventions and cultural sensibilities that have led toward an escalation of violent imagery? In short, violence sells! As Ruben Martinez, the former editor of the *Los Angeles Weekly* suggests, "Aren't all Americans after all, either consumers or perpetrators of violence?"[48] At the same time, the chapter examines charged questions about the specificity and politics of violent representation in the popular-cultural expressions of the marginalized and racial minorities. All three narrators use a range of formal and thematic strategies that are at times complex and productive, and offer revealing insights into historical events as well as post–civil rights identity and experience. While this chapter includes discussions of masculinity that are prompted by the warrior-style behavior of the narrators, masculinity can also be socially constructed in contrast with feminine ideals. This chapter will highlight how women are seemingly sidelined in the memoirs to permit room for boastful tales of machismo and male bravado. When women do appear, they are stereotyped as doting mother/grandmother or more frequently trophy girlfriend/lover. Tal, Brumble, and other scholars who have explored the memoirs simply do not address these fleeting female characters.

Chapter 4—"Brothers Who Could Kill With Words"—will conduct another close textual reading of the memoirs to address vital questions of language, literacy, and education. The chapter will explore how the memoirists appropriate and subvert language to establish identity and narrativize their lives. All three memoirists offer sensationalist tales while simultaneously presenting the sober reflection of politicized hindsight. They deploy the conversion narrative as an ethical framework to license their violent tales of the 'hood, claiming to be writing for personal fulfillment and to escape the gang. Questions of how, and to what end, these memoirists exploit language and genre form the basis of the chapter. Though textual readings of these memoirs form a crucial part of this study, the final two chapters are less concerned with the intrinsic properties of the texts and more interested in the structural responses of the readers who actively construct meanings from the memoirs. The focus will thus shift from textual operations onto media reception and reader responses, deriving new meanings from the texts.

Chapter 5—"Murderer, Monster, Novelist, or Nobel Nominee?"—will examine the press reception of these texts, analyzing a sample of book reviews and their thematic discourses and counter-discourses. Critical reception helps us understand how these texts engaged with prominent public debates of the time. The chapter will demonstrate how controversy at the time of release of the texts opens up a series of discourses about black masculinity, censorship, and celebrity (the publicity images of the memoirists), as well as expanding on previous debates over cultural commerce. Williams's unusual circumstances dictated that *Blue Rage*'s book reviews were frequently intertwined with press coverage of his fight for life and eventual execution. However, the press reception of these three memoirs does not address the potential role of such memoirs in pedagogical environments. All three narratives state they were writing with young, often vulnerable, people in mind, and my fieldtrips to LA revealed these books have a determined presence in the city's classrooms and libraries. Furthermore, pedagogical themes run throughout all three memoirs, whether the narrators are appraising their childhood schools or stressing the importance of education in their personal development. This prompts a turn toward those youthful readers in the final chapter.

Chapter 6—"Quick Reads for Reluctant Readers"—explores pedagogical concerns by analyzing lived responses to the memoirs in LA classrooms, exploring the role of Californian high schools in encouraging student engagement with these memoirs. I will consider whether the readers take such memoirs seriously and what their responses can tell us about the texts. Some of the blind spots in the press reception become subjects for critical discussion among high school youths and their educators. The particularities of LA as a site of gang violence and gangsta culture will be touched upon at various points in this study. But the critical importance of the city is fully addressed in this final chapter when certain neighborhoods are passionately referenced by readers. The chapter will incorporate discussions of the series of books that Williams published in 1996, specifically aimed at elementary schoolchildren who were learning to read, as well as *Life in Prison* aimed at middle school ages.[49] These children's books and his adult memoir appear to have a considerable afterlife in educational environments, but the reader will note that the chapter is dominated by *Always Running* because it is the most well-read by schoolchildren.

The tension between the rival impulses of violence and pedagogy that are at the heart of this book are witnessed in the loose pairings of chapters 3 with 4, and 5 with 6.

The reader will note that I refer to these texts as "memoirs" rather than "autobiographies." Technically the two are different, a memoir usually being narrower in focus and an autobiography covering a longer period of the author's life, often from early childhood until late adulthood.[50] Nonetheless, in chapter 2 the study of memoirs falls into the same critical category as autobiography theory and studies.

During the textual readings of chapters 3 and 4, I will use the nicknames "Tookie" and "Monster" for the actions of the characters, analogous to the narrator. (Hence *Monster* italicized refers to the memoir itself while "Monster" denotes the character within the narrative.) Though the protagonist of *Always Running* was assigned the moniker "Chin," the narrator makes no use of this nickname. "Tookie," "Monster," and the narrator are different from the authors Williams, Shakur, and Rodriguez.[51] Fundamental notions of narratology dictate that there are three individuals who together take responsibility for fictional storytelling: the narrator, the author, and the reader. According to literary critic Mieke Bal, the narrator—or "narrative agent"—is clearly distinguishable from the biographical author who inhabits the "real" world.[52] The author and reader are consecutively crucial in creating and interpreting the story, while the narrator exists only within the fictional pages of the book.

With regard to memoir, narrator and author are usually seen to share the same persona, as the worlds inside and outside the narrative are indistinguishable. Although the texts under exploration in this book are autobiographical, the subgenre of a conversion narrative renders it logical that the young, naïve gangbanging character and the older, reflective author be treated separately to some degree. Contemporary gang memoirs are themselves a mediated medium between their author and reader in which it may be in the author's interest initially to present himself as an immature and somehow "raw" character. The very nature of conversion or redemption is dependent upon this characterization as the author attempts to persuade the reader of their rebirth into a different identity. This becomes particularly relevant when considering the authors' actual situations in a "real life" context.

It is worth briefly noting the term "literary nonfiction." This phrase is sometimes applied to texts that are factual accounts of the writer's personal experience, but are presented with notable literary flair. A significant example would be Maya Angelou's *I Know Why the Caged Bird Sings*, which, as an autobiography, is written with publication in mind.[53] Yet Angelou has carefully shaped and crafted her text so that the reader's interest is retained. Literary nonfiction often engages with many techniques usually exercised by a novelist (including description, dialogue, and creative uses of language) to ensure it is a compelling read. While I am by no means definitively categorizing these memoirs as literary nonfiction, they do toy with some structural and aesthetic practices to persuade the reader of their conversion and present their "authentic" tales of the 'hood. This supports the notion that the teller of the tale be labeled the "narrator" in the textual (literary) readings in chapters 3 and 4. Though the handling of memoirists as their own characters may initially seem odd, the reason for this distinction will be highlighted in chapters 5 and 6 as I move into the reception of the memoirs and the reader's understanding of the "real" author.

Chapter One

FROM RAGE TO RAP AND PRISON TO PRINT
Social, Cultural, and Commercial Contexts of Emergence

One of the objectives of this book is to position gang memoirs within prevailing gangsta culture. To do so requires an exploratory chapter into how LA gang experiences and cultural practices came to be narrativized and sold in popular form. This chapter will highlight the complex processes at work in the production of contemporary black and Latino popular culture, particularly in written form. This chronology will commence in the early twentieth century with the history of Mexican American gangs and end with the emergence of the literary production trend under analysis. I will highlight the origins of the African American Crips in the early 1970s, whose establishment is generally seen to denote the point at which contemporary street gangs emerged. Social, economic, and political changes in inner-city areas at this time wreaked havoc among urban youth of LA and sparked massive gang proliferation among Mexican and African Americans. Membership of these urban gangs continued to grow rapidly throughout the 1980s. The reasons behind the explosion of gang warfare in LA will be explored, as will the suppressive tactics and media coverage that responded to such violence.

By the late 1980s thousands of former gang members were either dead or incarcerated, but their legacy and the gang subculture was celebrated and commodified through gangsta rap music and videos, film, and fashion. In the early 1990s this lucrative cultural trend sparked interest from potential authors and publishers. Such literary attention was partially fueled by public fascination with life in the ghettos following the 1992 LA riots. In 1993 two memoirs were released that would prove to be incredibly popular like their earlier musical and media counterparts: *Monster: The Autobiography of an LA Gang Member* by Sanyika Shakur and *Always Running: La Vida Loca—Gang Days in LA* by Luis J. Rodriguez.[1] More memoirs would follow over subsequent years including *Blue Rage, Black Redemption: A Memoir* by Stanley "Tookie" Williams in 2004.[2] I will consider the impact of existing gangsta trends on contemporary gang memoirs as well as other cultural expressions (such as the 1960s prison narrative) and the inclinations of the publishing industry that encouraged the production of these texts.

Monster, Always Running, and *Blue Rage* narrativize the street gang phenomenon in LA from the late 1960s to the early 1990s, but understanding their frames of reference requires a brief consideration of a longer history of gang activity and culture.[3] Mexican American gangs in LA, such as the Maravillas and the White Fence, have a long and rich history. In California during the 1920s and 1930s, Mexican youth asserted their identities by forming gangs. Their working-poor families were lured to East LA by jobs and cheap housing. The Mexican experience of immigration posed huge problems with acculturation and assimilation, and the barrios were segregated and overcrowded. Life for young people spilled out of the family home and onto the streets. Youths formed gangs as a protective, united front to racist, mainstream American society and the gangs gradually turned on one another as neighborhood rivalries flared. Forced by schools and other institutions to sacrifice their culture, language, and therefore dignity, the self-descriptive identity label "Cholo" was deployed by youth to reflect their own street language and style.[4]

These early barrio gangs were usually seen by the community as relatively harmless boys who wished to fight rival groups, rather than as criminal gangs.[5] The 1940s have been seen as the point at which Mexican American gangs took a turn for the worse, becoming more dangerous in character and beginning to defy law enforcement. Paranoia about the "Zoot-Suiters" (so called because of Mexican fashion trends among young men) boiled over in riots in LA in 1942. Racial tension flared as Mexican American men became the target of white marines who were stationed in the city in preparation for World War II. The police initially refused to intervene and newspapers attacked the "Pachucos." Indirectly attributable to the Zoot Suit Riots, the innocence of the barrio boys was lost and their competitive fighting at parties and on the streets was forced to evolve into more organized criminal gangs, partly for protection. As more Mexican American men than ever before went to prison in the early 1940s, prison gangs gradually evolved and would go on to become the foundations of the renowned Mexican Mafia, functioning from inside. Heroin was introduced to the barrios in the late 1940s and the use of violence (both on the streets and inside prison) gradually increased throughout the next two decades.

The Mexican American gangs emerged in early-twentieth-century LA as an oppositional response to cultural marginality, but in the late 1960s and early 1970s the African American Crips gang sets developed alongside the Black Panther party. The proliferation of modern-day gangs nationwide is often attributed to the founding of the Crips and their rival "Bloods" in South Central LA. Donald Bakeer offers one of many versions of the gang's history in a historical novel he wrote about the rise of the Crips.[6] In this popular version, a teenager by the name of Raymond Washington admires the politically active Black Panthers, who aim to protect communities from what they deemed to be racist police officers. Together with his friend "Tookie," Washington establishes the Crips in order to unite his neighborhood and defend it against the police, emulating Panther models of insurgent resistance. As one former gang member, Twilight Bey, explains, "During the time period, everybody in the city was in a revolutionary mindset. You had the Black Panther party, the US Organization, all these organizations doing things. So the youngsters that wanted to be Black Panthers but couldn't, they created their own organizations, which became known as gangs."[7] Joao Vargas's recent ethnography of African Americans in LA also uses evidence from former gang members to conclude that the Black Panthers and black power ideologies inspired street gangs in the 1970s.[8]

In a marginally different version of events according to urban historian Mike Davis, the gang phenomenon known as "Crippin" became "the bastard offspring of the Panthers' former charisma."[9] Rufus Schatzberg and Robert Kelly wrote a social history of African American organized crime which supports this version, maintaining that the Crips filled the void left behind when the Panthers were crushed by law enforcement. According to Schatzberg and Kelly, the Crips "inherited the Panther aura of fearlessness and transmitted the ideology of armed vanguardism—they began as a teenage substitute for the fallen Panthers—evolving through the 1970s into a hybrid of teen cult and proto-mafia."[10] In both historical versions, local violence soon expanded from skirmishes with the police to warring with rival neighborhood gang factions, particularly the Bloods. Despite such disagreements in contemporary gang history, most accounts stress the issues of the era: radical politics and responses to police harassment.

Social and economic changes in the 1970s gave rise to an increase in gang membership and a decrease in gang politicization. Regardless of the relationship the Crips may (or may not) have had with the Panthers, there is agreement that soon after the gang was established, as one anonymous social historian states, "the social fabric of LA began to unravel and disintegrate; solidarity lost out in a razor fight with survival."[11] There is a clear correlation between the disintegration of the ghetto and the massive government disinvestment and privatization policies that affected inner-city LA (areas such as South Central) throughout the 1970s. Employment in the barrios of East LA also took a turn for the worse, particularly with the area experiencing a tremendous increase in immigration from Mexico during the 1970s. Gang warfare became one symptom of the effect of mass de-industrialization in the 1970s as desperation set in, exacerbated by the loss of welfare under Reaganomics in the 1980s. This book will regularly stress the deteriorating urban circumstances for both Mexican and African Americans since the 1970s that stimulated gang growth in LA, highlighting the social relevance of studying gangsta culture.

When Reagan became president in 1981, in that first year his administration cut $35 million from budgets for education, housing, food stamps, and school lunches.[12] The situation for minorities was already grave before he came to power. According to the Department of Labor, in 1978 the unemployment gap between blacks and whites was the widest ever, the jobless rate among blacks being 2.3 times higher than the rate among whites.[13] Reagan exacerbated the problem, becoming the first of the last five presidents to fail to support affirmative action. Having won a popular victory at the polls without black or Mexican support, the president proceeded to propose legislation opposing the rights of minorities. He opposed renewing the Voting Rights Act of 1965 (though was overruled by Congress), and he cut funds for civil rights enforcement agencies such as the Equal Employment Opportunity Commission. African Americans encountered similar racial impediments to adequate housing. As sociologist James Blackwell elucidates with regard to Reagan, "His actions betray his public pronouncements decrying prejudice and abhorring discrimination."[14]

In his inaugural address in 1989, President Bush promised to substitute Reagan's America with a "kinder, gentler" nation that would be more sensitive to the poor and the disadvantaged.[15] During his first years in office, Bush and a Democratic-controlled Congress raised the minimum wage and voted to provide financial support to low-income families for childcare. However, these efforts were overshadowed by a prolonged economic recession that began in July 1990. By early 1992 over two million jobs had dried up; during 1991 approximately 20 percent of the labor force was unemployed at some point.[16] In December 1991 alone, General Motors, IBM, and Xerox slashed 100,000 employees from their payrolls.[17] Though the recession affected white-collar as well as blue-collar workers, it exaggerated an already dire employment situation for blacks and Mexicans. In 1992, 10 percent of whites were classified as "poor," but this figure was 26 percent for Latinos and 30 percent for African Americans.[18] The situation was particularly bad in California, which had gained more people than any other state during the 1980s, primarily due to Mexican immigration.[19] The state simply could not provide sufficient jobs and adequate housing to keep its minority residents out of poverty and prevent the widespread growth of the ghettos, especially in urban areas like LA.

With insufficient employment and declining welfare benefits, criminality became a viable option, as demonstrated by the crack cocaine epidemic. This alternative drug economy was first seen in LA in the early 1980s and provided "jobs" for Mexican and African American youth, inevitably infiltrating street gangs. Combined with increased access to firearms as a result of President Reagan's deregulation of guns, the drugs market resulted in a sudden upsurge in gang violence. Drive-by killings became commonplace tactics of warring gangs and the greatest cause of death among young black and Mexican men was the bullet.[20] Within a five-year period in the mid-1980s, the homicide rate among young urban blacks quadrupled.[21] Thus the 1980s are often seen as the point at which the "super-gang" was born.[22] Despite the dangerous circumstances of street gangs, by the late 1980s and early 1990s they had established themselves as extremely popular organizations among Mexican and African American young men.

Gang-related homicides in LA rose steadily from 212 in 1984 to 771 in 1991, and gang-related deaths accounted for 36 percent of the total homicide figure in the city in 1991. The peak was 803 murders in 1992.[23] Archiving of the statistics of the LA Police Department (LAPD) only commenced in 1993, but they indicate 418 gang sets with 61,362 members, compared with 407 sets and 48,289 members in 2003.[24] Comparative statistics of gang membership and related homicides from earlier decades are sparse. Gang expert Alex Alonso suggests there were eight Crips sets in 1972, which grew to approximately forty-five in 1978.[25] By 1982, the LA County Sheriff Department (LASD) claimed there were 109 Crips sets across the county.[26] Though these statistics reference Crips alone and not all LA-based gangs, they give an idea of the sudden growth of gangs.

The crack cocaine outbreak and subsequent rise in gang violence prompted stricter federal and state penalties for such crimes. Though Reagan had already declared a "War on Drugs," the vigorous response from police and officials toward gang violence led to the situation in LA also being described as "war."[27] Such a metaphor became commonplace in April 1988 when the LAPD and the LASD under the command of Chief Daryl Gates launched Operation Hammer on ten square miles of LA. Thousands of black youths were forcibly seized and found their names being checked against computerized files of gang members. Gates justified the "invasion" by stating: "This is war . . . we're exceedingly angry . . . we want to get the message out to the cowards out there that we are going to come and get them."[28] In a media article evaluating Operation Hammer, Mike Davis likened members of local black gangs to the "Vietcong"; the gang members were also compared to the "murderous militias of Beirut" by LA's politicians.[29] Such harassment, military-style maneuvers, and warring tendencies from law enforcement toward street gangs would come to represent the tense relationship that existed between the two institutions, particularly throughout the late 1980s and early 1990s.

As president, Reagan enacted the philosophy that figured in the later administrations of Bush and Clinton, that it simply was not good politics to be soft on crime. Reagan argued, "Disarm the thugs and the criminals, lock them up and if you don't actually throw away the key, at least lose it for a long time. . . ."[30] During the Reagan presidency nine new prisons were opened in California alone.[31] Both Mexican and African American youth in contemporary LA have endured the legacy of racist police chiefs and a discriminatory criminal justice system. In South Central and East LA of the early 1990s, incarceration impinged on numerous families. Even if one's own circle was not immediately affected, most knew neighbors, friends, or distant relatives who were immersed in the legal system. By 1992 one quarter of all African American men nationally were in prison or jail, on probation or parole.[32]

As a result of Bush's stringent legislation and Clinton's "Three Strikes and You're Out," that figure has today increased to approximately one-third of African American men aged twenty to twenty-nine.[33] The incarceration rate for Latinos has also been significantly higher than for whites, though it has remained lower than for blacks. The chance that a Latino male will be in prison at least once in his lifetime is 16 percent.[34] For African Americans that figure is 28.5 percent and for whites is 4.4 percent.[35] Such experiences of racist law enforcement and judiciary were reworked by gangs to discard negative connotations involving the shame of being a criminal and embrace positive implications, with prison sentences offering peer recognition and gang validation.

There is a clear street gang trend for telling boastful "war stories" about prison and street life. The traditional macho nature of the contemporary street gang has evolved into a ritual of storytelling with potential for bias and embellishment, as recognized by gang scholars.[36] These hyperbolic warrior tales—what Williams terms "bullology"—are central to gangsta existence both on the streets and in prison.[37] Eithne Quinn's cultural study of gangsta rap takes into account such high levels of gang violence, which provided exciting content for "powerful, realist tales about gangbanging conquests, murderous escapades, and tense, poignant stories about loyalty and allegiance, sacrifice and loss."[38] These war stories have since been converted into material for memoirs, both in terms of clashes with the LAPD and the LASD as well as internal gang strife.

Mexican and African American gangs have given symbolic meanings to their own styles and rituals. Mexican American gangs historically paved the way for many subcultural trends of contemporary African American gangbangers such as low-riding and smoking "the chronic." Another popular ritual was reworking the prison Pendleton shirt as a trend for the streets, coined by sociologist Joan Moore as the "prisonization of street life."[39] Since then, subcultural inclinations within both groups have included hand-thrown set signals and graffiti marking territory. Gang members even manipulated fashion, using colored neck bandanas and sports caps to signify set affiliation. The gang's personalized vernacular was particularly notable for cholos.[40] These trends corresponded with those found in scholarly studies of youth subcultures, which thrived in Britain in the late 1960s.

The rise of subcultural studies in Britain is usually attributed to the Centre for Contemporary Cultural Studies (CCCS), founded in Birmingham in 1964. Stemming from the CCCS, Stuart Hall, Dick Hebdige, Ken Gelder, and other cultural scholars explored the ways in which urban youth adapt and use emblematic rituals as symbolic responses to wider societal issues such as unemployment, poor wages, or educational inequality. The Crips responded to living in this climate of urban decay by giving structuralist meaning to their own style politics and rituals, as their Mexican American counterparts had done. Like their Mexican forerunners, yearning for identity (to acquire social status) is a powerful incentive for joining an African American gang, as explored by gang sociologist Malcolm Klein.

Gang monikers supplant birth names, creating exciting and playful new possibilities for individual identity, as part of identification with the larger gang unit.[41]

Cultural historian Robin Kelley explores Malcolm X's participation in the subculture (clothes, music, and dance) of black working-class youth during World War II as detailed in *The Autobiography of Malcolm X*.[42] According to Kelley, partaking in this subculture helped Malcolm X and other young men establish identities that resisted the hegemonic culture of the era with its ingrained racism and white nationalism. Kelley maintains that black youth constructed their own subcultural image as a direct response to prevalent social issues of the era. This research will similarly contextualize the development of the gangsta subculture in the wider economic, political, and social setting of America, California, and specifically LA.

Gang subcultures take on further social significance because of their marketability. The actual gang experience, with its traditions and customs, is converted into cultural form and entertainment. Hebdige notes that youth subcultures are initially highly creative in their rebellion against mainstream culture. Such inventive trends then frequently develop market potential.[43] The gangsta neck-scarf and Pendleton shirt became fashionable in the 1980s even outside the ghetto; they are what Hebdige deems "currency for exchange."[44] Kelley recognizes this potential in contemporary subcultural models. He proposes that urban play is "more than an expression of stylistic innovation—and/or racial and class anger—increasingly it is viewed as a way to survive an economic crisis or a means to upward mobility."[45] The gang's subcultural responses to societal hardship quickly became material for economically lucrative gangsta rap and its videos. As I will reveal, gang memoirists have similarly exploited subcultural appropriations as capital.

Contemporary street gangs became a sensational topic in the press in the late 1980s. A broad area of enquiry in gang studies has been the gang's problematic relationship with the printed media and news programs. Mike Davis was one of numerous journalists who subjected Operation Hammer and other urban gang wars to extensive coverage in newspapers and the printed press. The media soon became the public's principal resource for information about gangs, and exploited public fascination with the subject. The sensationalized portrayal of gangs in the media spread misinformation and created moral panics.

Street gangs could soon be seen in the print media and news, and also in entertainment media. The use of the subject of gangs in recreational forms was partially sparked by the immense popularity of urban gangs for marginalized youth. Malcolm Klein labeled this process "the cultural diffusion of gangs."[46] Now information about gangs could be garnered from various popular sources rather than just the press. Klein voices apprehension about MTV (the music television channel), which shows gangsta rap videos, as well as worrying about ghetto films such as *Boyz N The Hood*.[47] He argues that they have had a major impact on gang proliferation rather than serving as innocent entertainment. In an interview, Klein was critical of the photographic covers of the memoirs, particularly *Monster* and *Blue Rage*.[48] Both memoirs present images of their authors, stripped to the waist, flaunting extremely muscular physiques (see photo insert). In the photographs Williams dons a Crips headscarf, while Shakur carries an AK-47 machine gun and his gang tattoos are just discernible. From Klein's perspective, such gangsta-loaded imagery glamorizes and encourages the gangsta lifestyle by prompting excitement and fascination among impressionable young readers. Klein assists in raising awareness of the powerful and influential role of all media in affecting public opinion on gangs themselves.

Gang scholar Martin Jankowski, like Klein, criticizes the media's tendency toward sensationalized news coverage of gangs in order to stimulate audience interest. Jankowski's exploration of the media's "exploitation of the concept of violence" is a fundamental concept for this research, underpinning discussions of the violent imagery and commercial impetus of gang memoirs.[49] But Jankowski contentiously probes further than Klein, claiming that media exposure benefits gangs by assisting in the recruitment of new members, advertising for business, and getting threatening messages to rivals. According to Jankowski, gang members are aware of the media's clout, with their egos reveling in media attention, "hamming it up for glory and gain."[50]

Prior to contemporary street gang memoirs being released in 1993, rap proved how such secretive gangsta subcultures, inaccessible to the majority of the public, could provide captivating true-to-life material for popular texts. This intrigue was partially fuelled by a longstanding white fascination with black masculinity, which in the 1950s Norman Mailer branded "coolness envy."[51] Contemporary historian Kevin Starr attempts to understand the culture of modern-day California by quoting a white, upper-class seventeen-year-old who observed the trends at his high school: "Everyone is totally into inner-city street language . . . there is a lot of yearning to be black."[52] The likes of Eminem and Vanilla Ice have embraced and interpreted contemporary black rap styles, though white fascination with blackness has been traced back to the minstrel shows that gained popularity in the mid-nineteenth century. Longings for blackness certainly spurred the commercial success of rap, and its popularity was further fuelled by its candid first-person form. Quinn argues that such music satisfied the "vast appetite for 'black ghetto realness' in the popular culture marketplace," by "mobiliz[ing] the authenticity discourse."[53] Such "street-realist reportage" could offer white suburban audiences an immediate insight into black ghetto culture, feeding their curiosity.[54] The music's unruly and anti-establishment themes further attracted white audiences.

Hip hop, the musical genre that arose on the East Coast in the late 1970s, is often credited with paving the way for gangsta rap. This music involved rapped lyrics over backing beats, often accompanied by break-dancing and graffiti, and was popular among African American and Latino youth cultures. By the mid-1980s a distinctive version of rap, increasingly preoccupied with violent tales from the inner city, was becoming popular on the West Coast. The term "gangsta rap" was invented by artist Ice Cube in 1989 and his original band, Niggaz With Attitude (NWA), became the first gangsta rap act to reach number one on the *Billboard* top pop album chart in June 1991. The success of their album, *Niggaz4life*, suggests the point at which gangsta rap became truly mainstream; by late 1991 gangsta rap had generated an impressive $700 million in record sales.[55] Cultural studies scholar Todd Boyd stresses the influential role of rap in this era: "in essence to talk about gangsta culture is to talk about gangsta rap. The music provides the themes and ethos of this particular cultural movement."[56] Shakur demonstrates a keen awareness of this musical genre in his acknowledgments to *Monster*. He includes dedications to early rap groups Public Enemy and Boogie Down Productions (who had reputations for being politically conscious), as well as renowned gangsta artists Ice-T, Ice Cube, and Tupac Shakur.[57] Such dedications position gangsta rap as a significant and immediate precursor to and inspiration for gang memoirs.

In April 1988, two years after Ice-T and NWA's first singles and just as Operation Hammer was being launched, the film *Colors* was released. Though "white" (directed by Dennis Hopper), the film sparked the ghetto action movie cycle of the early 1990s.[58] Hollywood responded quickly to the commercial success of gangsta rap, channeling ghetto authenticity through another medium for popular consumption. The old white ethnic gangster and the black gangster of blaxploitation films were displaced with a new villain.[59] As one advertising tagline actually read, "They're a new breed of gangster."[60] These African American "gangsta" films would prove extremely lucrative despite being low-budget productions.[61] The success of *Colors*, with its graphic depiction of gang life, prompted further blockbusters with mostly African American directors, including John Singleton's *Boyz N The Hood*, Mario Van Peebles's *New Jack City*, and Matty Rich's *Straight Out of Brooklyn* (1991), Edward Olmos's *American Me*, Ernest Dickerson's *Juice*, and Stephen Anderson's *South Central* (1992), and Allen/Albert Hughes's *Menace II Society* and Allison Anders's *Mi Vida Loca* (1993).[62]

South Central was the film version of Donald Bakeer's prominent book, *Crips: The Story of the LA Street Gang from 1971–1985*.[63] Published in 1987 as a novel, *Crips* depicted historical characters including Raymond Washington. In 1992 the book was converted by Anderson into the provocative film (produced by Oliver Stone), which came out in limited release for fear of inflaming public violence following the LA riots earlier that year. Nonetheless, 50,000 video copies were sold during its first week, demonstrating the market for gangsta in filmic as well as musical forms.[64] The movie industry's swift response to the success of gangsta rap was certainly worthwhile. Such films would be critically acclaimed by film critics and journalists as original and factual portraits of gang life. Cultural scholar S. Craig Watkins interrogates the accuracy of such films in representing ethnic poverty and societal injustices, creating a theatrical reality that captured the public imagination.[65]

Cultural scholars have contended that gangsta rap and ghetto action films formed part of a black cultural movement that originated with those who have suffered most by the conditions of post-industrial America and years of deliberate race and class subordination.[66] While specific sociological subcultures—such as the contemporary street gang—have thrived in response to oppressive and restrictive mainstream society, Boyd identifies this distinctive "ghetto" black popular culture as a similar response. One of the most prominent theorists on contemporary black culture, Cornel West, notes the irony that "just as young black men are murdered, maimed and imprisoned in record numbers, their styles have become disproportionately influential in shaping popular culture."[67] The popularity of this "gangsta" trend in reaction to, and as a reflection of, political and economic climates reinforces the social relevance of studying the production trend of contemporary gang memoirs within this wider insatiable appetite for gangsta culture.

Contemporary street gangs were also a new and exciting subject for documentary films. In his book review of *Monster* for *Atlantic* magazine in December 1993, journalist Mark Horowitz notes, "it is now much in fashion to go to gang members in LA for the authentic voice of black experience—or at least the experience of the black underclass."[68] Horowitz argues that prior to *Monster* this phenomenon had been evident on television, citing Ted Koppel's interviews on news channel ABC in the wake of the 1992 LA riots. In the weeks following the uprising the public watched in fascination as gang members who had been archenemies called a truce. Commentator Koppel interviewed Lil' Monster (Shakur's brother) as well as rival gang members. On national television these young men criticized society's treatment of the lower classes and raised awareness of living conditions in the poverty-stricken ghettos of South Central and East LA. Yet even prior to Koppel's discussions, in 1989 three television documentaries on gangs had appeared: Dan Medina's *Our Children: The Next Generation*, Dan Rather's *48 Hours: On Gang Street*, and Tyne Daly's *Not My Kid*.[69] Each of these programs incorporated interviews with real-life gang members, and were widely promoted and watched nationwide by large audiences.

By the late 1980s, although the gangsta subject was firmly established in several media and popular forms, printed-word accounts of gangs remained limited. Boyd argues that the lonesome black gangster figure in the earlier literature of Donald Goines and Iceberg Slim was one of the precursors setting the stage for gangsta culture to prosper in the 1980s.[70] Although I contend that it is possible to see contemporary gang memoirs as their own distinct literary genre with their own definitive form of cultural production, it is necessary to acknowledge they may be distantly related to the longer history of ghetto pulp novels. Indeed, a parallel world of black urban experience fiction emerged in the early 1970s. Goines and Slim were the most popular writers among black youth that grew up to comprise the hard-core element of the hip hop generation. As Ice-T details in his gang memoir, "All through high school, I was reading Iceberg Slim. I picked up my street name, and later my rap name, from Iceberg Slim."[71]

Texts such as Slim's *Pimp: The Story of My Life* (1969) and Goines's *Whoreson: The Story of a Ghetto Pimp* (1972) offer a construction of street life with themes of ubiquitous violence and racism, and characters typically including the pimp and the hustler.[72] Though often not strictly categorized as autobiography, these "autobiographical novels" capitalized on their authors' firsthand experiences of urban crime and the penal system.[73] Chester Himes can also be recognized as a forerunner to this tradition of black ghetto writing. Goines paid literary deference in naming the protagonist of his prison novel *White Man's Justice, Black Man's Grief* "Chester Hines."[74] Himes most famously devoted himself to detective fiction in the late 1950s and early 1960s, and exploited the genre to rationalize black violence as a response to a racially repressive environment.[75] He also wrote several autobiographical tracts in the early 1970s that addressed his transformative experiences as a criminal, prisoner, and finally writer.[76] While Himes's work was being released by more mainstream "white" presses (particularly after his popularity soared in the late 1960s), both Slim and Goines were published by Holloway House.[77] Based in LA, Holloway was *the* independent publishing house for inner-city writers. Holloway nurtured such authors, helping them to overpower the plight of the criminal through the art of (semi-autobiographical) writings.

Authors such as Goines and Slim set the stage for contemporary gang memoirs to burst onto the literary scene by proving the popularity of fiction addressing life in America's ghettos. Though the tropes and form of these "black experience novels" (as Holloway marketed them), seem to be recycled by the gangsta memoirist of the early 1990s, the original versions remain popular.[78] These earlier authors are still well-liked among juvenile readers and available in high school libraries across California.[79] One high school librarian I interviewed referred to Goines's and Slim's texts as "African American popular fiction" while her colleague deemed them "ghetto or urban fiction."[80] Both agreed such texts were "full of sex, drugs, violence, very racy and extremely popular."[81] Yet despite setting the standard for generic black gangster writing, such authors did not specifically engage with contemporary street gangs as their primary subject.

There was another extremely important literary precursor to the emergence of gang memoirs. Over a period of three years up to 1992, while the movie *Malcolm X* was being made, sales of *The Autobiography of Malcolm X* increased 300 percent.[82] Gangsta rappers were already reporting on the story of the politicized black power hero whose memoir was originally published in 1965. African American interest in Malcolm X and his message was revived during the conservative Reagan presidency. Rapper Ice Cube, for example, frequently referred to Malcolm X, while Tupac often referenced the black power era.[83] Boosted by the publicity surrounding Spike Lee's film, *The Autobiography of Malcolm X* was the bestselling paperback book during the Christmas 1992 sales period. The memoir renewed an awareness of and fascination with the prison narrative genre that included works by Eldridge Cleaver and George Jackson and that had been so popular in the late 1960s and early 1970s.

Such earlier prison narratives were a significant influence on Shakur, Williams, and Rodriguez. Shakur admits in *Monster* to being "stunned" when he learns of his parallels to George Jackson, whose prison letters, *Soledad Brother*, were published in 1970.[84] Williams details in *Blue Rage* his reading of the dictionary in a way reminiscent of Malcolm X in *The Autobiography of Malcolm X*.[85] Williams and Shakur draw comparison with earlier prison writers due to their incarcerated status and, like Rodriguez, they are authors originating from the bottom of society with no education. Rodriguez did not publish from prison but similarly takes inspiration from prison authors or those who have experienced prison. Piri Thomas's *Down These Mean Streets* (1967) was cited as a primary influence in *Always Running*.[86] Such referencing sparks comparisons between the two groups of authors, in which earlier prison memoirs can be seen as literary precursors to contemporary street gang memoirs. Though the three gang memoirists do not pay specific homage to Goines and Slim, there is arguably a richer provenance to the gangsta memoir than just prison writings from the civil rights era. Perhaps the distinctive character of contemporary gang memoirs can be seen in literary terms as a hybrid of the prison narrative legacy and "true crime" urban fiction.

The Autobiography of Malcolm X was not the only success story among minorities in the literary scene of the early 1990s. The year leading up to the release of *Monster* and *Always Running* produced bestsellers from other African American authors including Toni Morrison, Alice Walker, and Terry McMillan.[87] According to *Book Industry Trends 1993*, booksellers were recognizing the growing Latino population of the United States and increasing their numbers of Spanish books.[88] Despite the general recession of the late 1980s and early 1990s, the publishing industry thrived, with two hundred book superstores opening in 1992.[89] The industry's optimism was further fueled by the election of President Clinton in 1993. Clinton, an avid book fan, was expected to encourage the expansion of the book market and increase library revenues. The trend for diverse multicultural projects continued through early 1993 with the popularity of Maya Angelou, Morrison receiving the Nobel Prize in Literature, and the founding of the American Writers of Color Literary Agency.

Additional trends in the publishing world at this time paved the way for *Monster* and *Always Running* to be released in 1993. In April 1993 an article in *Publishers Weekly* noted how "true crime" books saturated the literary market in the early 1980s and explored why the genre continued to be extremely popular.[90] True crime stories are generally assumed to be biographical rather than autobiographical, for example secondhand accounts of infamous serial killers, but the nature of the genre offers insight as to why gang memoirs are alluring. *Publishers Weekly* claimed "publishers and booksellers agree that psychological insight into the minds of killers, some rational explanation for monstrous behavior, and the fallout of such crimes on the community in which they occur are the strongest components of the genre."[91] Gang memoirs satisfy similar voyeuristic impulses, with protagonists justifying their passionate and aggressive behavior and discussing the impact of gangs on the ghetto. Violent gang memoirs thus fulfilled public reading demand for sensationalized crime.

When Clinton was elected, America was in shock over the beating of Rodney King in March 1991 and the LA riots in April 1992 that resulted from the acquittal of the accused police officers. Both Mexican and African American gang memoirists took advantage of these riots. Alex Alonso, a gang expert and founder of an online book club dedicated to urban culture, claimed that such texts are often quietly signed or released to little acclaim.[92] According to Alonso they often become well-known later, following adverse events. He cited the example of the riots aiding the popularity of *Monster* and the execution of Williams encouraging sales of *Blue Rage*. According to Quinn, general paradoxes can be viewed with regard to gangsta rap: "The ironies run deep: these artists turned the very social costs of urban poverty, violence, and social isolation into assets"; the idea that "horrible living conditions, and above all LA's brand of urban crisis, actually lent themselves to dramatization and exploitation."[93] Both *Monster* and *Always Running* address the riots in their prefaces and epilogues, using the 1992 uprising to frame their life stories.

Rodriguez was the first of the three memoirists to secure a publishing contract, although Shakur's memoir would be released first in 1993. Rodriguez wrote throughout the 1980s, finally being signed by Curbstone in July 1991. In the early 1980s Rodriguez decided to novelize his life story, only to receive rejections from twenty-two publishing houses.[94] The text only gained attention among publishers when he rewrote the book as a memoir rather than fiction. In one of many rejection letters that Rodriguez received from publishers in the mid-1980s, Bantam House informed him that they had released their current "quota" of Latino books and would not be undertaking any more for ten years.[95] When Rodriguez finally secured a book deal, Curbstone was a small, non-profit press that dealt with social subjects, human rights, and cultural issues.[96] It was familiar with the author, having already published some of his poetry.

Gangsta rap, ghetto films, and the media coverage of gangs were dominated in the late 1980s and early 1990s by African American artists and
producers, despite the successes of a few Mexican Americans such as rapper Kid Frost and the group Aztlan Underground. A few other Latino rap
artists also were commercial triumphs, including Mellow Man Ace and
Cypress Hill.[97] Frost's hits suggested there was some appetite for Mexican
American barrio tales and thus room for Mexican American artists to cash
in.[98] Edward James Olmos's film *American Me* (1992) was the first block-
buster to highlight Chicano gang life. *American Me* takes its name from
Beatrice Griffiths's 1948 text, which offers insight into early-twentieth-
century Mexican American history, depicting how the gang lifestyle in LA
was already entrenched.[99] Despite this longstanding history of Mexican
American gangs, popular culture trends of the late 1980s and early 1990s
manifested a clear favoritism for African American tales of the 'hood. To
some degree this rationalizes the attitude of Bantam House and others
who initially failed to see the lucrative potential of *Always Running*.

Although the stereotype of a California gang member is often an African American, recent studies have verified that LA's Latino gangs in the
late 1980s and early 1990s were greater in number than their African
American counterparts.[100] Notwithstanding the huge numbers of Latino
gangbangers, the racial profiling of Operation Hammer demonstrates the
way public imagination has remained fixated on the black gangbanger. In
an interview, Rodriguez spoke adamantly about "the urgent need for my
book" from a Latino viewpoint.[101] Rodriguez was concerned that media
coverage and literature ignored the plight of Latinos in gangs as well as
ghetto life more generally.[102] He claims "this story had to be told" because
"it's the first major account of the Chicano gang experience from an actual
participant."[103] Mexican Americans similarly experienced life in LA as
marginalized residents throughout the 1980s, so it was surprising that in
discussions of the 1992 riots Latinos should be omitted, particularly when
they were the largest minority group among the 18,000 arrested.[104] At
the time of the riots, the media coverage framed events as black/white,
interviewing solely African Americans as authentic authorities on the
occurrences in the inner city, and rendering Latinos voiceless. The media
coverage of these riots later came under extensive criticism for under-
representing the Latino contribution, including Cholo involvement in the
gang truce.[105]

An article in *Publishers Weekly* in December 1992 entitled "In aftermath
of LA riots, a lively diversity of voices" claims Curbstone went "all out"

for *Always Running* with a 7,000-copy hardcover printing and a national book tour that was unprecedented for such a small press.[106] The article acknowledges that it is difficult to ascertain solutions to racial tensions in the post-uprising period, but believes that "if understanding diversity is key to relieving ethnic and social tension, book publishing is doing its part to reflect a wide spectrum of opinion on just what happened in LA."[107] Such optimism is counterbalanced by Susan Faludi, writing for the alternative *Los Angeles Weekly*, who believes that this publishing industry was simply "eager for a piece of the marketable LA riots drama."[108] Whether for conscientious or profitable reasons, publishers proved their sensitivity to social and minority issues and readiness to exploit real-life drama. In an interview with Rodriguez, the memoirist joked that his friend accused him of starting the rebellion as a means of publicizing *Always Running*. Rodriguez disclosed that his contract had in fact been signed prior to the uprising in April 1992, but acknowledged that *Always Running* was released at a particularly appropriate point in social history: "the LA riots opened the door to my book . . . they came at just the right time."[109]

As Rodriguez was in the midst of negotiating his Curbstone contract in 1991, journalist Leon Bing released a book on the Crips and the Bloods.[110] Bing's short biographical accounts of street gang life, which usually included firsthand interviews with gang members, began to appear in newspapers and journals nationwide in the late 1980s.[111] She played a crucial role in instigating *Monster* and paving the way for written gang memoirs. Her book, *Do or Die*, became an instant bestseller in 1991 even though she was writing about a subject "before it was fashionable [in literature]."[112] The subtitle for *Do or Die* was compelling: "For the first time, members of America's most notorious teenage gangs—the Crips and the Bloods—speak for themselves." A chapter was dedicated to Shakur, interviewed by Bing while incarcerated, and his brother Lil' Monster. Shakur featured alone on the cover photograph of the text (see photo insert). Shakur pays homage to Bing in *Monster*'s acknowledgments for "writing about us when it was unpopular to do so," referring to the negative coverage that gangs were receiving in the press at that time.[113]

Bing subsequently introduced the still-imprisoned Shakur to William Broyles, a journalist who was seeking gang members from South Central for a television pilot. The program was never commissioned but Broyles saw the literary potential in Shakur, encouraging him to start writing his memoirs. Shakur claims: "believe it or not, as it is printed is how it was written. One draft, no rewrites," though he did have an editor who visited him in prison to go through the manuscript with him page by page.[114] Broyles was responsible for initial drafts being published in *Esquire* in April 1993 and instigating publishing interest in the whole text. While Broyles believed he had the only draft of *Monster*, Shakur quietly sent his manuscript elsewhere and a bidding war ensued before Atlantic Monthly Press emerged the victor. Atlantic had merged the previous year with Grove Press, which had an established reputation for publishing the work of radical political thinkers (including a collection of Malcolm X's speeches in 1969). When Shakur finally signed the formal contract in November 1992, Atlantic Press was deemed "a hip, independent publishing house."[115] Shakur explains "I just felt they [Atlantic] would allow me to express my point of view."[116] The substantial deal which Shakur himself negotiated with Atlantic (a $150,000 advance with the promise of additional payments of at least $100,000) was over double the amount Bing received for *Do or Die*.[117] Though gang memoirs can be deemed a distinct form of cultural production in themselves, there is also a need to recognize some degree of hip hop cultural entrepreneurialism more generally at play.

At the Frankfurt Book Fair in late 1992, publisher Morgan Entrekin of Atlantic Press announced that he had purchased the rights for a memoir by an incarcerated LA gang member. Excited interest spread throughout the exhibitors.[118] Curiosity about *Monster* was said to have eclipsed Madonna's infamous book *Sex*, as well as the latest offerings from bestselling authors John Clancy and Stephen King.[119] Within two days, seven publishers in varying countries had purchased the foreign rights to Shakur's memoirs, praising themselves for spotting a "culturally important work."[120] Like Horowitz, one of the original literary agents to view *Monster* defended this commotion, insisting that "we see so much of the violence of the American inner city; now here's a voice that comes from inside that can explain it to us."[121] Such justification echoed the demand for personalized gang tales rather than merely a book on gangs—as prompted by Bing—and also makes explicit connection between media interest in gangs and marketability of gang memoirs.

The memoir genre is encouraged by publishers who are working within an American tradition that autobiography sells. From Benjamin Franklin to modern-day sports stars, memoirs have regularly topped nonfiction bestselling lists. Genre can certainly function as a commercial device, for instance being used as a labeling method in bookstores.[122] Publishers interested in street gang tales are aware that life writing can be lucrative. It was only after Rodriguez reworked the text as an autobiographical account that he secured a publisher. Similarly, when Shakur informed his publisher, Morgan Entrekin, that he wanted to focus his book on the history and development of contemporary gangs, Entrekin specified that Shakur should persevere with an autobiographical approach. In author correspondence with Shakur, he classified his book as "social anthropology/sociology."[123] But Entrekin protested: "I'm not interested in gangs. I'm interested in you."[124] Shakur wanted to use the title *Can't Stop, Won't Stop*, but Entrekin fought for the usage of *Monster: The Autobiography of an LA Gang Member*, highlighting the power relations at play between author and publisher. Though Shakur could exercise independence in his initial search for a lucrative book deal, once signed, the struggle over the memoir's title stresses the dominance of the publisher. Entrekin's use of "autobiography" in the title demonstrated keen awareness that the success of such a text depends on its engagement with the autobiographical genre, reflecting the popularity of gangsta rap because of its (supposedly) true-to-life anecdotes in first-person form.

Like Curbstone, Atlantic used the gloomy social setting of 1992 to its benefit. Though Shakur had sent a chapter of his work to Broyles in 1991, it was following the 1992 riots that he secured a publishing contract and interest in his memoirs suddenly escalated. Entrekin was so assured of Shakur's prowess as a ghetto spokesperson and the sure success of his memoir in this atmosphere, that he originally announced he would publish *Monster* on the first anniversary of the riots (April 1993).[125] The release date was later pushed back by a few months.

Unlike *Monster*, the memoirs of Stanley "Tookie" Williams did not create an initial publishing furor. Like Rodriguez, Williams struggled to secure a publisher. On death row since 1981, the infamous former gang-banger began reading and writing in the early 1990s, encouraged by his friend Barbara Becnel. Becnel contacted Williams in 1993 when she was researching a book about the history of the Crips. She soon became a regular visitor and abandoned her initial research plans to help Williams fulfill his desire to promote gang peace. Together they published their first texts in 1996, a series of anti-gang books aimed at schoolchildren learning to read.[126] The following year Williams released his first independent book *Life in Prison*, which targeted young adults, deploying shock tactics to scare them away from prison.[127]

Becnel revealed that the way they collaborated on book projects evolved over time.[128] Just as my correspondence with Shakur divulged the protracted process of revising the manuscript little by little in prison with his editor, Becnel stressed a painstakingly slow manner of writing. Becnel disclosed that she would discuss the outline of a book with Williams and he then would draft the text one chapter at a time. Each chapter would be read over the telephone to Becnel, who would record and transcribe the chapters. Becnel would edit the manuscripts and return them by post for approval.[129] This raises questions as to why Becnel could not merely pick up the written drafts. Both stories are to some degree mythically founded to make the process more deliciously "covert." The production processes of Shakur and Becnel/Williams were hindered by prison and such tales serve to emphasize the "authenticity" discourse of such memoirs.

In 1998 Becnel encouraged Williams to start writing his life history; six years later his adult memoirs appeared, the delay a result of his struggle to find a willing publishing house. She stressed that by this stage the work was written entirely on his own and that she merely offered brief revisions: "Over the years, Stan learned to love words and developed his own style of writing and use of language."[130] Many publishers were reluctant to associate with Williams because of his controversial death row status (he had experienced similar problems with his earlier texts).[131] Eventually Williams suggested that Becnel establish Damamli Ltd. in 2004 for the sole purpose of releasing *Blue Rage*. He chose the Swahili word meaning "beautiful vision" as a title for the publishing house and its mission statement reflected a distinct outlook on William's death row status: "All books and other media from this company will be dedicated to and defined by the notion that redemption is possible—that adults and kids can—create real personal and spiritual growth."[132] Damamli only issued the memoir in a paperback format, aware that the California prison system banned inmates from receiving hardback books.

Damamli included an email address at the front of *Blue Rage*, also listed on the website that Williams and Becnel had established (www.tookie .com), prompting a flood of responses from readers of the memoir. It is difficult to ascertain the target audience and exact readership of such memoirs, which, while not a primary intention of this book, are relevant. Some of my interviewees, such as gang scholar Malcolm Klein, believe the books were written for black and Mexican youth.[133] Others, such as gang expert Alex Alonso, argue they were intended for European and Australian audiences (implying a commercial impetus).[134] Rodriguez commented in an interview that he wanted to make his memoir "literary enough for anyone who knows literary works can say it has some, but also accessible so some kid down the street can read it."[135]

The email responses provided Becnel with some idea of who was consuming *Blue Rage*: "the readership is very diverse. It's composed of students at the high school and college level, as well as parents, teachers, law enforcement officers and librarians. The readers are black, white, Hispanic and Asian. Finally, the readers are from all over the world, particularly from Australia, Britain and Canada."[136] This multiracial and mixed-class audience of the 1990s and 2000s is vastly different from the 1960s and 1970s, when Goines and Slim initially found a blacks-only audience.[137] Nonetheless the unwavering presence of the gang memoirs in libraries at schools across South Central and East LA, as well as being taught in many of those classrooms, reminds us that there is a significant number of young black and Mexican readers.

Once *Blue Rage* had been released and shown a certain degree of popularity among its variety of readers, it was commercially logical for a larger publisher to step in and reap further benefits. Having sold 10,000 copies of *Blue Rage*, Damamli struggled to cope with the huge surge in demand for the memoir following Williams's execution in 2005. Having been asked by Williams to ensure that his memoir received wide distribution and having been named executor of his estate, Becnel sold the posthumous rights to Touchstone, an offshoot of Simon & Schuster, in 2007. Becnel believed the larger publishing house had a similar agenda to Damamli's for publishing *Blue Rage*, claiming the two companies both "saw Stan's autobiography as a modern classic that would be read by students and adults for many, many years."[138] Becnel confirmed that she did not have final input on the marketing and design for the Simon & Schuster cover, though she did fight to prevent the company from using a picture of Williams in handcuffs for the newest edition of the memoir (see photo insert).[139]

In 1994 Touchstone issued the first of many paperback editions of *Always Running*. According to Rodriguez, "eight big publishers initially bid for the paperback rights—the rebellion and all this attention spiked the sales of the hardcover and this meant [they] could do a paperback."[140] Rodriguez received an initial payment of $60,000, a sum significantly larger than he had received in 1991 from Curbstone.[141] In 1994 an article in the *Washington Post* addressed the contemporary climate of the publishing industry and its treatment of African Americans, raising accusations of exploitation. The journalist criticized publishers for being most interested in texts such as *Monster* and former gang member Nathan McCall's *Makes Me Wanna Holler*.[142] The article expressed disappointment that publishers correlate black writers with tales of criminality. Such concerns over representational responsibility did not discourage Penguin Books, who would rerelease *Monster* in 1994. Penguin marketed the book along similar lines to Atlantic, keeping the same image of Shakur on the cover that had initially been taken for the cover of *Do or Die*.

Since *Monster* was published in 1993, the publishing industry and the reading public have continued to seek out books that describe from first-person perspectives the ghettos and barrios and their gangbanging residents. Other bestselling gang memoirs in addition to *Monster, Always Running, Blue Rage,* and *Makes Me Wanna Holler* include those by Geoffrey Canada (1996), Mona Ruiz (1997), Snoop Dogg and Bill Lee (1999), Reymundo Sanchez (2000 and 2003), Colton Simpson and Terrell Wright (2005), and DaShaun "Jiwe" Morris (2008).[143]

Literary scholar David Brumble has begun to define a body of gang memoirs. He cites twenty-seven authors who should be classified together, including the contemporary street gang memoirists mentioned in this chapter.[144] However, Brumble's bibliography also incorporates prison narratives from the 1960s and 1970s, which suggests that 1993 may be seen as a point of *re*-emergence of gang memoirs.[145] From this perspective, it could be argued that the street gang memoirs that appeared from 1993 onwards sprung from the juncture between the historical popularity of the prison memoir and the new demand for gangsta cultural stories. The latter was proven by gangsta rap and ghetto films and intensified at a particular historical moment thanks to the Rodney King riots.

The continuing demand for gangsta stories in pop culture is evident. A docudrama about *Monster* entitled "The Pen and The Gun" was released in 2009 as part of the Black Entertainment Television (BET) Channel's popular *American Gangster* series, while Shakur is in negotiations for a major motion picture deal.[146] Shakur currently resides in solitary confinement at Pelican Bay State Prison, from where he released a novel entitled *T.H.U.G. L.I.F.E.* in August 2008.[147] *Blue Rage* was made into a high-profile television movie in 2004 (starring Hollywood celebrity Jamie Foxx), while Williams formed the subject of the first episode of the *American Gangster* series in 2006. Rodriguez has also been offered significant sums for the film rights to *Always Running.*[148] A 2009 documentary, *Crips and Bloods: Made in America,* explores the growth of contemporary street gangs through the eyes of former gang members, demonstrating an ongoing fascination with the subject.[149] Though gangsta rap is often considered to have reached its zenith in the mid-1990s, artists like The Game, 50 Cent, and Eminem are still signing multi-million-dollar record deals and topping the *Billboard* charts.[150]

Just like the earlier deployment of gangsta in popular music and film, these autobiographical narratives that first appeared in 1993 provided gripping insight into life as a resident in the ghettos and barrios of LA. The Mexican history of social struggles in LA is in fact longer than its African American counterparts. Life in the so-called "City of Angels" was not easy for Mexican residents in the peak periods of immigration early in the twentieth century, and Mexican and African Americans towards the end of the century. The predicament of minorities in LA at this time served as evidence of the urban malaise that would blight barrios and ghettos across the country and spawn gangs and later gangsta culture. There is some irony that this city with its difficult socio-economic circumstances could simultaneously be known for the vast entertainment system that was significantly responsible for producing and promoting gangsta culture. Despite some disputes in their work, gang scholars tend to agree that LA has a gang problem unique in size and nature.

As well as detailing gang styling and the reasons for gang membership, the memoirs include exciting anecdotes of warring with other gangs and riveting tales of altercations with the police. Like gangsta rappers before them, the narrators of these memoirs voice resentment at the criminal justice system and their marginalization in contemporary American society. These artists, both musicians and authors, turned their negative experiences into positive resources. Despite popular culture's initial preference for African American gangsta tales, publishing houses and other entertainment industries happily incorporated both Mexican and African American slants on the gang lifestyle. Their experiences were converted into cultural form as part of a larger popular penchant for gangsta that could also be witnessed in films and the news.

Chapter Two

HOMEBOYS BETWEEN HARD COVERS
Scholarly Approaches to the Study of Gang Memoirs

This book will examine the emergence of these memoirs as a popular cultural phenomenon and a commercial production trend while also considering their complex textual politics in terms of both theme and form.[1] Furthermore, I intend to explore how gang memoirs are constructed in the media and interpreted by audiences. In an attempt to understand the many aspects of these under-studied memoirs, this book takes an interdisciplinary approach. The theoretical frameworks which have informed my research can be divided into three (sometimes overlapping) areas: scholarly debates in the field of autobiography theory (form, narration, identity); debates in the field of the cultural studies of race (representational politics); and, scholarship on both media reception and reader response.

In broad terms, the main field of this project is cultural studies. This chapter will reflect on some of the early but still relevant work in this discipline and will also encompass recent interventions and developments. The discipline of cultural studies is often identified as being split between structuralism (operations of discursive power and constraints on individuals) and culturalism (looking at the practices of everyday people to understand how they might comprehend and ultimately overcome structural constraints). Structuralism, according to cultural scholar James Procter, is "concerned with the linguistic structures that underpin, enable and govern meaning," while culturalism is quite simply "a less exclusive, more democratic understanding of culture."[2]

The structuralist/culturalist divide has already been identified in gangsta culture, including gangsta rap and ghetto action films.[3] On the one hand gangsta can be deemed groundbreaking, even revolutionary; on the other, such culture can be critiqued as co-opted and commercial. Rap, for example, can be seen to give voice to and therefore empower the marginalized, or conversely as exploiting black criminal stereotypes for profit. These competing paradigms that underpin the discipline of cultural studies are both in evidence in this study and provide an organizing principle for this chapter. Culturalism is a more obvious fit with this project because these are, at least in ostensible terms, memoirs of the oppressed and the subcultural. However, the structuralist constraints of the memoirs—of their emergence, genre, and media reception—are also very much in evidence in contrast to the culturalist, grassroots dimensions of the books.

Autobiography theory is naturally central to this study into gang memoirs. In particular the contemporary turn toward the marginalized forms a valuable part of my conceptual approach to the gang memoirs. Though scholarly work exploring memoirs as a literary form is vast, I will highlight the specific formal dimensions of memoirs (narrative personas, identities, and trajectories) that are imperative for studying Mexican and African American autobiography. Many diverse theories of autobiography help to assist this project due to the experiential versus formal nature of gang memoirs. Memoirs by definition are essentially based on practical experience, and most of the scholarly studies of these memoirs have been empirical (that is, sociological) rather than formal (textual). Yet I contend that the formal features and dimensions of these particular memoirs are equally crucial and that consequently there is a need to acknowledge a variety of theoretical approaches.

Contemporary autobiography theorists note that autobiography is everywhere.[4] Modern-day developments such as the internet and email mean that private lives are conducted in public spaces. Prison autobiographical writings can now be found on the internet (consider Stanley Williams's website), in magazines, radio and television shows, rap lyrics, and advertisements.[5] New topics for autobiography scholarship have also included reasons for lying, controversially suggesting that all autobiographers are unreliable narrators simply because all humans are naturally liars.[6] According to Timothy Dow Adams, the audience reads with the assumption that the complete truth is not feasible and thus lying in autobiography is rendered impossible.[7] Furthermore, there have been ethical dilemmas in contemporary autobiography criticism. As Paul Eakin asks, are memoirs now offering *too* many graphic details?[8] Recent life writing offers these new materials for analysis, but Laura Marcus argues that, in fact, contemporary theory is similar to older criticism regardless of con-tent. According to Marcus, both old and new schools of thought main-tain that autobiography is an unstable genre because of the complicated relationships between self and world, literature and history, fact and fic-tion, subject and object.[9] These are some of the most compelling ques-tions in cultural studies more broadly. Critics differ as to whether, and to what extent, autobiography acts as a means of compromise between these oppositions, or whether life writing fuels such conflicts.

Scholarly studies of contemporary autobiography reflect critical con-cerns prevalent in cultural studies that emerged in the late 1980s. Under the terms of reference for so-called "cultural populism," cultural studies became even more concerned at this time with issues of "difference." The field had previously focused on the experiences of the working class as a site where society's structures of domination could be explored, particu-larly in British cultural studies and the research that stemmed from the Centre for Contemporary Cultural Studies (CCCS). By the 1980s cultural studies in Britain similarly began to discuss the oppression of minor-ity groups. In line with this new focus on marginalized people (women, gays and lesbians, racial minorities), the scholarly study of autobiography turned its attention to the sheer cultural and political power of life writing.

The "culture wars" of the United States in the early 1990s stemmed from these marginalized groups realizing the potential power of their own agency and establishing their own politics. Bitter political debates raged over issues including feminism, gay activism, AIDS awareness, anti-racism, and multiculturalism. These cultural conflicts were set in opposi-tion to structuralist lines of thought, whereby structuralism showed the limited parameters of individual agency. Cultural studies began to affirm the notion of "otherness," becoming an academic site to explore the ways in which cultural texts either promoted oppression (including sexism, homophobia, and racism) or resisted and struggled against it. This new cultural front line, with its politics of difference, encouraged critical dis-cussions about previously invisible identities. Within a memoir, the author could metamorphose into an alternative identity, coming out as feminist, gay, disabled, or ex-criminal, while placing their individual experiences in the wider context of women's, gay, or prisoners' rights. Scholarly work on autobiography explored these new materials.[10]

As the term "globalization" came to the forefront of cultural stud-ies in the late 1980s, literary studies were also nurturing a new term that would appear regularly in contemporary discussions of autobiography:

"postcolonialism." Interest in giving voice to the oppressed (consistent with a culturalist approach) that was developing in the United States also was happening internationally, becoming fertile areas for analysis. Postcolonial criticism notes how oppressive states often discouraged or even prevented suppressed groups from writing. The intent of postcolonial literature to resist such oppression, and its confidence in doing so, conforms with contemporary cultural studies' fascination with the ways in which marginalized groups voice and valorize their experiences. Postcolonial writings tackled subjects of unequal political, economic, and cultural relations as well as ongoing processes of resistance and reconstruction—issues that are similarly raised in gang memoirs. Postcolonial literature often struggles with questions of identity living between the old, native world and the invasive new culture, notions that have captivated postcolonial scholars like Edward Saïd and Gayatri Spivak.[11] As cultural scholars Andrew Milner and Jeff Browitt explain, "the argument commenced not so much with a celebration of subordinate identity as with a critique of the rhetoric of cultural dominance."[12] Like scholarly criticism that stemmed from the cultural wars in the United States, global postcolonial criticism presented new intellectual questions of marginal voices and hybrid identities.

One leading form of narrative expression in both contemporary postcolonial and minority memoirs is the conversion trajectory. Historically, conversion narratives concerned spiritual as well as material growth dating back to Benjamin Franklin, in which the subject tended to be in search of a transformed or redeemed self.[13] Contemporary conversion narratives involve subjugated people, frequently young, starting as oppressed and ignorant and coming into awareness and empowerment. The conversion narrative is thus used to exercise what Eakin deems the "expressive freedom" that was previously denied to members of oppressed and silenced groups.[14] However, the trajectory of conversion raises narrative dangers that, according to Marcus, primarily revolve around the problem that in the process of conversion, "the present, 'reformed' self will be overwhelmed by the past it ostensibly seeks to put behind itself."[15]

More specifically, the narrative form of conversion is the popular style for oppressed groups such as prisoners, as exhibited among prison narratives that stemmed from the 1960s and 1970s. It is a style the gang memoirs in question have in common (especially *Monster* and *Blue Rage*, whose authors were writing while incarcerated). Life writing by incarcerated authors such as Eldridge Cleaver and James Carr that were released in the wake of *The Autobiography of Malcolm X* in 1965 often detail the narrators' lives before and after their incarceration.[16] Contemporary gang memoirs concentrate not merely on the narrators' experiences of prison but also on life before criminality and after their prison conversion. Prison scholars like Brian Jarvis argue that *The Autobiography* identifies Malcolm X's imprisonment as his formative experience, while cultural scholar Robin Kelley believes that it is X's pre-prison years that are the most crucial.[17] Kelley contends that although *The Autobiography of Malcolm X* is often viewed as a prison narrative whereby conversion occurs while incarcerated, the importance of his text lies outside prison. For Kelley, it is the early, illicit stories X offers that are "not a detour but an essential element on his road to radicalization."[18] Kelley's interpretation of the conversion narrative offers an important twist on traditional scholarship surrounding such trajectories; the importance of this attitude will be witnessed in the textual readings of gang memoirs.

The conversion arc sparks related narrative discussions of persona and identity. The subjugated histories of Mexican and African Americans more generally also lend themselves to such narrativization. There is much autobiography criticism that explores the oppression of these two groups and their subsequent political postcolonial-style awakenings. Since its inception in the slave narrative form, African American autobiography has been used as a means of both asserting individual identity and addressing sociopolitical realities of the collective black experience, a practice that can similarly be applied to contemporary prison narratives. According to Henry Louis Gates Jr., the "narrated, descriptive 'I' was put into service as a literary form to posit both the individual 'I' of the black author and the collective 'I' of the race."[19] Autobiography offered the silenced slave and the imprisoned gang member a chance to voice their own unique experience and speak on behalf of all those sharing a common identity and experience (within the institutions of slavery or prison). These scholarly approaches carry potential limitations, for not all African Americans were slaves (or indeed prisoners) and slave experiences varied greatly. Nonetheless, cultural studies of gangsta rap have referenced Gates's "I," paying heed to the form of the music and the content.[20] Eithne Quinn aptly elucidates the importance of such direct accounts, not simply because narrators had themselves lived through such ordeals, but moreover "because this perspective enhanced reader identification, thus personalizing the institutionalized violence and exploitation of the slavery system."[21]

Autobiography theorist Genaro Padilla prompts parallel debates surrounding Mexican American autobiography. Padilla expands on Gates's

"I" concept by arguing that Mexican American autobiography, just as much as African American, functions as representative of both individual and collective experiences.[22] Questions of identity within Mexican American autobiography criticism often have been prompted by authors drawing on traditions from both sides of the border. Padilla argues that the resulting narrative becomes a cultural battleground, predominantly manifested in language usage.[23] Within these Mexican American narrative battles, English and Spanish (representing the American/Mexican narrative personas) wrestle for ultimate control of the author's identity. Memoirists have voiced their struggle to find a comfortable position between the two languages and cultures (a problem similarly examined by gang scholar Diego Vigil in Cholo gang identity).[24] As Marcus claims, this "trying-on" of alternative identities is central to ethnic autobiographies, helping to shape personal and political narrative identities. Marcus's concerns with autobiographical instability and oppositions can be witnessed in her discussions of vernacular, in which she claims language can be either "a magical instrument of reconciliation" or a "dangerous double agent," moving precariously between two opposing cultural forces.[25]

Within African American autobiography, the slavery (spiritual) conversion narrative and the prison (criminal) conversion narrative have sparked lengthy discussions surrounding evolving identities that are not innate. Gang autobiographies often draw attention to the constructed nature of identity while at the same time laying claim to an unmediated and authentic vision. This book will apply traditional discussions of autobiographical conversions and identities to contemporary gang memoirs and consider alternative readings of African American gang identities as presented by literary scholar David Brumble. Brumble engages with mythical stories like Beowulf and Achilles to examine contemporary gang memoirs.[26] He draws links between these legendary warrior cultures and contemporary gang subcultures, arguing that issues of identity are prevalent in both. In *Monster*, he contends, this warrior identity is particularly expressed through language and narrative features. Brumble's essays, offering a comparative analysis of canonical versus "ephemeral" literature, serve as an example of cultural studies' challenge to orthodox parameters of traditional academic discipline.

Autobiography theory traditionally has focused on thematics, but Brumble explores the formal structures and linguistic detail of *Monster* in depth. His emphasis on style reflects recent trends in autobiography criticism that have also shifted from theme to form. The autobiography scholar, Herbert

Leibowitz, argues that it is in fact literary style and technique rather than content that form the crucial interpretive link to understanding an autobiography. In order to comprehend the text, the reader must become a "secret agent" or "literary sleuth" who analyzes the "slippery clues" that an author leaves behind.[27] Leibowitz classifies different elements of style (diction, syntax, rhythm, and form) and states that the reader must inspect the evidence, arguing that differences in narrators' temperaments will determine discrepancies in style. Memoirists thus expose themselves to the reader through style, even when trying to be reticent. This exploration of gang memoirs will place emphasis on stylistic features to understand the memoirists' social, political, and cultural messages.

It is important to draw brief attention to my use of other forms of gangsta culture as a point of comparison and reference. There are clear analogies and divergences between gangsta rap, ghetto film, and gang memoirs. Of particular importance is the similarity of content across all three forms: violent tales of life among marginalized young men in the ghettos and barrios of LA. Rap and film scholarship is where most of the cultural debates on gangsta have occurred. Since these gang memoirs share many of the generic themes of gangsta culture, this body of analysis naturally informs my study. Yet this research contends that form is extremely important, and memoirs are vastly different from rap and film in structure and aesthetics. In his cultural study of gangsta rap, Robin Kelley is concerned with style and form more than content, just as autobiography criticism has shifted in focus from theme to form. Kelley explains, "What counts more than the story is the storytelling."[28] But if form carries the burden of the message, then can we equate different cultural forms so readily? At the very least, we need to note the advantages and limitations of engaging with gangsta rap and ghetto films, and their associated scholarship, as a model for discussing autobiography.

In addition to thematics, there are further parallels between gang memoirs and music or film on a formal level. Certainly, there is a shared narrative style of young gangsta versus "mature" rapper or writer. The conversion narrative energizes and organizes much rap and many memoirs (though it is more sustained in the latter). These shifting perspectives and identities, as well as the use of similar narrators or personas ("eye/I" ambivalence), are prevalent in all forms of gangsta culture. Like gang memoirs, most gangsta rap utilizes the first-person form.[29] This is integral to reinforcing the ghetto realness of the music, with its tales of poverty, police abuse, and gang warfare. The first-person perspective quite simply heightens the drama, particularly when the narrator is not merely a witness but an active participant. As the rap group the Geto Boys have explained, switching from "I saw" to "We did" makes their urban experiences more shocking, offensive, and memorable.[30]

Yet many rap songs are metaphorical—for example, in which the narrator fantasizes about a bloodbath of police officers or acted the role of murderous gangbanger eliminating entire rival gangs. While gangsta rappers do invite listeners to take their music as autobiographical, the clearly exaggerated stories and frequently mocking tone highlights the fact that, as Jon Pareles wrote in the *New York Times*, "Gangsta rap, for all its first-person machismo, is not a simple or naïve narrative form, and it's certainly not autobiography."[31] By comparison, written autobiography—like the contemporary street gang memoirs under scrutiny in this book—is founded on the premise of truth, even though (as we have seen thus far in this chapter) contemporary autobiography theorists have challenged the extent of that veracity. Despite crucial shared features, there are also profound differences between memoirs and music or film.

That rap has been the victim of censorship more so than film is perhaps surprising to the extent that visuals lend a sense of immediacy and authenticity to a text. Arguably, the filmic narrative is restricted by the ratings systems, in which studios often encourage directors to tailor violence sufficiently to gain an "R" rating (anything more restrictive makes the distribution of a film difficult). The cycle of ghetto action films did not spark as many complaints as gangsta rap; to some degree this fact serves as testament to the extent of the violence in rap.[32] As Pareles explains so succinctly, rap "prides itself on bluntness, and it doesn't provide consolation or tie up loose ends. Unlike action movies, the rap refuses to let listeners off the hook."[33] The content of gangsta rap and film, as well as their scholarship, remain important for my purposes. This book simultaneously recognizes the differences in cultural forms of gangsta, which provide important points of contrast for understanding the role of gang memoirs.

While the previous section dealt with issues of narrative identity, particularly in relation to ethnic autobiography and criticism, it is also necessary to consider the politics of identity in a periodized framework. Important questions over the politics of identity, both individual and collective, were raised during the Chicano and black civil rights movements of the 1960s and 1970s. These important decades spawned the contemporary prison literature that has prompted extensive scholarly research, essential for the study of gang memoirs.

Critical readings of Mexican American popular culture and representational responsibilities are not as exhaustive as their black equivalents. This is partly explained by the fact that black American history is arguably longer and more brutal than the Mexican experience and this has given rise to the circulation of many more high-profile narratives of oppression. Scholarly debate about African American autobiographical expression and other black cultural paradigms is consequently far more extensive than for Latino cultural expression. Furthermore, in contemporary cultural frameworks, the dominance of black theory stems from the inspiration fellow marginalized groups took from African Americans during the civil rights movement. The movement had vital consequences not just for blacks but for Mexican Americans, Native Americans, women, and gays, all of whom were motivated and encouraged by the effective model of black civil rights. The civil rights movement transformed the way subjugated African Americans saw themselves, with many varied groups engaging with the civil rights paradigm of collective identity and mobilization to claim their rights. Though Mexican American autobiography and its criticism has made a significant contribution to the canon, this project will logically be dominated by black approaches and black-specific criticism, much of which can be applied to other marginalized groups with similar histories of oppression.

Autobiography critic William Andrews claims that since the mid-1960s, spurred by the civil rights movement, African American autobiography and its criticism has shifted from an emphasis on bios (life) to autos (questions of the self).[34] Autobiography theorists and cultural studies scholars acknowledge that, in the United States in particular, racial identity politics were inextricably linked with the radical politics of both civil rights and the Chicano movements.[35] More than any other ethnic group in the United States, Mexican Americans have been given a multitude of identity labels including Hispanics, Latin Americans, Spanish Americans, Texicans, Mexicanos, Californios.[36] The "Chicano Generation" of the 1960s argued for shedding previous labels and pursuing a new identity and power characterized by militant and radical politics, rather than being assimilationist and accommodationist. Identity was becoming an antonym of difference.[37] Like black power, brown power promoted racial pride and self-determination, and questions over identity formed a fundamental part of a surging sense of racial nationalism.[38]

The term "identity politics" became popular in the late 1960s as a result of both black and brown protest movements. The notion that identity is inextricably linked with politics has been continually revisited and revised by contemporary autobiography studies. For instance Kenneth Mostern's *Autobiography and Black Identity Politics: Racialization in Twentieth Century America* argues that "identity" and "politics" are not independent variables: "solidarity always stands in the complicated relationship between the two."[39] His research includes *The Autobiography of Malcolm X* as a primary textual case study. The rise of the phrase "identity politics" coincided with the sudden increase in autobiographical literature appearing from American prisons. In 1965 as X was releasing his memoirs, Eldridge Cleaver, George Jackson, and James Carr were all drafting their own narratives.

My research adheres to a definition of contemporary American prison literature that was put forward by the most prominent commentator on prison literature. H. Bruce Franklin's *Prison Literature in America: The Victim as Criminal and Artist* is rightly considered a landmark work in prison studies. He identifies contemporary American prison literature as a body of work commencing with the publication of *The Autobiography of Malcolm X*.[40] This research will respect Franklin's classification and also engage with prison literature scholar Bell Gale Chevigny, as well as Auli Ek, Peter Caster, and Brian Jarvis, who have produced cultural readings of both literary and cinematic prison texts.[41] In a recent scholarly contribution, Caster argues that though Franklin and Ek are important entries in the field of critique of representations of imprisonment in American literature, analysis is still insufficient.[42] The work of these scholars suggests prison autobiography is no longer merely a subgenre of American autobiography and prison films are no longer a marginal categorization of action or crime films.[43] Prison texts are now an established genre, receiving critical attention in their own right.

Just as discussions of identity have a longstanding history in autobiography studies, prison scholars agree that issues of identity are prevalent in prison culture. Prisoners are deprived of names and identified instead by numbers and forced to conform to institutional regulations in which they all behave the same. Prison thus strips prisoners of their sense of self. Under such conditions it is difficult to identify "who am I?" Franklin deems it important to trace the historical development of this relationship between prison culture and identity. He considers the songs of slavery as an art of an imprisoned people, highlighting that the dominant political structures of both slavery and the contemporary prison system have quashed identity and resulted in artistic forms that attempt to liberate traditionally excluded voices.[44] The discussions of identity surrounding prison culture are important because gangsta culture is similarly preoccupied with issues of identity, as demonstrated in the memoirs through the use of monikers and gang affiliations. Moreover, prison culture itself is an integral part of the lifestyle of contemporary street gang members.

For Franklin, the most crucial period in the prison cultural history is the late 1960s and early 1970s. He argues that Malcolm X's *Autobiography* and subsequent prison narratives appeared as a result of the thriving black liberation movement.[45] Like Chevigny, Franklin spends much of his text detailing the changing history of prison policies and prison writings over the past forty years, changes that stem from these activist movements and broad-minded attitudes. During this time, political ideas were brought into prison while the common criminal inside was thrust into political activism.[46] Along with a growing prisoners' rights movement and encouragement of rehabilitative programs, there was huge interest in prisoners' writings. Malcolm X wrote alongside a whole generation of African Americans who were politicized while incarcerated, many of whom turned to the Nation of Islam and became black Muslims, inspired by the black nationalist movement that was thriving outside prison. Certainly, black power attracted criminals and the black underclass. Huey Newton was rumored to admire "brothers" like Eldridge Cleaver and Malcolm X who had served time in the penitentiary.[47] Since its inception, contemporary cultural studies has been likewise sensitive to political circumstance, focusing on the potential for powerful resistance in oppositional subcultures. Black nationalists of the 1960s and 1970s, like the urban youth subcultures of the 1950s and 1960s in Britain, can be seen as creating individualist identities by defining themselves against standard models, acting and looking different from those in the mainstream. In America, such oppositional identities easily thrived in the liberal atmosphere of the 1960s.

While I am interested in the genre of prison memoirs, I am more concerned with the politics of writing and of literacy itself that enabled the writing of these literary texts by incarcerated black and Mexican men. This includes the significance of prison, as addressed by Mostern. Mostern combines Jarvis's emphasis on the prison experience itself with Kelley's attention to X's pre-prison years. It is comprehensible that contemporary gang memoirs hold appeal for many readers on the basis of their firsthand access to an inaccessible street authenticity. Yet it can be argued that these accounts actually are involved in the construction of reality, which is not the same as being immediately authentic.

Mostern contends that X's criminal past endorses everything else that occurs thereafter; that his street life makes X a reliable narrator along the lines of "trust me because I represent your (actual or potential) untrustworthiness. I have known it and I have lived it."[48] The implication is that X's knowledge holds conviction because it is not institutionally based. The traditional site of erudition has been inverted: "While Malcolm Little stops looking to school as a place for learning, he continues to seek the locations of learning—indeed, *schools*—which, unlike the public school, are there to train him."[49] Mostern's seemingly paradoxical approach to questions of (criminal) authenticity, as well as his assertion that the prison is the most significant educational institution for X, is similarly important for my research.

By the 1980s, as the writing of prison memoirs was being suppressed by the prison authorities in accordance with Reagan's increasingly punitive attitude, contemporary prison scholars became more fascinated with the significant feat of writing itself. While autobiography criticism often supported the notion of the free agency of the individual (through the act of writing), prison literature suggested that individual experience was in fact always politically and culturally constrained. Ek, Jarvis, Chevigny, and Franklin all highlight the suppressive legislation of the 1980s that restricted prison writing, resulting in authors "smuggling out manuscripts" to publishers.[50] Such injunctions prompt immediate comparisons with the situation of slave narrators, for whom learning to read and write was an illegal act. The first political gesture of slaves within the Anglo-American literary tradition was often seen to be the very act of writing in view of such illegality.[51]

Moreover, the act of writing, in humanist tradition, demarcated the ultimate sign of difference between animal and human. As a result, writing became a potent means of resistance or even "a weapon" for both slave and prison narrators.[52] There is a huge amount of political power in literacy for slave narrators as well as prison authors, and prison literature scholars repeatedly return to the historical and cultural significance of slave narratives when discussing contemporary prison literature.[53]

As well as holding relevance with slave historians, prison literature scholars share with contemporary cultural scholars their fascination with the sheer political power of culture. Along these lines, culture is seen as political rather than artistic. In the words of cultural scholar

Francis Mulhern, culture becomes "a contested terrain, a space for politi-cal struggle."[54] In the 1970s cultural studies showed interest in the politics of cultural texts in relation to wider political influences. By the 1980s, as prisoners were being discouraged from writing by the authorities, con-temporary work in prison cultural studies reflected the domineering sys-tems at play both in prison and in wider societal structures. Gang memoirs follow the tendency of earlier prison narratives to critique (and therefore resist) dominant society whereby the narratives speak on behalf of those who have been victims of political injustices.

Franklin views prison literature as a window through which to view American society with its underclass and victims of discrimination.[55] In an author interview with Angela Davis discussing gang memoirs written from prison, she contended that these texts "offer us a different window into social realities."[56] Likewise, Kelley sees much gangsta rap as "a window into, and critique of, the criminalization of black youth."[57] Yet despite these attitudes, within scholarly studies of prison literature there is a distinct lack of critical engagement with gang memoirs as evidence of prison life, by victims of a racist judiciary or wider societal injustices. The exception to this rule is Ek's work, *Race and Masculinity in Contemporary Ameri-can Prison Narratives*. Similar to Jarvis, Ek offers critical discussions on the "business" of prisons, but is primarily concerned with how cultural forms mediate state power. Both scholars use literature and film as texts to explore punishment and the cultural responses to the American penal sys-tem. Jarvis stretches to a much longer timeline, while Ek focuses on con-temporary America, paying considerable attention to questions of black criminal representation. Ek admires Franklin's work for suggesting that prison narratives not only reflect changes in society but also "induce those changes by offering a window through which to look at American society, as if from the outside."[58] She then expands on Franklin's work by viewing issues of modern-day bias (race, class, gender) using gang literature as the porthole in one of her case studies.[59] I am interested in these approaches of prison scholars, tracing contexts into the text and culture itself.

By the time of the emergence of gangsta rap in the late 1980s and gang-sta memoirs in the early 1990s, the vehement people politics of the 1960s and 1970s that had spurred prison literature and African American and Chicano protest movements had dissipated. This notable waning in pro-test has been documented by black cultural scholars and seen as a partial explanation for the content of contemporary gangsta texts. In her study of gangsta rap, Quinn maintains that the thrust of her analysis is that the music's political energies "lay in the struggle to come to terms with an age in which there was a dramatic decline in popular protest politics, precisely for a community that had a vital protest history."[60] Kali Tal argues that contemporary black popular texts have undergone "the erasure of explicit political ideology" since the resistive texts loaded with political-meaning that came out of the politicized black power and civil rights movements.[61] Using *Monster* as an example, Tal believes that this text reflects the wider political disinterest of the era and is representative of a larger trend in film, music, and literature. Such concerns are also voiced by Boyd, who recognizes that many ghetto action films have replaced their overtly political messages with themes of self-destruction and nihilism.[62]

A central critical opposition that is being explored in this book is between the subcultural, marginalized, "organic" voicing of oppressed people on one hand, and on the other, the constraining patterns of power that put limitations on these oppressed people. This second slant, deemed structuralism in cultural studies, literally determined the underlying structures that made meaning possible, exploring how meaning was produced and reproduced by dominant ideologies within a culture. In terms of gang memoirs, their production of cultural texts under subjugation suggests a culturalist victory. However, the structuralist stereotyping that surrounded such gang authors, as well as gang members or young black men in general, soured any signs of a clear culturalist cause for celebration. Structuralism played a crucial role in the representative debates of contemporary black cultural studies, a field indebted to the work of Stuart Hall, Paul Gilroy, and other scholars at the CCCS. Black cultural studies has been the most productive area for discussing the politics of racial representations.

When using cultural studies as a framework for analyzing gang memoirs, it is valuable to consider Hall's research into how the mass media's messages could influence popular opinion. Hall dedicated much time to studying the mass media, contending that the media's representation of people and events help shape our understanding of reality. For example, Hall deliberated the series of social crises in Britain in the 1970s, with muggings and union unrest. The media played a huge role in defining "normal" and "deviant," and the cultural discussions that emerged considered how such sociological classifications of deviance were constructed by the media. The media presented such crises as moral panics, demanding a firm response from the courts and politicians. Hall's work often explored the sheer power of the media in influencing popular political, social, and

cultural opinion in response to those subcultural practices and subversions that might threaten the state's legitimacy.[63] He saw media texts,
rather than a conventional "artistic" text, as "moments when the larger
social and political structures within the culture are exposed for analysis."[64] Hall's critical work from the 1970s greatly assists my own exploration
into the media's interpretation of gang memoirs. By the late 1980s, Hall's
interests had evolved into the role that the media played in racial representations, which becomes further crucial support to my own research.

Hall tends to view structuralism as superior to culturalism, favoring
theoretical analysis over empirical audience studies. What is at stake for
Hall is the "cultural power" of the media—the power to define things and
to give something meaning. He thus conducts close textual readings using
semiotics, the communicative power of the system of signs and symbols
within the text, paying particular attention to issues of representation. His
innovative essay "New Ethnicities" (1988) debates the shifting politics of
racial identity at that time. It explores how the British media "normalize"
black culture, presenting it as inferior and marginal. The black experience
is often absent or, when it does appear, stereotyped. The crux of the essay
lies in what Hall sees as a shift from this "struggle over the relations of
representation to a politics of representation itself."[65] The "relations" reveal
the binary approaches to critiquing racialist representations, relations
normally cast as less complex than politics of representation. For instance,
when a "bad" black image is replaced with a "good" one, the positive image
still shows complicit racism by assuming all black people are either "good"
or all the "same." Instead, the "politics of representation" involves "looking
behind the relations of individual media representations and self-repre-
sentations of blackness in order to explore the wider structures and deeper
determinants" that shape popular culture.[66] "New Ethnicities" exacerbated
the tension between existing debates over representation as a process of
artistic depiction and representation as a form of delegation—for example,
making a documentary film to explain life "as it really is" or alternatively
speaking on behalf of the black community.[67]

Following "New Ethnicities," Hall remained preoccupied with cultural
representations and their signifying practices (those practices including
the production and reading of texts). Hall's edited collection *Representations* (1997) explores how visual images, language, and discourse (especially
film, advertising, and photography) produce and perpetuate stereotypes
and fantasies of racial identity and "otherness."[68] The work was criticized
for assuming that historical reality can be deduced simply from close

textual readings using semiotics. Nonetheless, *Representations* forcefully continues the debates Hall had opened up in "New Ethnicities," as well as his essay "What is this 'Black' in Black Popular Culture?" (1992), in which he revised the ideas from "New Ethnicities" for an American audience.[69] In that essay, Hall argues that the simplistic nature of the debates surrounding black popular culture are no longer sufficient, that the simplistic binaries ("high and low; resistance versus incorporation; authentic versus inauthentic; experiential versus formal") that had previously been used to map out black culture are no longer appropriate.[70] According to Hall, such binaries are "a crude and reductionist" way of establishing meaning and representing race.[71]

Gang memoirs work very much in terms of the depiction discourse that was initially presented in "New Ethnicities." The memoirists proffer their stories as an authentic slice of gang life, dedicated to "keeping it real." Hall's essay informs my own research, which considers this act of depiction—particularly in the case of *Blue Rage*, whose author marketed himself as an authentic role model for conversion and escaping the gang life. Of the binary oppositions that troubled Hall, the discourse of authentic versus inauthentic is the most pertinent for this research. All three memoirs invoke the powerful discourse of authenticity (the authentic voicing of the street), only to have it further imposed on them in the media reception.

The work of Hall was very influential in contemporary American black cultural studies, which continued and evolved the research that originally stemmed from the CCCS. Just as contemporary street gang scholars such as Malcolm Klein and Martin Jankowski revealed the sensationalized and stereotyped attitude of the printed press and entertainment media toward gangs themselves, the binaries presented by Hall have been deployed in press/media discussions of gangsta rap and film.[72] Hall argues that this politics of representation is "a struggle over meaning which continues and is unfinished."[73] The subject has been tackled in the United States by black pop culture critics who have explored the burden routinely placed on black artists to fight against limiting or damaging black representations. Gangsta, like prison literature, is an excellent source for studying the discourse of stereotyped "otherness" in American culture and has been addressed by Boyd and bell hooks, among others. Boyd has praised black artists and texts such as *Monster* for their discourse of authenticity, voicing the marginalized.[74] Meanwhile, bell hooks worries that gangsta culture furthers the stereotypes (the lazy and insolent slave, the criminal) that African Americans have for so long struggled against.[75] Gangsta culture provides excellent materials to apply to Hall's conceptual ideas over both the reproduction of popular images (black men as criminals) and the ways in which the subjects themselves resist those stereotypes and marginalized representations.

While Hall's work on representations, as well as studies by American scholars Boyd and hooks, have been squared in black frames, I will apply their theories to Mexican American typecasting, too. African Americans have fought hard to erase stereotypes that have existed since slavery. In contemporary American society the black man regularly has been seen as the archetypal criminal, prompting more critical analysis than their Mexican counterparts. Within such representational debates over contemporary popular culture in the United States, there has been notably more scholarly work in the realm of African Americans and masculinity specifically.

That is not to say that Mexican Americans (and other marginalized groups) have not been the victims of stereotyping. White America's literary and cinematic imagination has typecast Mexican Americans, centering upon the white "gringo" winning over the contemptible "greaser."[76] Over the past half century, Mexicans have been stereotyped as violent knife-carriers. As former FBI director J. Edgar Hoover famously remarked in 1970, "You never have to bother about a president being shot by . . . Mexicans. They don't shoot very straight. But if they come at you with a knife, beware."[77] Stereotyping of Mexican Americans today, like their African American counterparts, is not as prejudiced and extreme as it has been historically, but there remains a pressing cultural need to continue to address their under- and misrepresentations in pop-cultural forms.

Meanwhile, prison scholar Auli Ek concentrates on issues raised by the black male body. Male body building is familiar to gang life and prison culture. Ek probes lines of thought pertaining to black hyper-masculinity that were previously opened up by scholars such as Hall and Kobena Mercer. Mercer addresses the legacies of black super-sexuality and hyper-masculinity, but also highlights that the traditional attributes of masculinity have been denied to black men since slavery and they are deemed to have the potential to be a sexual predator.[78] In his considerations of contemporary black masculinity, Hall's *Representations* cites the example of a tabloid newspaper that commented on Linford Christie's "lunch-box."[79] The term can be seen as racist stereotyping of a black man. While Hall and Mercer have explored the negative cultural and social aspirations toward black men, Ek's research has furthered scholarship in this area by addressing the ways in which black male authors have autonomy and agency to rework these stereotypes and encourage a positive image of black male sexuality. This book is informed by certain racialized gendered discourses, both Mexican and African American, as will be revealed in the textual readings of the memoirs, raising specific critical questions around feats of hyper-masculinity.

Cultural and literary scholars who have begun to conduct analyses of contemporary gang memoirs stress the very feat of writing an (African American) autobiography (Boyd and Ek) and the form of the text (Brumble).[80] Other scholars have addressed the lack of political ambition in gang memoirs, situating such narratives in a wider popular and political context (Tal).[81] But none of these studies has considered any reception of the memoirs through the cultural studies paradigm, which suggests that both the media and people are important and therefore should be incorporated and studied.

Hall's theories of structuralism, and the role they have played in contemporary black cultural theory, are crucial for my research into the response of the printed media to the memoirs. To approach the subject of media reception, my research combines Hall's research on black representation with that of Janet Staiger, one of the leading scholars in the field of reception studies. Because of its interest in how meaning is produced, structuralism often treats the reader as the site of underlying codes that make meaning possible. Staiger acknowledges this, contending that reception studies then asks: "What kinds of meaning does a text have? For whom? In what circumstances? With what changes over time? And do these meanings have any effects? Cognitive? Emotional? Social? Political?"[82] My exploration of the media reception of the memoirs relies heavily on inspiration drawn from Staiger's work.

Some cultural studies scholars argue that the textualist approach (in which the voice of the literary theorist is often privileged) is too limiting.[83] Simultaneously, semiotics has been censured for not incorporating feelings or practices. Hall's work, for instance, has been seen as relying too heavily on the presumption of the critic.[84] This project is concerned with both textual readings and structuralist models for examining the printed press and mass media, exploring how the media came discursively to frame the meanings of the memoirs. The everyday practices of people themselves are also extremely important. To understand what the memoirs mean to people, it is necessary to adopt culturalist approaches to reception. How do people respond to these texts and use and interpret commodities and meanings? Cultural studies has shown particular concern with subordinate groups, so politically engaged scholars examine those very social groups who are suffering oppression and explore their practices. This awareness will then hopefully lead to better understanding of people and ultimately to change. To conduct such culturalist studies, scholars frequently deploy ethnographic fieldwork techniques that stem from anthropology. This rationale and approach clearly lend themselves to the study of gang memoirs.

Since the early 1970s cultural studies has concentrated on textual analysis, but has extended the definition of a "text" beyond its traditional domain to include readings of cultural practices. As demonstrated in the previous chapter, the subcultural studies of street gangs suggest the meaning of "text" can be expanded to include urban youth's fashion and language. Put simply, cultural studies contend that everyday meanings of things are important. Cultural studies scholar Graeme Turner asserts that one consequence of the previous concentration on traditional textual analysis was that it deflected attention "away from the sites at which textual meaning was generated—people's everyday lives."[85] An active interest in extra-textual responses to texts, particularly that of public audiences, was seen to break down the line between textual and contextual approaches. By the late 1980s, audience studies had become the major new field of inquiry in cultural studies.[86] This book is inspired by these trends in cultural studies that have taken reader responses increasingly seriously.

David Morley's renowned *The "Nationwide" Audience* (1980) is often seen to be one of the first mainstream contemporary cultural studies of audience reception.[87] Morley declared that scholars needed to travel into the field to investigate exactly how people interpreted texts. He studied the viewers of the popular *Nationwide* television show and stressed the notion of culture as "polysemic," meaning different things to different readers. Under the "dominant" reading, the reader recognizes what a program's preferred or offered meaning is and broadly agrees with it, so the central meaning of the text is emphasized. The "oppositional" reading is where the dominant meaning is rejected for political, cultural, or ideological reasons and the text is read in a manner contrary to its intended meaning. The "negotiated" reading is where there may be slight disagreements, but the main meaning of the text is accepted. Negotiated readings are therefore where the reader accepts, rejects, or refines elements of the program in light of previously held views. Though I acknowledge Morley's work was concerned with reading practices of dominant discourses and I am concerned with the readers of non-dominant memoirs, his study is invaluable in paving the way for further audience work.

Morley's work has since come under criticism. His methods have been condemned for removing audiences from their usual site of viewing and bringing them into his research world. By no longer viewing the program in their own home and in the early evening, critics complain that Morley was changing the very nature of the program and that audience responses would therefore be different from "usual."[88] Morley even criticized his own *Nationwide* project in a further study six years later for similar reasons.[89] However, his research was important for opening up debates about the importance of conducting fieldwork to discover what people really think and feel. Morley's early studies were significant in enabling the focus of cultural studies to move smoothly from the text to the audience.

Throughout the 1980s, audience studies were almost exclusively of television audiences. Nonetheless, in 1984 Janice Radway produced a seminal study of literary audiences, *Reading the Romance: Women, Patriarchy and Popular Literature*.[90] Radway's intellectual agenda is similar to that of Morley, seeing readers as proactive consumers and emphasizing the importance of readers' interpretations, then applying the significance of their readings to the practices of their everyday lives. Her aim was "to deal with literary production and consumption as complex social processes."[91] Radway engaged with a group of forty-two readers of romance fiction, with whom she conducted formal interviews, written questionnaires, open-ended group discussions and simple observations of reactions within the group. She justified her methodology by stating: "empiricism would guarantee a more accurate description of what a book meant to a given audience."[92] *Reading the Romance* became another major contribution to the field of audience work within the wider body of cultural studies. Her approaches stimulated my own fieldwork techniques and practices.

In recent years cultural studies scholars Greg Dimitriadis and Robin Means Coleman have produced audience studies on gangsta music and films.[93] Their research has built on earlier methods of those such as Morley and Radway to pave the way for their own contemporary audience studies with innovative texts. Where Radway looked at the operations of patriarchy and the reading practices of women readers, these scholars have focused principally on black youth as audience members, using black texts by black authors as their subjects for audience analysis. They draw attention to the shortage of audience studies in the field of contemporary black popular culture, which are central to a fuller comprehension of the lives of urban youth. There have been no similar studies engaging Mexican youth culture, but Coleman and Dimitriadis raise themes of identity, race, place, class, history, and community that can be applied similarly to other marginalized youth. When I started addressing fieldwork approaches for this book, I was keen to venture into the "actual" world to conduct studies with "real life" youth, and wanted to do this with both Mexican and African American audiences. Too often, black cultural studies rely on scholarly readings of racial texts and speculative claims about the responses of and effects on marginalized readers. The importance of audience studies is paramount.

Coleman's collection, *Say It Loud! African American Audiences, Media and Identity*, makes a case for understanding how the mass media present images of African American identity and then how these portrayals are interpreted in African American communities. As black cultural scholar Herman Gray substantiates in the collection's introduction:

> As some of the exemplary and innovative research on audiences in general indicates, scholarship and discourse about the representation of Blackness as well as discussions of Black audiences begin by viewing Black audiences as active meaning-making agents. Blacks read, listen, view, and engage with media in the context of complexly organized social lives, circumstances, and social relationships. Thus, Blacks' lives and circumstances must be socially located and made visible discursively by scholars as subjects of complex life ways and practices rather than reduced to a potentially attractive segment of a consumer demographic that can help media and entertainment companies gain an advantage in market share.[94]

Of particular note is Coleman's study of the gangsta film *Menace II Society*, in which she used an incarcerated youth as the audience member. Caryon was serving a life sentence for a murder that was inspired by events of the film. Though he was hardly a typical audience sample, Coleman wanted to understand Caryon's "identification with the characters, behaviors, lifestyles, messages—how Caryon views the symbolic world as it informs and merges with his own African American male teen identity."[95] For example, whether "good" characters can provide Caryon with an alternative identity, or whether he opts for "thug life identification" because it is closer to his own lived experiences.

Dimitriadis's work enlisted hip hop music to investigate how young people engage with texts in order to make sense of themselves. His study,

Performing Identity, Performing Culture: Hip Hop as Text, Pedagogy and Lived Practice (2001), and a follow-up project two years later, stress that his own reading of these popular texts might be very different from those by young black men. He seeks to investigate how young black people's individual sense of self and localized identity is "linked to shared notions of what it means to be black and marginalized in the US."[96] Like Coleman, he considers the ways in which the power structures outside a text (such as class, gender, race) could shape the audience's views. Crucially, Dimitriadis moves further than Coleman to open up questions of popular culture texts as pedagogues. Throughout his study, conducted at youth centers rather than in the classroom, he considers the implications of popular culture for education, particularly the education of young people for whom traditional texts may hold little relevance in their daily lives.

Coleman and Dimitriadis's studies form crucial foundations for my own research in these areas of marginalized youth as readers of the memoirs. The existing critical work into gang memoirs by Tal, Ek, Brumble, and Boyd pay no heed to audience readings. This book will address such absences, replacing Coleman and Dimitriadis's films and music with memoirs. Part of the scholarly intervention of this study is to consider some of the intended readers of the memoirs, non-white youth. But while the work of Coleman and Dimitriadis concentrates on overarching social issues that are relevant for such audiences, their studies have tended to neglect the formal dimensions of texts, something to which my research offers a corrective.

This chapter has considered the longstanding divide in cultural studies between culturalism and structuralism and used it as a way into examining the scholarly debates about gang memoirs. Indeed, this key binary of culture versus structure informs the chapters to come. Chapter 4 will consider how much agency a subject can have in the act of writing a memoir, while chapters 3 and 5 address the structuring regimes of representation that reproduce stereotypes of young black and Mexican men. Proceeding from the subject matter about memoirs of the marginalized, this project almost necessarily takes a more culturalist approach. Nevertheless, to avoid the pitfalls of an overly culturalist approach that might exaggerate the resistive potential of these memoirs, I need to incorporate a structuralist angle and have hence also presented important theoretical concepts concerning structuralism. After all, these authors, all three of whom have a lot at stake in producing work that will allow them to earn a living and better their immediate material circumstances, are working within genre conventions and commercial expectations. As we will see, it may be, ironically, these genre and commercial imperatives that enable the authors to expose the power relations at work in their stories. Nonetheless, the authors are exploring their own identity and agency within conditions of structural constraint and that echoes my cultural studies approach and the frameworks that are utilized.

The analysis of stereotyped representations of gang members as "murderous thugs" presented in the news and print media lend themselves to structuralist lines of thought. The grassroots essence of gang memoirs, whereby imprisoned authors acquire an education and write to reclaim autonomy as well as protest the marginalized status of all gang members, aligns gang memoirs with culturalist terms. These competing concepts illuminate the key themes of violence and pedagogy that will be contrasted in the following chapters.

Chapter Three

KILLER BOOKS
The Representations and Politics of Violence in Gang Memoirs

Violent behavior is an integral characteristic of contemporary street gangs, as has been regularly illustrated across different forms of gangsta popular culture. Graphic and shocking acts of violence are routine in, and expected of, both gangsta rap and ghetto action films. Cultural scholars have explored at length the representations of violence that permeate such popular texts, the public demand for those aggressive images, and the controversy generated.[1] Gangsta rhymes, for example, have been condemned for cop-killing lyrics ("Fuck Tha Police!") delivered by those who were proud to call themselves "bad niggas."[2] The image of Caine dying in the street following a shootout at the end of the film *Menace II Society* is memorably uncomfortable for its bloody representations of death and typically seen as excessively violent.[3] Violence is similarly a vital component of contemporary street gang memoirs; I will interpret these texts' use of violence as an exploratory tool. It is important to explore the ways in which violence is expressed in contemporary gang memoirs, with subtle and intricate differences in their representations, framed within socio-historical factors that have led to changes in the nature of violence.

Chapter 1 demonstrated that violence has escalated and become depoliticized in LA, and that this is partially attributable to the social, political, and economic forces that have taken hold since the peak of the civil rights movement. As Ice-T once rapped, "My life is violent, but violent is life."[4] This chapter will contrast the late 1960s and early 1970s on one hand (the setting for *Always Running* and *Blue Rage*) and the 1980s and early 1990s on the other (*Monster*).[5] The chapter maps these eras to provide a context for the ways in which the narrators describe and attempt to justify their violent pasts. The periodic changes in the style and amount of violence have found their way into gangsta culture, changes that also can be credited to expressive trends in popular culture more generally. Certainly since the late 1960s popular culture norms have shifted, with increasing audience appetites for violence across all genres. Legal codes and regulations in the media toward violence have become more relaxed in their standards in response to this demand. This chapter will consider ways in which the escalation of violence in the memoirs are supported by evolving cultural sensibilities that permitted the violent lyrics of gangsta rap to flourish prior to the release of *Monster*. Though social contexts and popular trends are important, this chapter, fueled by textual evidence, will also analyze how that periodization is being presented in the narratives and the complexity of their presentations. I will deliberate how violence is framed in terms of narrative operations and development, considering how and to what effect violent imagery is used.

The chapter opens by exploring state violence as a backdrop to society in the two eras: *Always Running* and *Blue Rage* as one period, *Monster* as the other. All three memoirists include lengthy critiques of the authorities suggesting that they deem their struggles with the state as important to understanding their violent lives. I then move into a critical analysis of what the narrators do with their representations of violence, whether relying on the metaphor of war to discuss their actions or pointing towards feats of hyper-masculinity. Finally, this chapter will consider how the narrators, in constructing themselves and describing their violent acts, mirror variants on the cultural template of "bad niggers," in their behavior as motivated and politicized warriors or depoliticized thugs committing senseless violence.

The main narrative action of these contemporary gang memoirs revolves around tales of violence: that of the narrators toward other gang members, and that committed against them by the state. Descriptions of state violence are included to rationalize and explain the behavior of the narrators. Violence is viewed through the lens of a war in which the system is the enemy, and as warranted because the rules of war make combat temporarily acceptable. As social scientist Michael Walzer explains in *Just and Unjust Wars*, "All aggressive acts have one thing in common: they justify forceful resistance."[6] The three memoirs demonstrate that, though state violence was already thriving in late 1960s California, it would become increasingly oppressive in LA over the next two decades. The images of gangsta violence in the memoirs are at times extreme, as is the enactment of inappropriate and illegal violence in the courtrooms, prisons, and police departments. The LAPD and LASD feature regularly in the critiques of violence in the memoirs. The narrator of *Blue Rage* anticipates the reader's disbelief that such tales of state violence may seem "unbelievable" in view of the police pledge to uphold moral order and protect law-abiding communities (*R*, 136). The memoirs highlight the perceived incompetence and corruption of LA's police forces and judiciary.

In the discussions of state power in *Always Running*, the narrative emphasizes that police brutality was not reserved for gangbangers, drawing attention to the aggressive behavior of the state toward Mexican political protests of the late 1960s (*AR*, 72). The narrator was torn between his gangbanging inclinations and the empowering group violence of the Chicano movement, battling against the state for ethnic pride. The police are presented as "just another gang" and even given monikers by gang members (*AR*, 72). The narrator refers to specific police practices for gangs, such as abducting members and dropping them off in rival territories resulting in escalations in gang warfare, a custom referenced in *Blue Rage* (*AR*, 72, 112; *R*, 136–37). Yet the narrator is also at pains to detail the behavior of the police in the 1970 Chicano Moratorium Against the War. The event saw Chicano gangbangers join 30,000 Mexican American demonstrators, including "young mothers with infants in strollers, factory hands—a newly-wed couple in wedding dress" in a supposedly peaceful protest (*AR*, 160). When the LASD leads an offensive against the demonstrators, the narrator is roughly handled by the officers and arrested. The reader witnesses his innermost thoughts—"Come on, then, you helmeted wall of state power. Come and try to blacken . . . this festive park"—exuding contempt for the dominant social order and defense of his community (*AR*, 161). The narrative repeatedly stresses that the 1960s and 1970s history of racial activism, reaction, and reform sparked huge amounts of state violence and conflict for all Mexicans, not just gangbangers.

When describing his treatment at the hands of the authorities, the narrator of *Always Running* fondly evokes the collective and compassionate outlook of racial minorities in this era. In jail following the narrator's arrest at the Moratorium, an African American recalls the Watts Rebellion of 1965 and shakes the narrator's hand in solidarity for racial protest (*AR*, 162). The narrator's final encounter with the police in the memoir is for supporting a female stranger who is being punched by police officers. As a result, he receives a beating with a blackjack club and is arrested.

Such an act elucidates the communal concern that pervaded civil rights movements of the 1960s, encompassing the rights of women and other minority groups in addition to gangbangers. As he explains, "they'll do it to somebody else . . . I just couldn't let these deputies get away with it" (*AR*, 231, 232). Though the memoir was released in 1993, the narrative's discussions of the 1992 Rodney King riots in the epilogue are still very much in tune with the collective feeling of the civil rights era. The narrator looks outside his immediate circle of young Mexican men to other marginalized groups, noting "this book is part of their story" (*AR*, 10). In an interview with Rodriguez, when asked to classify his memoir, he claimed it was "a book of the post-industrial world," thus including all racial groups who struggled to deal with the socio-economic circumstances of the 1970s.[7]

Despite the narrator of *Always Running* being charged with assaulting a police officer, his punishment is not as harsh as that received by his two memoirist successors in the 1970s and 1980s.[8] The judge gives the narrator "a break" in the form of a fine and a short period of incarceration in the county jail (*AR*, 233). This is partly because the narrator approached a judge who had previously helped him when he was a juvenile offender. This judge wrote a supportive letter to the court on his behalf, resulting in lenient sentencing (*AR*, 229). His lack of punishment and experience of the state's penal system, particularly in the early 1970s, was more compassionate than that of the other two narrators. By comparison, in the epilogue of *Monster* in the early 1990s, the narrator is back in prison for a seven-year sentence for assault and into his third year of solitary confinement (*M*, 379). These two diverse experiences point toward increasingly punitive patterns taking hold in American society, particularly during Reagan's presidency.

By 1970, when the narrator of *Always Running* faced his final arrest, Reagan had firmly established his conservative base as the governor of California. His election to this position in 1967 reflected the right-wing politics that would grow to conflict with the progressive rhetoric and ideology of civil rights as depicted in *Always Running*. The immediate aftermath of the civil rights era has been a complex area of political and economic debate for historians, demonstrating multiple agendas rather than simple polarization of increasingly vocal white conservatism versus seemingly decreasing black radicalism. The angle of importance for this research, without compressing and simplifying a complicated story, is that there were undeniably conservative currents infiltrating and challenging radical fervor and even mainstream "Great Society"–style liberalism.

Historians such as Clayborne Carson have labeled 1968 as the beginning of this "post-revolutionary era" in which black militant politics waned and conservative political power burgeoned.[9] The narrator of *Monster* astutely observes that the "fixed expression of hopelessness" worn by his mother and others is "not just the result of four years of Reagan [as president]" but political forces that had been growing for some time (*M*, 252).

Throughout his time in both offices, Reagan encouraged the repressive tactics that would become fodder for the memoirs' critiques of state violence. The definitive exercise of state power is exhibited in *Blue Rage* by the death row status of its narrator. Reinstated in California in 1977, the death penalty was the ultimate response in tackling crime. It was assigned to Williams in 1981, the first year of Reagan's office as president. Williams's punishment represents the shift from the liberal sentencing seen in *Always Running* toward a wave of legislation that promised to "get tough" on crime.[10] *Blue Rage* mocks: "This was a bad time for the disenfranchised. California's criminal judiciary was handing out death penalties like government food stamps in a depression" (*R*, 262). The narrator is clearly aware that such sentences are not aimed at addressing the root causes of crime, instead being "constructed for punishment and execution, not for reform" (*R*, 294). He voices grievance that the ultimate penalty of death does not address the "systematic injustices" (poverty, racism, police brutality) that are inflicted upon residents of South Central and turn young black men toward crime (*R*, 208). The severe state punishment becomes an extreme form of violence in its own right.[11]

Just as *Always Running* is fascinated by the state's violent retorts to political protest, *Blue Rage* shows a preoccupation with the criminal justice system. Historically, after Emancipation whites turned to the law to regain economic control of blacks. Criminalization is a jurisprudential process: a person becomes a criminal through a declaration in court, not by actually committing a crime.[12] The narrator reminds us that "by no means was I born a criminal," yet he is clearly mindful that his supposed deviancy has influenced the opinions of the staff in the court and jail, justifying their violence during his trial (*R*, 4). The narrator maintains that officers "sought to emasculate me and to destroy my sanity" by leaving glass in his food, drugging him, and treating him "worse than an animal" (*R*, 210–11). *Blue Rage*'s narrator appears fascinated by this relationship between supposed black deviance and white exertion of power by law enforcement on the streets. The narrative depicts harassment from police officers as "business as usual," and describes "walking while youthful and black" as a criminal offense (*R*, 183, 102). However, it is in the courtroom that the narrator conducts his most detailed and telling critique of state violence, constructing himself as prey and a victim of the white legal system. The Civil Rights Act of 1964 was a legal affirmation of African American rights as citizens, and one of the intentions of the movement was to address inequalities in the judicial system. The experiences of the narrator in *Blue Rage* imply that this intention did not become reality.

In several chapters involving the courtroom and jail, the narrator of *Blue Rage* draws a fine line between supporting and dismantling archetypal images of the unlawful black predator. Tookie is acutely aware of the frequent misrecognition of blacks with criminality, noting that his "racist voyeurs" in jail deem him a "gargantuan black beast" and "subhuman" (*R*, 210, 216). As a result he verbally attacks the officers, throws objects, and even "sometimes I lowered myself to primitive levels of retaliation by spitting on them" (*R*, 211). On one occasion the narrator fuels their animalistic stereotypes by exploding with rage and breaking his handcuffs in two, sparking an onslaught from a mob of sheriffs (*R*, 211). Black cultural critic Kobena Mercer acknowledges that prevailing stereotypes promote the black male as engaging in illegal behavior and to be feared. Mercer is concerned that this becomes a never-ending cycle of violence. He argues that this regime of representation is reproduced and sustained hegemonically because black men have to resort to "toughness" as a defensive response to white aggression and violence.[13] The narrator of *Blue Rage* certainly believes his abuse in jail and the courtroom is sufficient to rationalize his hostile responses. Instead of solving problems of violence, the courtroom is presented in the narrative as being a prime source of sparking further violence.

Monster shows particular fascination with the police, discussing the LAPD in the most detail of the three narrators, portraying how by the 1980s the LA police forces played an intrusive and aggressive role in the ghetto. The crack markets led to sharp increases in violent crime, with guns needed to regulate and control the drug system. Crack also provided sufficient profits to purchase guns, which were easier to access following Reagan's gun deregulation policies. This perpetuated the cycle of violence. Gang scholar Malcolm Klein notes that in LA, gang homicides jumped from 212 in 1984 to 554 in 1989 and 803 in 1992.[14] Such increases in street violence justified greater police repression with "war zones" and "fortresses."[15] The chief of the LAPD throughout the 1980s, Daryl Gates, is presented as a dangerous character in *Monster* (M, 371). Under Gates the LAPD became the most technologically advanced force in the country, demonstrating a penchant for security and surveillance.

Monster references the Community Resources Against Street Hoodlums (CRASH) scheme, organized by Gates to gather intelligence on gangs and memorably described by the narrator as just another gang. During his first trial for murder, "three gangs filled the court—the Crips, the Bloods, and the LAPD CRASH unit" (*M*, 24). *Monster* implies that gangs were forced to evolve as a result of the CRASH tactics; thus surveillance campaigns found their way into the military buildup of the Crips and the Bloods (*M*, xiv). The opening sentence of the narrative—"Helicopters hover heavily above . . . staccato vibrations of automatic gunfire crack throughout the night"—sets the tone for the military nature of LA that resonates throughout the 1980s, in terms of both gang and police violence (*M*, xi). Monster maps violence, suggesting that such intense levels of gang and police violence were specific to the circumstances of LA. He states that the streets of South Central made the violent film *New Jack City* "look like a boys' club" (*M*, 261).

Though Monster cannot evade the physical threat of Gates and the LAPD, the narrative opportunity is exploited to ridicule and psychologically resist his oppressors. In addition to CRASH, Chief Gates was responsible for the LAPD's developing record of racial violence, epitomized by the infamous choke hold of which *Monster*'s narrator is highly aware. The narrator claims that the police were only concerned with giving the impression that they were trying to stop the violence: "Shit, if they [actually] wanted to stop the killings, they would have begun by outlawing the choke hold!" (*M*, 111). The only point in the memoir at which the police attempt to uphold the law and establish moral order is following the narrator's shooting. When he is being interviewed by two police officers while lying in the hospital, he amusingly decides "to have a little fun" (*M*, 185–87).

During this unforgettable episode, Monster observes the tensions between the younger and older officers: "I was careful to be nice and respectful to Clipboard, while agitating Donut Cup with my feigned stupidity" (*M*, 185). He evades their questions about the scene of the crime with lies, even claiming not to be a gangbanger.[16] The narrator temporarily presents himself as a trickster figure, making the officers appear utterly incompetent and demonstrating his sheer disdain for the law. Folktale tricksters in the African American cultural tradition often overcome oppression by using shrewd language and playful speech to challenge subjugation. The reader is entertained by Monster's antics, simulating helplessness and ignorance while deliberately goading the officers, culminating in a final moment of sheer amusement:

> When the soldier-cops had completed their report and were walking toward the door, I decided to use one of my old acting skits, which I had seen on an old TV show.
> 'Officer, officer,' I said faintly, my voice barely audible.
> 'Yes, son?' answered Clipboard.
> 'You—you will get them, won't you, sir?'
> And then just like in the movies Clipboard solemnly said, 'Yes, son, we'll get them,' and they left the room. Shit, that little episode threw me for a loop. (*M*, 188).

In *Monster*, scenes concerning police officers provide material as dramatic and entertaining as the gang tales themselves.

Just as police violence features prominently in *Monster*, so does prison violence, with worrying images of racial beatings and abuse from some prison deputies (*M*, 139). Prison forms the backdrop for much of the narrative and symbolizes the soaring incarceration rates for African American men throughout the 1980s, partly stemming from strict new penalties for possession and use of crack cocaine. In the other two memoirs police officers are unanimously white; in *Monster*, "Negro deputies" in prison signal the new hiring quotas of the state for minorities in the 1980s in both the police and prison systems (*M*, 139). The presence of African American officers does nothing to stop the violence. Instead, they participate in both physical and verbal maltreatment of black prisoners (*M*, 139). Their participation in the cruelty becomes the ultimate black-on-black violence.

Violence experts have long since been aware that provocation has been a popular tactic in the arsenal of state violence, with members of the state encouraging mayhem in order to excuse their own aggression toward certain groups and leaders.[17] In *Monster*, prison staff abuse inmates, and of equal concern is that rapes and beatings among prisoners themselves are rife (*M*, 141, 198). *Monster* implies that neighborhood gangs thrive in prison rather than being dispersed: "it has got to be the most blatant exercise the state has ever devised for corrupting, institutionalizing, and creating recidivism in youths—clearly a way to breed a criminal generation" (*M*, 136). *Monster* depicts the seriousness of such provocation. Prison staff actively encourage black-on-black aggression by attempting to force the narrator to paint the cast on his broken arm red, the affiliated color of the enemy Bloods gang (*M*, 126). Deputies deliberately place rival set members in the same cells (*M*, 292). The state no longer has to punish (what Michel Foucault deems the old regime practice), because inmates themselves take on responsibilities for physical torture.[18] By highlighting such provocations, the narrator criticizes the state for its role in escalating levels of gang violence, even when these marginalized young men are not on the streets.

The Rodney King riots of 1992 feature in the preface and epilogue of *Always Running*, indicating how the frustration of LA's minorities at the hands of the police grew steadily throughout the 1970s and the 1980s before erupting. The uprising also figures in the opening and closing pages of *Monster*. Cultural scholars have noted that the riots incorporated "classic badman ingredients," not merely in the construction of King as a dangerous black man and the destructive responses from the community, but in the act of police violence that initiated events.[19] In *Always Running* the events of 1992 hold particular social relevance. By commencing and closing his memoirs with 1992, then returning for the bulk of the memoir to the late 1960s, the narrator stresses the lengthy, ongoing history of police brutality in LA. He explains that, in 1992, in dispatching the National Guard and the Army, the government was demonstrating its aggressive intolerance of anyone protesting structural violence or challenging the "economic and political underpinnings of poverty in this country" (*AR*, 248). In spite of his personally lenient experience, the narrator recognizes in the epilogue that problems with state violence have continued and intensified.

Despite his emphasis on the 1992 riots as a result of a collective class-based frustration, the narrator of *Always Running* highlights the role of gang members in the discussion contained in the epilogue of the post-riot truce when gang members were temporarily politicized. He then contrasts this with the response of the authorities. He argues that although deindustrialization was the root cause, the riots became inevitable due to the addition of a brutal police force into the mix (*AR*, 248). In the aftermath, graffiti flourished boasting "Mexicans and Crips and Bloods together" (*AR*, 249). Instead of reveling in the peace and encouraging a sustained truce, the state's response to the politicization of the gangs, according to *Always Running*, was to remove the empowering graffiti, break up unity rallies, arrest truce leaders, report Latinos to the Immigration and Naturalization Service for deportation and send in FBI agents to investigate the gangs (*AR*, 249). These attempts to depoliticize gang members continued the trends in which the state's policies worked against young blacks and Mexicans, illustrated by harsher prison sentences with no right to vote upon release. The Rodney King riots provide a neat point of closure for two of the narratives and for this chronology of increasing gang and state violence since 1968.

All three memoirs deploy the metaphor of war in various ways including both real (physical) and imagined (mental) battles. They are fighting a war against the state but also other gangs, the death penalty, poverty, and stereotyping. The narrators present themselves as hardened warriors, telling boastful war stories about their weapons and parading their masculinity. The degree to which the memoirs deploy martial rhetoric varies greatly, as does the degree to which they present themselves as warriors. For example, the narrator of *Always Running* describes himself as a "war veteran" (*AR*, 251). Though a man is often thought to be more manly if he has been to war and seen violent actions, the narrator is not ashamed to present himself as a damaged and defective warrior, suffering from a "sort of post-traumatic stress syndrome" (*AR*, 251). This is in stark contrast to the boastful warrior tales of the other two memoirs.

Military metaphors are exercised the most in *Monster*, which like *Always Running* makes reference to gang members being subjected to the "same mind-bend" as Vietnam veterans needing similar psychiatric attention (*M*, 104). Rather than including himself in this injured category, the narrator uses Vietnam references for historical purposes. From the outset the narrative is permeated with militaristic vocabulary, describing South Central as a battlefield and gangbangers as armed soldiers (*M*, xi–xv). The narrator cites Vietnam as a means of explaining this lifestyle, constructing his militaristic imagery around a war that took many young and innocent   • lives and provoked extensive criticism of the American government. Yet within this futile imagery for gang strife, the narrator sees himself as a triumphant warrior. He proudly returns to his gang after shooting some rivals "like a Native American on horseback retreating back to my camp after slaying the enemy" (*M*, 174). The references to Native Americans and Vietnam in *Monster* underline that violence has a lengthy history in American culture.

The militaristic attitude pervades *Monster* to the closing pages, where the narrator views assaulting a crack dealer on his street as a warrior's mission to clean his community (*M*, 379). The narrator moves precariously between being interpreted as a war hero or a criminal. He boasts about the number of victims he has claimed (both killing and maiming), laying claim to at least twelve different shootings (*M*, xiii, 9, 25, 41, 46, 48, 50, 52, 83, 110, 146, 269). In the first chapter, aged only fifteen, he has already succumbed to the "total warrior mentality" of "Do or Die" (*M*, 27). To the narrator such gang violence makes perfect sense, as illustrated by his non-chalant tone, which generates pleasure for the reader. In stark contrast to the other two narrators, who project a sense of themselves as civilians, Monster remains committed to his role as a soldier.

Blue Rage similarly establishes its narrator as a respected warrior who leads by example and exhibits strong leadership skills. In terms of being a gang warrior, he lets others outline and interpret his behavior. Following an incident in prison in which he is involved in a violent fight, instead of boasting of his victory he lets fellow inmates conduct the bragging and praising: "I was greeted as a warrior by a group of blacks who proudly shook my hand" (*R*, 108). He becomes heroic because of his crimes and the story is told and retold among prisoners, though not by himself, "hyper-bolized with Biblical overtones" (*R*, 108). Yet once the narrator has left the gang lifestyle, he presents himself as a guiding warrior for vulnerable gangstas: "I could act as an African *griot* or Paul Revere, warning youths about what is coming down the crooked path" (*R*, 273). He encourages young men to copy his dedication to studying (as will be detailed in chapter 4 of this book). This warrior, unlike Monster, has psychological and spiritual discipline and training rather than being merely physically and violently adept. Such transferable skills of the warrior point toward the genre of memoir as conversion narrative.

Contemporary gang behavior as illustrated in *Monster* demonstrates numerous similarities with ancient tribal warrior customs. In his essay on *Monster*, literary scholar David Brumble maintains that the narrator cleverly composes his violent tales as an opportunity to establish his reputation and define his gangsta identity.[20] Brumble understands that warriors gain prominence in proportion to their amount of military glory and hence need to embellish and exaggerate their war deeds. Of the three memoirs, *Monster* travels to the greatest lengths to do this, with potentially dangerous results. Brumble contends that such coup tales inspire and instruct younger warriors for whom the narrator's violent rhetoric becomes inspiration to literal emulation. Gang scholars such as Malcolm Klein voice similar concern over such representations in these memoirs.[21] The jailed narrator in *Monster* can continue to fulfill his imperious leadership role despite not being on the street with his subordinates. He can use the narrative to market his gang—the Eight Trays—boasting of his violent war deeds on their behalf, literally still "employed" by his set, even "putting in overtime" (*M*, 40).

Brumble declares it similarly "worrisome" that *Blue Rage* be recommended as reading for young people.[22] In a second essay, Brumble asserts that "gangbanger autobiography" (identified by warrior traits) can be divided into three categories: "those told from inside the life, those told from outside, and those told by those who are outside the life but whose sense of self is inextricably connected with gangbanger deeds and the respect/status won by those deeds."[23] Brumble argues that *Blue Rage* is firmly situated within the third grouping. He also positions *Monster* in this "moral/psychological demilitarized zone (DMZ)."[24] According to Brumble, autobiographers in the DMZ offer their tales as warnings to vulnerable youth and to highlight societal tribulations that spawn gang warfare. Yet he maintains that such positive connotations are outweighed in the DMZ by literary implications that suggest Williams and Shakur "remain proud of their hard-won reputations," demonstrating little empathy for their victims.[25] The conversion is not complete and instead the narrative is somewhat of an exercise in cynicism. It could be argued however, that evidence suggests Tookie is distanced further from the DMZ than Monster. These two narrators appear hostage to the warrior code, though one more so than the other, as demonstrated, for example, through discussions surrounding weapons and women.

Weapons play an important role within warrior cultures, as Brumble stresses. The narrator of *Monster* details "a weapon in South Central is a part of your attire, a dress code" (*M*, 89). For him, "the medium of exchange in my life has [always] been gunfire," pointing to the massive increase in the use of firearms since the late-1960s setting of *Always Running* (*M*, 31). In 1968 there were 80 million guns in the United States, a figure that rose to 120 million in 1978 and 200 million in 1990.[26] The term "the handgun generation" was coined by gang memoirist Geoffrey Canada to illustrate their familiarity with guns and the resultant increase in violence from carrying firearms.[27] Monster highlights his participation in the latter era by offering extremely detailed descriptions of weaponry: "Two 12-gauge shotguns, both sawed off—one a pump-action, the other a single shot; a .410 shotgun, also a single-shot; and a .44 magnum that had no trigger guard and broke open to load" (*M*, 9–10; see also 48, 50, 115). Monster regularly alludes to gun stashes, highlighting that weapons played a significant role in his gangbanging career from the outset.

In stark contrast to *Monster*'s fondness for firepower, guns are not as prevalent (though by no means absent) in *Always Running* and *Blue Rage*. *Always Running*'s sole reference to a weapons collection appears toward the end of the narrative (*AR*, 207). Most of the fighting involves fists, chains, sticks, and bumper jacks, and the narrator happily admits, "I loved fighting" (*AR*, 100, 93, 58, 244). In *Blue Rage* too, "fighting was part of growing up in South Central," presented as necessary for survival (*R*, 15, 31). Tookie casually details fist-fighting as a hobby just like "partying," "girls," and "hustling" and is only just succumbing to guns as an alternative to fists (*R*, 54). The fist-fighting brawls of *Always Running* and *Blue Rage*, set in the earlier era, are eclipsed by the graphic violent escapades of *Monster* whereby the "desired effect" is "funerals" (*M*, 57). Set in the 1980s, the opening pages of *Monster* explain that "Gangbanging in the seventies was totally different than what's going on today," boasting that the gangs of the following decade "set a decibel level in violence that still causes some to cringe today" (*M*, 15, 56). In comparison to *Monster*, references to guns in the other two memoirs are relatively infrequent.

Guns and their phallocentric associations have long been used to demarcate and assert maleness, with the gun metaphorically reinforcing both the power and sexuality of men. Gang memoirist Nathan McCall candidly explains that shooting as a youth made him "feel like God."[28] Years later McCall read an article by a psychologist that equated the feeling of shooting a gun to ejaculation. McCall agrees: "That's what it was like for me. Shooting off."[29] In the three memoirs at stake, brief sexual dalliances are incorporated to substantiate the narrators' manhood. Women feature only sporadically in these narratives, while gangsta rap is regularly misogynistic and abusive of women. This underscores the image of gangbanging and gangsta culture as a "man thang," despite the success of several high-profile female rappers, a handful of female gang memoirists, and significant statistics for female gang membership (*M*, 259).[30] Within warrior cultures men must perform certain acts of fighting and bravery in order to be labeled as manly by others, particularly when the act of writing and expressing one's emotions is not traditionally a macho act.[31] I contend that, in the memoirs, the narrators seek ways to rebalance or even overcompensate for this unmanly act, such as their treatment of women. Women, like guns, provide the narrators with another means of exuding hyper-masculinity.

Though mothers and grandmothers are held in high esteem in *Always Running* and *Blue Rage*, female characters in all three memoirs are most memorably presented as young, voiceless sexual objects. Tookie eluci-dates that "My struggling mother was a true warrior for motherhood" (R, 306). In contemporary America the white norm remains the two-parent household, while more than 50 percent of black households are headed by women.[32] Tookie is extremely respectful of his co-author Barbara Bec-nel, whom he met in 1992, calling her his "human angel" (R, 271).[33] But he argues that his fatherless household caused him to overcompensate as a youth in "an effort to establish my manhood" (R, 306).

The "Criplettes" warrant a chapter to themselves in Blue Rage, albeit only two pages long. But gangbanging is presented as a primarily mascu-line entity in which "it was absurd for any woman to adopt the dangerous lifestyle of ganghood like hard heads" (R, 94). Tookie details that Bonnie (the mother of one of his sons) was merely someone for whom "I periodi-cally showed up to have sex with" (R, 307). He openly desires to be ogled by women and when recovering from a shooting he boasts of the numerous "attractive Criplettes" who rally around him (R, 166, 306). He has a fling with an older married mother who likes being pelted with fruit. Despite her unusual fetishes, he justifies the ongoing tryst because "I wasn't the weirdo—plus the sex was excellent" (R, 105). This aptly captures his stereo-typing of women during his gangbanging prime as merely serving sexual purposes, interchangeable, and subservient to men.

In Always Running the temptation of sex poses a threat to the narrator's gangsta duties. A girl seduces him and he ditches his fighting responsi-bilities for a sexual encounter (AR, 92–93). It could be argued that Tookie and Monster would be unlikely to confess (or hesitant to admit) that a woman could ever replace a man's allegiance to his gang. And yet the nar-rator of Always Running manages to keep his credentials by emphasizing the dangers of the situation because the girl is from a rival neighborhood. Homegirls provide the opportunity for men to become fathers and the narrator of Always Running plainly states that having children "is a source of power, for rep, like trophies on a mantel" (AR, 199). Monster boastfully declares as early as page three of his narrative that he has fathered three children (M, xiii).

The presence of children is often complicated for gangbanging fathers by the threat of death or incarceration. Traditional patriarchal responsi-bility for families has been affected by deindustrialization and reduction of welfare. According to black cultural critic bell hooks, under advanced capitalism in contemporary society "with the emergence of a fierce phal-locentrism, a man was no longer a man because he provided care for his family, he was a man simply because he had a penis."[34] hooks argues we are now witnessing a "dick thing" masculinity.[35] Furthermore, critics maintain that men are traditionally more shamed than women at being dependent on the welfare state.[36] When released from prison, Monster describes his "muscles bulging from everywhere" that prompts his girlfriend's "gaze dripping with lust" (*M*, 238). When eating at a restaurant that evening, his girlfriend is embarrassed to realize she is short of money for the bill. The narrator feels inadequate that he has no funds to assist. His momentary masculine lapse is reasserted when the waitress flirtatiously slips him her telephone number (*M*, 243). Monster is subscribing to two classic stereotypes of African American males as oversexed and on welfare.[37]

Monster even flaunts an openly sexualized cover photograph (see photo insert). Shakur pumped weights immediately prior to the photo shoot to emphasize his muscular physique, was stripped to the waist, wore sunglasses, and carried a machine gun. As the memoirist revealed in a post-publication interview: "It was some sexual shit. Here's this black dude with his shirt off, with his gun extended like a phallic symbol. Yeah, it was menacing; it was menacingly *sexual*."[38] *Monster* conforms to hooks's theories that a sexual conquest could bring as much status as being a wage earner and provider in today's society.[39] Within the specific framework of black performance, scholars have argued that sexual superiority is another legacy from slavery.[40] Because male slaves were physically unable to achieve full manliness in the workplace and were powerless to protect their black women from the sexual advances of white slave masters, they attempted to compensate by over achieving in the bedroom. When *Monster* was first published, Shakur received thirty to forty love letters daily.[41] Reviewer Mark Horowitz argued that there is very little in the book about the narrator's mother (or his childhood family) because it does not "fit with Monster's version."[42] Women serve sexual purposes; his mother does not suit these accounts and is therefore omitted.

Aside from its connection to masculinity (which reinforces the notable lack of female presence in the memoirs), the gun carries significance because of contemporary trends in popular culture. The cover photograph of *Monster* shows Shakur wielding a machine gun, presenting the narrator as a firm member of the handgun generation and moreover pointing toward a relaxation of standards over violent imagery.[43] The extreme exploits of *Monster* reflect changing genre conventions that permit such violent tales. Increasingly shocking popular culture texts in contemporary society can be attributed to two factors. Commencing in the 1960s, there was a distinct move toward increasingly violent and sexual imagery, as well as profane language, in the content of American films.[44] The viewing public grew ever more accepting of explicit content and desensitized to violence, with filmmakers using more close-ups than ever before and sounds of blood splattering.[45] The malaise of such contemporary popular culture is that its violent images are devoid of meaning. As criminologists Michael Lynch and Lenny Krzycki note, "it seems safe to say that the message no longer seems to matter as much as the economic viability of mass-produced popular cultural imagery."[46]

1968 was a landmark year in the history of film entertainment as Hollywood adopted a new, relaxed ratings code to replace the old, more conservative code in use since the 1930s. It permitted filmmakers the right to show almost anything. Similarly, cable television channels are not regulated by the Federal Communications Commission (FCC) and have exercised the right to show whatever material their directing boards deem suitable. Since the late 1960s, American society has grown increasingly violent. In cities with populations over one million like LA, the total violent crime rate nearly doubled between 1973 and 1990 alone.[47] The violence represented in contemporary popular culture texts has been strongly determined by this increasingly violent American society. This leads to a never-ending circle in which the increased violence in pop culture texts reflects an increasingly violent society, which in turn leads to the public finding violence more acceptable. This results in more violent movies, which then affects the society.[48] The violent, warrior nature of gang members, depicted through contemporary gang memoirs like *Monster*, is a classic example of such popular trends. The decline in standards of appropriateness means that more violent imagery can be used to make the narratives attractive.

Like weapons, male bravado and machismo goes hand in hand with violent warrior cultures, often flaunted among contemporary gangs by physically hardened bodies. Tookie states that bodybuilding was a "pinnacle of Crip-dom"; he makes regular references to lifting weights, takes off his shirt and flexes his muscles in public places, and signs autographs for women in awe of his macho physique (*R*, 166, 170). Only once in *Monster* does the narrator admit that someone might be superior to him. His description of the Crip boss is memorable: "Tookie was huge, beyond belief at that time: Twenty-two-inch arms, fifty-eight-inch chest, and huge tree-trunk legs" (*M*, 246–47). Despite such awe for his mentor, Monster also stresses his own size: "Swoll like a motherfucka!" (*M*, 239). The extreme act of violence in which Monster's gang chop the arms off a rival gang-banger with a machete now carries symbolic rationale, removing signs of manhood. Once Monster leaves prison and states his departure from the Crips, he gives up bodybuilding (*M*, 356).

The image of the muscular male body as circulated in pop culture has prompted two competing discourses. On one hand, the figure represents heroism and health, a triumphant assertion of discipline and control.[49] Such exaggerated gangsta masculinity has been interpreted as a gesture of defiance for young black men who feel helpless in a harsh society.[50] Tookie presents himself as extremely dedicated to his weight-training, setting a disciplinary example to fellow Crips (*R*, 252). On the other hand, the muscled body is seen as a grotesque and excessive distortion of a normal or "real" man. The narrator of *Blue Rage* is acutely aware of this second interpretation and knows his representation will be further marked by racist ideologies.[51] As he explains when the police raid his house: "I probably looked liked a huge black beast to them, shirtless and sweating from my workout" (*R*, 143). He acknowledges that this was the key point at which the police began to see him as "a super-nigger" who could "perform the impossible, even steal their guns while they were looking at me" (*R*, 143). His enormous size "frightened the hell out of the authorities" (*R*, 209). The narrator occupies a complicated position between these two discourses, being a role model for Crips and young black men, yet illustrating the negative possibilities of stereotyping muscular black men. The narrative suggests there is a fine line between black men asserting their masculinity in the face of this punitive culture and coming across as too dangerously masculine.

In *Monster*, prison holds special significance as a site of masculine cultures. Within prison, bodybuilding serves as a means of reasserting manly qualities in a space where the state attempts to emasculate marginalized men. Like the historical institution of slavery, prison denies masculine attributes of power, control, and authority. Monster memorably describes a favorite trick of certain prison officers being "to attack our private parts" (*M*, 139). Hyper-masculinity offers a means of resisting this repressive and violent system of black subordination. Hence it is understandable that Monster boasts of being "physically the second biggest in the institution" (*M*, 208). His size gains the respect of fellow inmates and, as in *Blue Rage*, often distances wary or nervous guards: "My size added to the Monster image, and I capitalized on it at every opportunity" (*M*, 208).

Auli Ek's study of prison texts suggests that prison tattoos are equally symbolic.[52] Like bodybuilding, tattoos can be read as a means of demarcating one's maleness.[53] Moreover, tattoos establish Monster and other inmates as individuals rather than generic prisoners, despite wearing mandatory prison uniforms (*M*, 233). But Ek argues that by constructing his masculinity around a corporeal image, the narrator is reproducing popular representations of African American criminal "otherness."[54] Monster retains and even fuels the image of black masculinity as violent, sexual, and corporeal.

Expectations of Latino male toughness have similarly permeated contemporary Mexican American gang culture; yet in *Always Running* the construction of masculinity revolves around failure and weakness.[55] The narrator's attempt at bodybuilding lands him in the hospital with a ruptured intestine, one of a number of incidents that suggest he has chinks in his warrior armor (*AR*, 60). He is encouraged to join a boxing club, proves to be unskilled, and embarrassingly loses an important fight (*AR*, 148–55). Suicide has traditionally carried cowardly connotations and has been seen as a violation of the codes of hardened masculinity, but the narrator is not ashamed to reveal that he contemplated slitting his wrists on more than one occasion. He contends that some gang members "stand on street corners, flashing hand signs, inviting the bullets" so they can, in appearance, remain on "the warrior's path" (*AR*, 9). Yet he honestly and openly portrays himself as gutless, not being able to self-harm for fear of his mother cursing about the bloody mess on the floor (*AR*, 81). His success with women to some extent compensates for other failures of manhood. But such ambivalence toward the construction of masculinity creates tension between the inwardly honest and unmanly narrator and the toughened physical gang behavior he outwardly conducts.

To narrate traumatic experiences, the narrator of *Always Running* uses the memoir to act as a confession for his physical actions, unashamedly showing a lack of bravado. He discloses that "killing for stealing didn't sit well with me" and he "didn't want to do this" when his gang plans to firebomb a rival's house (*AR*, 76, 119, 123). The narrator engages with extreme violence to demonstrate the true horrors of the gangsta lifestyle, but can avoid reprimand or make his narrative more acceptable by drawing clear distinctions between right and wrong. When conducting an armed robbery, he fails to recognize his own voice; when stabbing an enemy in the eye with a screwdriver, he experiences an out-of-body experience, not remembering the actual act (*AR*, 77, 111). His discomfort engages the reader emotionally and establishes narrative acceptability on grounds of his responsibility for his actions. The narrator's prolonged and conscientious confession establishes him as a psychologized badman who consequently demonstrates clear character development in his conversion from violent gangbanger to reformed individual.

The screwdriver incident furthermore serves to demonstrate ways in which gang members self-absolve responsibility by dehumanizing their victims. Invoking the Marxist concept of reification, the rival has his identity as a fellow human-being erased, becoming merely another gang member and hence a permissible target.[56] The narrator of *Always Running* exposes the way in which gangbangers kill and maim rivals simply as gang members rather than as fellow Mexican and African Americans or even actual humans. In hindsight, the narrator of *Blue Rage* vehemently concludes that "there is no bigger fool on earth than a man who destroys his own people" (*R*, 131). But at the time of events, the narrator of *Always Running* effectively pardons himself for the screwdriver assault because it is against another gang member.

Always Running and *Monster* detail homeboys who have been symbolically shot several times in the face (*AR*, 58; *M*, 28). This subplot—in which gangbangers dehumanize their victims in ways partially analogous to the ways in which the memoirists see the "system/state" dehumanizing inner-city dwellers—is present to some degree in all three memoirs. In the process, the perpetrators are also dehumanized. From this point of view, there is no sense of bravado or boastfulness in the narrators' gangsta behavior, merely nonchalant, desensitized narration. This serves to reveal the psychological horrors of gangbanging, in many ways worse than the detailed descriptions of torturous physical violence that appear throughout the narratives.

In *Monster*, the narrator also indicates what the reader should think during violent passages, imposing his censorious judgment on events rather than withdrawing to lend these scenes more immediacy. However, instead of conveying a moral conscience like the narrator of *Always Running*, Monster is boastful and macho. Following his first mission "to rid the world of Bloods" in the opening pages of the memoir, that evening he "feels guilty and ashamed" and sleeps little (*M*, 11, 13). In the next paragraph, however, he acquires his "Monster" moniker, and for the bulk of the memoir he seeks to maintain that image as a hardened Crip warrior. Monster now needs to shoot Bloods in order to sleep soundly and professes to numerous shootings simply because he "liked to see the buckshot eat away their clothing, almost like piranha fish" (*M*, 174, 83). Just as the narrator physically puts on a "mad dog" mask to "stare down rivals," he narrates such explicit violence in a similarly cold manner, keeping the reader at a distance and discouraging emotional involvement (*M*, 71). He can conduct a retaliatory shooting and casually return home to watch comedy, *The Benny Hill Show*, feeling "much better" (*M*, 65).[57] Neither the gangsta as a young man nor the mature narrator exhibits a conscience during such narrative episodes.

Instead of demonstrating principles or ethics, the narrator of *Monster* excuses his bravado behavior on account of the normality of this lifestyle by the 1980s. The flippant attitude with which he can commit murder and then watch a comedy show is shocking on account of its "banality of evil." Revenge, a common theme in warrior cultures, is portrayed as a customary component of the street gang lifestyle, as typical as watching a comedy show on the television. In hospital after having been shot, his roommate was "totally taken aback by LA's madness"; for Monster "it all seemed quite normal" (*M*, 99). He maintains a semblance of innocence and ordinariness amid all this madness by referring to popular television detective series *Baretta* and *Barnaby Jones*. *Blue Rage* too refers early in the narrative to *The Beverly Hillbillies*, *The Little Rascals*, *Family Matters*, and even *The Brady Bunch*, all popular television shows (*R*, 39, 5, 30, 32, 47). As the narrator of *Blue Rage* explains, "I was a normal child in an abnormal environment" (*R*, 203). Their (abnormal) normality is established using this series of accessible popular culture citations—which paradoxically also works to render their extreme violence more shocking. At the same time, such pop references do militate against the idea that the black experience is somehow separate and essentially different. In *Monster* in particular, the narrator constructs himself both as a normal American kid and as monstrously abnormal.

The "bad nigger" or "badman" has a long and rich expressive history in African American folklore. Subsumed within the broad term "bad nigger" are various stereotypes and caricatures, including a politicized figure who enacts violence for revolutionary purposes, or a depoliticized and destructive thug who commits senseless violence. The different personas are not necessarily polar opposites; there is some fluidity and overlap between them. These mythical templates have been used by several cultural scholars to explore contemporary black cultural forms including blaxploitation films and gangsta rap.[58] Such personas are similarly useful in examining gang memoirs and, though stemming from black folklore, can appropriately be applied to contemporary Mexican American gang culture. The narrators of all three memoirs mirror variants on the cultural template of bad niggers. When the bad nigger is presented as a murderous and nihilistic gangsta, it raises problematic questions surrounding issues of responsibility and representation.

The narrators initially construct themselves as warriors fighting for a noble cause against the state and other gangs. However, the metaphor of a "justified" war becomes less appropriate as time progresses—and the narrators are aware of this. The myth of the warrior or motivated badman, in some cases more than others, is challenged by the destructive bad nigger. These two frames of "badness" provide a means through which to interpret the kinds of violence presented in the three memoirs. The eras of civil rights and the Chicano movement witnessed numerous motivated acts of violence by Mexican American and African Americans that can be interpreted as legitimate responses to living in a society deemed to be racist. Cultural historian William Van Deburg contends that black "social bandits" of the era were hailed as heroes by fellow African Americans, while simultaneously frightening and bewildering whites.[59] For instance, while African Americans interpreted the calls for "black power" as empowering and courageous, the white mainstream was petrified and branded black power activists as subversive villains.[60] The revolutionary violence of blacks and Latinos during the 1960s and 1970s is aligned with the behavior of the historical badman of slavery, an outlaw hero who, despite murderous and violent tendencies, is celebrated by the black community for resisting dominant white culture.

For the politicized bad nigger presented by Van Deburg, violence was justified because the establishment was corrupt and unlawful. *Blue Rage* similarly focuses upon issues of structural violence, with the narrative conducting an exhaustive socioeconomic critique. Tookie admits that he cannot condone his past behavior, but attributes the violence he inflicted on rival gangbangers to being a "display of my frustration with poverty, racism, police brutality" (*R*, 207–8). Describing violence as a "display" of physicality, the narrator implies he was not a criminal or perpetrator at heart but rather a victim of deeper, often invisible structural forces that were outside his control.[61] The narrator widens his analysis to stress that such "systematic injustices" were experienced collectively by residents of urban black ghettos such as South Central (*R*, 207). He contends that such inequalities are extremely dangerous, offering himself as evidence of "what a black child can evolve into when he is ignored by society" (*R*, 121). *Blue Rage* proposes that the socioeconomic conditions that give rise to street gangs are more pertinent and informative than actual violent behavior.

Blue Rage stresses that the narrator was oblivious to the structural determinants of his life as he rose to his gangbanging prime in the mid-1970s (*R*, 207). As he succinctly explains: "I was duped into believing this toxic environment was normal. I was unaware of the violence being done to my mind" (*R*, 13). The teenaged Tookie demonstrates no interest in activism or politics like the narrator of *Always Running* at the same age, with the former confessing he was "unconscious" of the battle being fought on a higher level for black survival by civil rights organizations (*R*, 64). Considering the situation and circumstances with hindsight ("the problem, I now believe"), the narrator suggests his physical behavior as a gang member in fact carried weighty, political grievances (*R*, 41). The memoir thus carries two narrative voices: One narrates violent actions as a bad nigger, depicting a criminal guilty of senseless violence. The second explores badman behavior with politicized hindsight, arguing it was a motivated form of violence in response to a racist society. These two competing narrative threads are used effectively alongside one another to elucidate and explicate the violent imagery. The current narrator often reprimands his former self, creating friction between his old and new selves. His positioning as a reformed badman in his memoir lies tensely alongside his readiness to recount violent exploits from his depoliticized bad nigger phase.

Confined to death row and appealing his sentence, the narrator of *Blue Rage* has more at stake than the other two memoirists in his depictions of violence. The rhetoric of resistance has a long-standing history in African American culture, forming an integral part of the badman's character. Van Deburg contends the badman of the black power era exuded contempt for the system. Fighting his sentence appeal with vigor, Tookie exhibits classic badman characteristics of resisting white law. There is a motivated dimension to the memoir, fueled by the narrator's desperate wish for penal clemency that censors the narrative's representations of violence. This is not to say that the other two memoirists were not inspired, but instead that the motivated dimensions of Tookie arguably hold more weight. While writing his memoir, the narrator of *Blue Rage* was fighting a murder charge in which a shotgun was used. He uses the opportunity to protest his innocence and states in bold that, ever since he became involved with gangs, "we wanted to beat our enemies into submission, not kill them" (*R*, 74).

Tookie explains that the "horrors of gunplay" disturbed him to the extent that he never had a reputation for carrying a gun (*R*, 74, 153). Black cultural scholars have argued that despite the extensive control of the media and dominant commercial culture, artists do have some control over their image within contemporary black popular culture.[62] The narrator of *Blue Rage* relinquishes all responsibility for the increasing use of firepower by claiming the Crips only began to arm themselves when forced to do so by other gun-toting gangs (*R*, 86). He manages to maintain warrior respect by insinuating he was an excellent fighter and that carrying a gun was cowardly.

Rather than merely justifying his involvement with gangs on account of structural violence, Tookie lays the blame for his actions elsewhere. Though the other two memoirists also do this to a lesser degree, the narrator of *Blue Rage* in particular manipulates the narrative to underplay his own participation in an extremely violent culture that ultimately leads to a death sentence. For instance: ". . . force and violence. This was the American Way! Neither the Crips nor our rivals invented greed or violence, the basic capitalist theme of man-eat-man" (*R*, 148). Such bold critiques of the system attempt to incite sympathy in the reader for his complicated predicament in which he is caught in a cycle of violence that he did not instigate but for which he will receive violent punishment. As a seemingly redeemed man who is executed by the state, the narrator's victimization becomes a literal embodiment of his critique of state violence.

The narrative voice of *Always Running* similarly regulates the violent exploits, acknowledging representational responsibilities. Autobiography critics have noted that memoirists are aware of their duties to readers, family members, and future generations and hence often "police" their accounts.[63] The narrator of *Always Running* asserts that he drew the boundary of his criminal activity at sexual assault, refusing to partake in the rape quests of his homeboys (*AR*, 124). In the preface, the memoirist describes his emotional pleas with his son Ramiro, to leave the gang lifestyle, dedicating the memoir to "the Ramiros of this world" (*AR*, 11). In trying to set an example to his gangbanging son, the narrator makes light of some aspects of his violent lifestyle, soothing the tension between representations of violence and the genre's anti-gang message. In *Blue Rage*, the narrator states that the criminal acts he avoided were rape, drug-dealing, and burglary (*R*, 154). By including these brief but loaded statements the narratives claim a certain moral authority. They attempt to elicit the reader's trust by admitting to failings as human beings while demonstrating certain moral lines they will not cross.

The narrator of *Monster* seemingly has less moral accountability. His moral standards are questionable despite proudly proclaiming they treated female victims better than men. The statement that "We'd never rape the women, nor would we take the whole purse," seeks to justify his actions (*M*, 179). To counterbalance his maltreatment of others and make his own abusive behavior more acceptable, the narrator recites more horrific acts of violence enacted by others. In prison, fellow Crip Fat Rat extensively tortures a weaker inmate; during his final violent act of sodomizing the victim, Monster insists that Fat Rat refrain (*M*, 300). The narrator depicts prison rape as the ultimate crime, attempting to make his own exploits seem permissible and manly in comparison by commenting that "the only language Fat Rat knew—was violence" (*M*, 295). The narrator sets representational standards in violence that supersedes the other two memoirs in extremity but simultaneously positions himself in a morally superior position in order to present those images.

Monster dangerously provides fuel for racial profiling in the narrator's deployment of his gang moniker. "Monster" is a classic archetype of a criminal, and the narrator revels in such tagging.[64] After "stomping" a victim, the police inform bystanders that the person responsible for this was "a monster," reflecting the sensationalized use of the "gang-member-as-monster" trope common in police and media coverage of street gangs in the late 1980s and early 1990s (*M*, 13).[65] Though "monster" is applied in the memoir by white law enforcement, the narrator readily embraces the label as his gang moniker. The name becomes synonymous with fear, encouraging associations between blackness and criminality, as well as prompting peer respect and establishing individual identity within the gang. Respect and identity were likewise sought by the badman of black folklore. The moniker tale is crucial for setting the violent tone that pervades the entire narrative. All subsequent violent images are centered on his role as a monster, for under his new alias he must "consistently be more vicious and live up to the name" (*M*, 12). He subscribes to, rather than resists, the popular image of black man as criminal that could reflect badly on the wider black community, just like the depoliticized bad nigger of slavery who, in white eyes, committed random acts of futile violence. In black eyes, even gratuitous violence against whites could be deemed political.

Despite his lack of morals, toward the end of the memoir Monster suggests he has undergone a political awakening that can potentially counterbalance his earlier violent antics. He claims, "I took revolutionary premise seriously" (*M*, 349). The narrator is aware that "by not being a good black American I was resisting," and knows this resistance was "retarded" until it takes on a more meaningful form when he discovers George Jackson and other political mentors (*M*, 330). As with his morals, his politicization is

disputable. Black cultural scholar Kali Tal challenges the narrator's political conversion. Tal contends that it is only on page 348 out of a total of 383
that the narrator discusses his revolutionary edification, at which point he
merely recites a list of books without conducting meaningful economic and
social analysis.[66] It can be argued that *Monster* fails to express genuine radical and political rage, as prison memoirs had done during the civil rights
era.[67] The narrative consistently favors violent gangsta rhetoric over meaningful politicized or socioeconomic commentary. The epilogue of *Monster*
closes with remarks concerning the Rodney King riots and life for the "New
Afrikan man in this country" (*M*, 389). Yet this final chapter is dominated
by the haunting image of the narrator committing another violent assault
(*M*, 379). Though constructing himself by the end of the memoir as a social
revolutionary, the narrator has not distanced himself sufficiently from his
violent former self to lay claim to a full political and moral conversion. It is
a hollow and generic move without depth or narrative motivation.

Monster's excessive violent imagery with a lack of moral or political conscience points toward the "hip hop generation." The term, used by black
cultural critic Bakari Kitwana, identifies young black men born between
the mid-1960s and mid-1980s, disenchanted with activism and having no
interest or faith in politics.[68] Born in 1953 and 1954 respectively, Williams
and Rodriguez evade this grouping, Rodriguez in particular on account of
his activism while young. Williams can potentially be labeled a member
of the "bridge generation," too old to be a hip-hopper and too young to be
defined by civil rights and black power, yet playing a pivotal role in linking
the two groups.[69] In retrospect, *Blue Rage*'s narrator projects a sophisticated sense of the wider political forces that contextualized his childhood.
By comparison, the narrator of *Monster*, born in 1963, can be aligned with
the hip hop generation on account of his "don't give a fuck" attitude. Monster is clearly aware of these different cohorts, acknowledging "the language of older people, people I didn't know" (*M*, 263). The whole notion
of a hip hop generation can be heavily criticized for its reductive view of
a whole cohort. How do more politically conscious rap groups like Public
Enemy and KRS-One, or figures like Barack Obama, fit into this typology?
Yet there are a significant number of young black men within this generation, demonstrated by Monster and other characters in the narrative, who
exude a nihilistic attitude that can be aligned with the violent contemporary variation on the bad nigger of slavery.

The violence of the hip hop generation reached such extreme levels that
in *Monster* it is flaunted as sheer entertainment. As well as inflicting harm

on the black community, the destructive bad nigger of slavery often acted as a neighborhood bully. Such community damage is clearly witnessed in *Monster* when inmate violence within prison prompts lockdowns and punishments for all prisoners, not just the instigators. Monster unashamedly discusses his physical and mental intimidation of a fellow prisoner, proudly stating "This one was worth detailing" rather than being "a standard beat-down" (*M*, 148). He boasts of forcing the rival gangsta to drink a cup of urine and states his sustained bullying reduced "Tangle Eye to a basket case and [I] enjoyed the sight" (*M*, 150, 156). Though the episode is not essential for propelling the overall events of the narrative, it offers crucial insight into the narrator's character. Violence is a leisurely pursuit for the narrator in prison, and in turn he uses that violence as a narrative operation to entertain the reader, testing the limits of his narrative responsibility.

For the hip hop generation, black solidarity of previous decades was gradually replaced with an individualist fight for survival by any means necessary (despite the label "generation" ironically implying a kind of unity). This is again illustrated most clearly in *Monster*. According to the narrative, only the toughest and most aggressive men will survive prison, what bell hooks deems a "modern jungle."[70] Monster justifies his excessive aggression toward Tangle Eye and other inmates in terms of simple human nature: "The Darwinian theory of survival of the fittest continued to rule our existence" (*M*, 156). Prison is presented as the ultimate test of survival where, unlike the streets, you cannot flee your gang enemy. More so than in the other two memoirs, if the narrator does not fight his fellow black man he will die, because "it was kill or be killed, live and let die, law of the land" (*M*, 295). Such reasoning explicates his behavior on the streets, too. He states that he has shot numerous people, but the confession is offset by his subsequent comment that he has been shot seven times himself (*M*, 11).

The violence of *Monster* is further stressed as extreme and excessive in underlining the nature of the aggression as black-on-black. Such ethnic violence is referenced in all three memoirs: white subjugation has prompted a pathological misdirection of rage in which oppression is turned inward and violence inflicted on one another.[71] *Always Running* briefly refers to gang members targeting their "mirror reflection," while *Blue Rage* notes that "other black people became my prey" (*AR*, 9; *R*, 207). But in *Monster*, the haunting image of black genocide is explored further and this again occurs in prison. The violent acts of the motivated badman during the Chicano movement and black power era were more dangerous to the state because they challenged the status quo. By the 1980s Monster's spiritual advisor, Muhammad Abdullah, notes that gangbangers are less of a threat to the state when they fight one another: "as you kill each other, the real enemy is steadily killing you" (M, 219). Abdullah, as well as the memoirs more generally, point toward the ironies of the state system allowing (even encouraging) these rebel cultures that threaten the state's equilibrium to destroy one another. Monster explains that revolutionaries such as Muhammad want to stop black-on-black violence by proving it a result of white-on-black violence (M, 276). The narrative offers the shocking statistic that the biggest killer of Crips is in fact other Crips but validates such displays of black brutality and black bullying with a mind conditioned by white forces.

Monster presents the contemporary bad nigger as an outlaw figure who is now a menace to white society and also to his fellow African Americans. He is no longer a revered archetype, instead purely bad. This contemporary phenomenon of black-on-black violence is presented in *Monster* as having no political dimension and no collective characteristics. In contrast, the Watts riots of 1965 led to African Americans' collective protest against white police abuse. The black street gangs of LA in the late 1960s joined together to fight against the police oppressor, resulting in peace in the ghettos from 1965 to 1968. The description of events in *Always Running* throughout the Chicano movement, such as the high school walkouts—the "blowouts"—(1968) and the Moratorium Against the War (1970), reveals politicized, collective violence in the interest of the community. As the narrator of *Always Running* explains, "for a time, for a most productive and wonderful time, gang violence stood at a standstill" (AR, 166). During these periods, it was noted that "we had something more important to fight for" (AR, 166). By Monster's heyday, the revolutionary bad nigger has evolved into a more sinister character that kills fellow Crips for entertainment rather than self-defense, posing a threat to the moral value of the black community and increasing the paranoia surrounding the black ghetto male in the 1980s.

The presentation of violence in these memoirs rests on two narrative constructs. First is a self-conscious narrative trajectory to incorporate deteriorating social circumstances (resulting in more violence and different forms of violence) into their texts. It is interesting and important to consider the ways in which the memoirists build this periodization into their narratives. For instance, the narrator of *Always Running* tries to make sense of state power and abuse in the 1960s, building to a narrative climax of 1992 with the events of the LA riots telling much about the modern-day urban environment. The narrator reflects on the past two decades since his revolutionary experiences and highlights the displacement of progressive politics with gangsta culture, implying the two are incompatible.[72] Framing violence in these historical contexts is not surprising, and nor is the second narrative strategy of justification of their violent acts. The narrators' rationalization of violence creates interesting narrative tension and distance between the violent gangbanger and the reformed politicized narrator. It also offers the narrators permission to present their violent imagery. Their justification (and even apology in the case of *Blue Rage*) provides an ethical license to present their tales of the 'hood.

Though characters such as *Menace II Society*'s Sharif and *Boyz N The Hood*'s Furious Styles offer political scraps of commentary throughout the films, their ideologies are cynically rejected by violent characters such as Caine and O-Dog (*Menace*) and Doughboy (*Boyz*).[73] The films remain memorable for their depressing portrayal of marginalized men desperately trying to survive in a world of gang violence and poverty. Some rap artists in the late 1980s, like Public Enemy and Ice Cube, proffered politicized and socially profound rap lyrics, but were simultaneously preoccupied with vitriolic assaults on fellow gang members. These memoirs, somewhat surprisingly, only partially align themselves with the unmotivated, black-on-black violence of the bad nigger. Instead, as this chapter has revealed, the memoirs are less depoliticized than might be expected, offering detailed social critiques of state brutality and structural violence. Though the memoirs do offer some evidence of the same bad nigger who permeated rap and ghetto films (particularly *Monster*), such materials are counterbalanced by emphases on social analysis.

Even *Monster*, the most depoliticized of the three memoirs (and arguably carrying the most violent imagery), offers an extensive critique of state violence. To some extent this can be attributed to form: the memoir has more room for analysis than the restrictive limits of a rap song. Rap artists and producers were aware that public appetite for their music was likely fueled more by violent imagery than political commentary.[74] Two of the memoirs were written inside prison, their narratives invigorated by firsthand experience of state violence. Numerous rappers were familiar with the police forces, jails, courthouses, and prisons of LA and may well have written lyrics while incarcerated. The performative nature of rap required artists to be outside bars (and possibly not even on parole, if promotional travel was required). By comparison, the imprisonment of the authors readily became a commercial strategy for publishers. Tookie's circumstances, housed in the ultimate prison, further energized his critique of the state.

Nineteen sixty-eight was a crucial year in the shift from politicized badman toward nihilistic and dangerous bad nigger.[75] The year was a particularly violent moment in American history, with the assassinations of Martin Luther King (with subsequent riots) and Robert Kennedy, the Tet Offensive in Vietnam, and fighting at the Democratic National Convention in Chicago. The nation's fastest-growing minority group, Latinos, had begun to demand political and economic equality, and in 1968 the infamous Chicano "blowouts" were taking place at schools across LA. The narrator of *Always Running* exudes classic badman behavior in his tussles with the police to protect women and in his defiance of state power at rallies of the Chicano Movement. His justified violence is juxtaposed with the senseless violence that would be described in later years of gang memoirs. Also in 1968, Ronald Reagan infamously commented: "If Eldridge Cleaver is allowed to teach our children, they may come here one night and slit our throats."[76] Cleaver's prison memoirs gained popularity in that year, and Reagan's comment marked the tension between the revolutionary possibility of the politicized criminal versus the black man as criminal and incorrigible. His statement captures the themes of pedagogy and violence, the two premises that compete throughout this book.

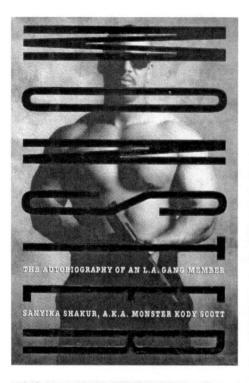

THE AUTOBIOGRAPHY OF AN L.A. GANG MEMBER

SANYIKA SHAKUR, A.K.A. MONSTER KODY SCOTT

DO OR DIE

For the first time, members of America's most notorious teenage gangs—the Crips and the Bloods—speak for themselves

BY LÉON BING

The images were all taken by photographer Howard Rosenberg in 1991 for the cover of Leon Bing's book. Rosenberg asked Shakur to take his shirt off and pump weights in the studio immediately prior to shooting the photographs to make him more "menacing." See Susan Faludi, "Ghetto Star," *Los Angeles Weekly*, 6 October 1999.

For the 2005 version the traditional Latino sketch was replaced with a photograph of a Mexican American gangbanger, not Rodriguez himself. Exuding stereotypes about gangsta and Latin male toughness, the subject's muscular back is in fact humbly consumed with tattoos of the Virgin of Guadalupe, the Virgin Saint of Mexico and a symbol of Indian/Mestizo pride for Mexicans. Though the long chain tattoo suggests a previous lengthy prison sentence, the religious presence of the Virgin Mary implies a request for forgiveness. Thus the reader can observe elements of sinning as well as faith and remorse, all key ingredients in "classic" prison conversion narratives.

ALWAYS RUNNING
Gang Days in L.A.
Luis J. Rodríguez

'**Fierce and fearless.**'
— New York Times

In written correspondence with Rodriguez, he
confirmed that he did not have any input on the
cover of the Marion Boyars edition and "personally
didn't think it was compelling." When Rodriguez
looked for the book in London many years ago, he
saw it in the True Crime section of a bookstore and
felt it may have been marketed wrong.

In an author interview, Barbara Becnel (Williams's friend and co-author of some of his books) explained that Williams and she were responsible for designing the original Damamli cover of his memoirs.

STANLEY TOOKIE WILLIAMS

CRIPS CO-FOUNDER AND NOBEL PEACE PRIZE NOMINEE

BLUE RAGE,
BLACK
REDEMPTION

A MEMOIR

EPILOGUE BY BARBARA BECNEL

FOREWORD BY TAVIS SMILEY

In an author interview with Becnel, she explained that she did not have final say on the Simon & Schuster cover, though "I did fight—and prevailed—to prevent Simon & Schuster from using a picture of Stan in handcuffs for the cover."

"A fascinating and frightening read" *FHM*

REDEMPTION

The Last Testament of
Stanley Tookie Williams
Gang Leader turned Nobel Prize Nominee

Milo would rerelease a posthumous edition in the
UK that included a prologue by Becnel detailing the
execution itself. Note the slightly different title.

Chapter Four

BROTHERS WHO COULD KILL WITH WORDS

Language, Literacy, and the Quest for Education in Gang Memoirs

Gangsta rap and ghetto films both savor graphic and aggressive imagery. Film scholar Jonathan Munby describes the ghetto action movie cycle as "uncompromisingly violent," contending that these films "struggled to provide a positive message about the fate of America's black urban communities."[1] Violence is certainly an integral and typical characteristic of gangsta popular culture, and one aim of this book is to consider whether contemporary street gang memoirs fit readily into that gangsta ethos. But in contrast with the gangsta penchant for contentious subjects such as extreme violence, the memoirs diverge from their musical and filmic counterparts by engaging with more positive themes, including self-help (learning to read and write by oneself) and conversion through education. The memoirists deploy narrative tactics and approaches to make moves toward becoming pedagogical rather than violent narrators.

Formal education is the traditional portal for acquiring language and literacy skills; the narrators of *Blue Rage* and *Always Running* discuss their childhood schools at length. Educational institutions are depicted in all three narratives as sites of conflict, whereby the right to language and literacy must be forcibly negotiated, suggesting these marginalized young men fought an uphill battle to acquire the skills to narrativize their experiences. Language and literacy skills undertake a symbolic role, serving as a figurative alternative to guns. They are also deemed structurally prerequisite for survival and success in mainstream American society. They can fuel playful identities, hold historical significance, even save lives.

This chapter will explore how themes of pedagogy are developed in the memoirs. The lack of conventional education acts as a narrative springboard working to expose and critique unequal social relations in the United States. Working-class non-white youths are frequently sidelined, often receiving a substandard education. For example, in 1988 the high school dropout rate for the entire LA Unified School District (LAUSD) was 39.2 percent, but for schools in South Central the dropout rate was significantly higher, estimated at between 63 percent and 79 percent.[2] This launches a potent social critique of the failings of educational institutions. The chapter will consider whether these authors were actually failed by school, how they construct these disappointments in their memoirs, and what insights such experiences may reveal.

At the same time, the rejection of conventional education opens up space for personal trajectories. The failure of state structures leads to dramatic stories of informal education and advancement on the street and especially in prison, where conversion usually takes place. The narrators demonstrate personal strength and the ability, against the odds, to overcome this adversity. Through using unconventional and improvised resources (the gang, the street, and the prison, among other means), the narrators can gain status and ultimately write their own life stories. While these accounts of overcoming difficult odds offer certain traditional American narrative pleasures of self-reliance and rugged individualism, the difficult and unpredictable journeys told in these memoirs also expose the faultlines and inequalities of living in the contemporary United States. The generic expectations in American culture—and in memoirs themselves—of mobility and uplift are followed by true-life or actual dimensions that are far less teleological, creating tensions that will be addressed in this chapter.

Like the previous chapter, this one is driven by textual evidence. It will commence with an exploration of the representations of formal education in the memoirs, followed logically by the depictions of informal education on the street and in prison. Though the chapter is primarily concerned with how the memoirists narrativize their identities and lived experiences using language, literacy, and education as frames for discussion, it will close with a consideration of how the narrators construct themselves as authorial educators. The textual focus is the three memoirs; however, when discussing the possibilities surrounding the narrator as teacher, the final section of this chapter will make brief reference to the children's series of books that Williams released to help elementary children learn to read.

In all three memoirs schools are presented as a site of crisis in which schooling is portrayed as unconstructive and unsupportive. In *Always*

Running the narrator describes high school in East LA in the late 1960s and early 1970s as a place where speaking Spanish was deemed a punishable offense that could lead students to be classified as mentally disabled by impatient teachers (*AR*, 21, 26–27). The narrator's participation in the Chicano movement later prompts slightly more positive experiences of schooling. An early chapter of *Blue Rage* details the narrator's experiences in the early 1960s at an elementary institution in South Central LA. In this account, pencils and erasers were absent, shelved books were used to decorate the classroom rather than for reading, while engagement with physical-play items such as clay and papier-mâché took priority (*R*, 26). And by the time Monster was admitted to juvenile hall aged sixteen in 1980, he admits, his reading and writing skills were substandard (*M*, 68).

The narrators engage with the subject of deteriorating schools to provide social insight into life as a Mexican or African American young man in urban California in the period 1965–90. As governor of California from 1967 to 1975, Ronald Reagan slashed education budgets; per capita student expenditure in California fell from ninth to thirty-third place nationally, or merely a third of the per capita level of New York.[3] He would continue this budgeting trend on a national level during his time as president throughout the 1980s. When Reagan took office the federal share of total education spending was 12 percent; when he left it was 6 percent.[4]

By 1990, according to social historian Mike Davis, the LA school system was "travelling backwards at high speed."[5] Davis notes some irony in the use of the word "unified," for in reality the LAUSD operated separate systems for blacks, Latinos, and whites. Educational sociologists have addressed such problems, noting that policies such as grade retention and reliance on standardized testing have disenfranchised minorities at school.[6] Black and Mexican youth are disproportionately placed in special-education classes and more likely than white students to be subjected to extreme disciplinary measures.[7] Davis stresses that the consequences of failing schools can be devastating, stunting mobility and denying mainstream access to life.

Of the three narratives, *Always Running* is the quickest to illustrate the potential power of education and the narrator's respect for educated people. The preface details the memoirist's struggles to save his own son from gangbanging; his plan to do so involves assistance from school officials and teachers. He contends his son needs "complete literacy," using the phrase to denote reading and writing skills (*AR*, 9). Complete literacy is furthermore presented as a tool that enables children to become adults who can

function independently in society, participating "competently and confi-
dently in any level of society one chooses" (*AR*, 9). In chapter 1 the narrator proudly announces that back in Mexico his father was an educated
man—"unusual for our border town"—who became principal of the local
school (*AR*, 14–15). After the family moves to the United States and the
narrator commences high school, the teacher insinuates he is not wanted
(*AR*, 26). As he explains, "in those days there was no way to integrate the
non-English speaking children" (*AR*, 27). These opening pages present the
pedagogical dilemma that runs throughout the memoir: education is crucial for life survival, yet one will struggle to obtain that education.

Though formal schooling fails the narrator of *Always Running* and
numerous Spanish-speaking children in California in the early 1960s, the
memoir progresses to portray certain achievements of the school system. Such successes are attributable in the narrative to the heated Chicano movement of the late 1960s and early 1970s. From the outset, the
narrator's prose smoothly incorporates Spanish words or phrases, with
a glossary provided. His inclusion of Spanish marks the fierce loyalty of
Mexican Americans to their traditional culture (language being a defining feature of culture), reflecting social and political events that were taking place throughout the United States at that time. Being forced to speak
English at school was deemed an insult to Mexican heritage and an assault
on civil rights. This posed a serious cultural dilemma that was, according
to the narrator, "the predicament of many Chicanos" (*AR*, 219). The narrator elucidates his heavy involvement in the 1968 East LA school blowouts,
becoming leader of the Chicano student organization at his high school
and organizing several walkouts. He is also voted the Movimiento Estudi-
antil Chicano de Atzlán (MeCha) organizer for East LA schools. In these
roles he demanded the inclusion of Spanish in high school curricula, and
his triumphs are symbolically represented by the use of Spanish in his narrative. By incorporating Spanish the narrator triumphantly rebels against
the linguistic rules his own school had sought to enforce.

The requests of high school protestors during the Chicano movement
were not limited to the inclusion of the Spanish language in the classroom. *Always Running* illustrates that, as their frustration continued to
build, they insisted on strict academic commitment at both high school
and college level to the study of Chicano literatures and the recruitment
of Chicano faculty. The narrator is concerned that his school's curriculum centered on the Western canon. His request to write a book review
of Beatrice Griffith's famous study of Mexicans in California, *American*

Me, is overturned and he is instead required to write about Wordsworth (*AR*, 139). He states that the authors they read in school were either dead or English and hence of little relevance for these youths (*AR*, 91). The successes of the Chicano movement in improving access to education for Mexican Americans is ultimately marked for the narrator by his enrollment at California State University with its professors of Chicano studies. A college education is widely recognized to be the fastest route out of poverty for marginalized young men.[8] Though the narrator later quits university, he insinuates that his participation in educational protests contributed to his formal qualifications, educational feats that surpass those of the other two narrators.

The educational achievements of the narrator of *Always Running* are ultimately superior to those of the other two in the way the narrator points himself toward literary greatness, an unusual tendency for this genre of gang memoirs. The narrator introduces himself as a "poet" as well as a "journalist, publisher, critic," all highly literate roles that demand to be taken seriously (*AR*, 4). He is frank about his literary pretensions, asserting the narrative is "in keeping with the integrity of a literary, dramatic work" (*AR*, 11).[9] He often uses expressive and magical similes to describe sights and sounds: "descending like a torrent of leaves, like the blaze of dawn," "like old men's whiskers," "like a raven's wail" (*AR*, 39, 5, 25). As a result, in literary critiques of the text, scholar Tim Libretti refers to it as "an autobiographical novel" while Vincent Perez's essay compares it with a novel (Ronald Ruiz's *Happy Birthday Jesus*).[10] As a means of legitimizing his new position as a literary artist, the narrator cites prestigious authors, stressing his knowledge of the classic canon. He is proud of the literary traditions that inform his narrative, for example referencing Piri Thomas's *Down These Mean Streets* as one of his foremost influences (*AR*, 138). On the first Touchstone edition of *Always Running*, a Thomas quotation even graces the back cover, praising Rodriguez for his "strong singular voice."[11] The narrator of *Always Running* is complicit in recognizing an exclusive literary canon and wanting to be part of it.

Blue Rage likewise shows concern with a lack of cultural awareness in schools, for example, no encouragement of African American history (*R*, 35). The need for appropriate education in hindsight forms the basis of much of the educational discussions in *Blue Rage*. The narrator of *Blue Rage* does briefly mention two black women who were "exceptionally kind to all the children" at elementary school (*R*, 29). Their compassion however, is not sufficient to counteract his "dys-education"—a term the narrator coins to depict "the abnormal, impaired, and diseased knowledge I received in life and from the public school system," emphasizing that this is different from merely being "uneducated" (*R*, 14, 25). The narrator is shocked in retrospect that by age thirteen he had not been introduced to any African American writers at school. Despite Williams being born one year earlier than Rodriguez, Tookie explains that he had no knowledge of and no involvement with the black civil rights movement or black power at that time. It can be argued that the civil rights movement did not infiltrate schools in LA to the same degree as the Chicano movement. However, the narrator of *Blue Rage* now argues for "a valid psychoanalytic model for black people and the black experience" that includes black history and black social studies (*R*, 41). He believes such a model should form a crucial part of the education of all black youth.

The LA education system in the late 1960s and early 1970s is further criticized by the narrator of *Blue Rage*, who implies that his dysfunctional schooling propelled him toward a life of crime. At elementary school the narrator informs us that he was "a darn good reader for my age" (*R*, 27). Being particularly fascinated with an encyclopedia about dogs, he reflects that in this reading world "there was no poverty, no discrimination, no violence, no racism, no pain" (*R*, 27). Reading was "a way of escaping from my often-riotous thoughts" (*R*, 27). Yet with no reading permitted in the classroom, he is forced to pilfer books from the school library shelves, resulting in punishment. With a lack of books to occupy him both inside and outside the classroom, he is soon submerged in the underground world of illegal dog fighting (*R*, 15). The supposedly respectable institution of school is paradoxically established as the trigger to his criminal career.

The narrator's critique of his education incorporates a theme of blame that resonates throughout the memoir. He attributes his rage to "mainstream society and white people," and his self-loathing is "based on my black skin and my historical place at the nadir of America's social system" (*R*, 301, 207). The narrator constructs himself as much a victim of the system as a perpetrator of gang crime, encompassing bold statements such as, "Because I am guilty of being black" (*R*, 301). His first official experience of second-place citizenship takes place in the school. Tookie explains they were denied access to the American Dream on account of color and class and thus began a "Crip-walk toward self-destruction" (*R*, 93). Being established while still a child as an outsider to reading symbolically reflects the bigger picture of what is yet to come—becoming an outcast to mainstream society as an adult. Tookie carries his critique further than that of the narrator in *Always Running* by not merely criticizing the pedagogical curriculum but forging explicit links with the potential outcome.

Blue Rage continues to censure the LAUSD throughout the narrator's secondary education, now for its failure to curb violence. Regularly expelled for fighting, the narrator is moved from school to school and the name "Tookie" becomes synonymous with "troublemaker" for most local teachers (*R*, 98). Both *Always Running* and *Blue Rage* detail pages of fights at school where even the teachers run for cover (*AR*, 44). In the eighteenth and nineteenth centuries, public schools were considered a preventative method and actual solution to urban violence and disorder. The belief that schools could serve as a cure for delinquency persisted well into the 1960s.[12] By these narrators' school days, schools are presented as no longer able to provide youth with a promise of freedom and protection. School days are now injurious and even potentially deadly when the catchment area of institutions includes students from rival gang turfs. As *Always Running* details, "Bloody kotexes on the hallway floor. Gang graffiti on every available space of wall. Fires which flared from restroom trash bins. Fights everyday . . ." (*AR*, 44). Such precarious conditions stir concern that children are subjected to such experiences and, in the case of *Always Running*, incite respect that the narrator should actually graduate despite such barriers.

In contrast to *Always Running* and *Blue Rage*, the high school in *Monster* is practically nonexistent. In the opening pages of the memoir, the narrator is suspended from elementary school for throwing a gang sign during a class photograph (*M*, 4). School thereafter plays a minor role in the narrative. Brief references explain that Monster sporadically attends to satisfy his probation officer, while his mother screams that the purpose for attendance is "To learn, dammit, to learn!" (*M*, 70). The narrator states that "being ignorant, is to me the equivalent of being dead," but shows indifference to high school, stating "Academics just couldn't hold my attention" (*M*, 117, 71). He implies the blame for his disinterest and thus educational failures lies with the system itself. By the 1980s, when Monster should have been in school and with Reagan's slashed budgets, fewer youths than ever were attending schools. Though education has long been considered an escape route out of poverty, time spent at school was considered wasteful when youths could be making money in the illegal drugs economy. Cultural studies scholar Eithne Quinn notes that in these changing socioeconomic times marked by government disinvestment in schools, gangsta rappers "rejected the conventional notion that formal education leads to economic success and to the eradication of racial inequality."[13]

It is therefore predictable that Monster dedicates little narrative space to schooling, as school simply did not figure in the lives of many urban youths in the early 1980s. The dropout rate for senior high school students in South Central in 1988 was over 60 percent, and 25 percent for junior high students, the institution Monster should have been attending for much of the narrative.[14] My reasoning varies from David Brumble's literary analysis of Monster. Rather than contextualizing the memoir in the failing school system of the 1980s, Brumble states that Monster offers sparse detail of childhood schooling because the narrator is aligning himself with warriors from tribal cultures. Such (gangbanging) warriors "characteristically think of the story of their life as being the stories of their great deeds, their coup tales."[15] Thus, the opening chapter of Monster deals with the narrator's first shooting. Brumble makes a case for classifying both Monster and Blue Rage as memoirs that are not fully "outside" the gangsta lifestyle. Yet perhaps Tookie's extended accounts of school indicate he is not as hopelessly connected with gangbanging (re classic tribalism) than his younger counterpart.

The failure of formal education is thus illustrated in the three memoirs through a variety of resources, including cultural discrimination or a lack of any education at all. Regardless of the type of pedagogical failings, there is a recognized correlation to gang growth, suggesting Tookie does have the right to accuse his school of propelling him into a life of crime. As gang scholar Diego Vigil explains, the gang and its urban context can become a substitute for conventional education as well as other traditional institutions: "with stressed family experiences and poor schooling experiences, many youths are pushed out into the streets for their education—[the gang] remains the socialiser of last resorts and fills the void in parenting, schools and policing."[16] Sergeant Wes McBride, formerly of the LASD, argues for teaching youths to read and write, claiming this will immediately reduce their chances of becoming involved with gangs.[17] In the year before Monster and Always Running were released, gang members themselves acknowledged the importance of educational intervention when, in the aftermath of the Rodney King riots, several demands were made by the Crip–Blood truce directed at the LAUSD. Despite such educational setbacks as children, all three gang memoirists acquired an education sufficient to author a book, the symbol of linguistic fluency and literate success. But before they reach their authorial status, the failing schools push them into the streets leading to crime, delinquency, and an unusual form of education.

Though school is the conventional portal for acquiring use of standard English (verbal, reading, and writing skills), for gang members the streets themselves become an informal place for learning vocabulary, albeit an unconventional one. The distinctive subculture of contemporary street gangs includes a vocabulary that has been created for their own private usage. As Tookie explains, "words were coined for our madness" (*R*, 92). Subcultural slang has been widely acknowledged by gang scholars, and the narrative presentation and discussion surrounding this street vernacular offers important insight into the narrators' characters. The streets are specifically depicted as the location for this linguistic development in the two African American memoirs. Monster claims the streets are "the only thing in this life that has ever held my attention for any serious length of time"; Tookie explains, "Downtown Los Angeles became our institution of higher learning" (*M*, 5; *R*, 37). The school as an institution of education is displaced with the informal urban setting of the gangs' streets.

The re-spelling of "nigger" into "nigga" serves as an example of how language is subverted by contemporary gang members, as demonstrated in the two memoirs. According to the narrator of *Blue Rage*, in the early 1970s the word "nigger" conveyed racist connotations toward blacks (*R*, 45). But the two narrators demonstrate acute awareness of the politics of language in which one can identify, subvert, and challenge the power relations in traditional language. By the 1980s, Monster's use of the refashioned "nigga" in South Central suggests the word is a term of endearment. Within cultural studies, "nigga" has been seen to signify the depressing social realities of the young black experience of the late 1980s and early 1990s in America caused by deindustrialization, loss of welfare, and escalating punishments.[18] Its refashioning from "nigger" has been explored by contemporary black cultural scholars, who reveal the complex and ambivalent meanings of the term.[19] The respelling of the ethnic "gangster" into racialized "gangsta" has similarly been seen as key to understanding the current functions of this contemporary linguistic, urban movement.[20] This is notably prevalent in *Monster*, in which the narrator is incessantly yelling "gangsta" when he pulls a trigger, calling his friends "nigga," swearing using "motherfucka" and encouraging others to call him "Monsta" (*M*, 64, 17, 240).

Within street speech there is distinctive wordplay and a tendency to develop insiderist language and signs. From the outset of *Monster*, standard English and the gangsta vocabulary compete for space, providing literal narrative battles. Military jargon, comic book violence (BOOM! CLICK! DOOM! KABOOM! POW! POW! SWOOSH!) and gangsta vernacular are interspersed with descriptive narrative in standard English (*M*, 92, 174, 179, 240, 272–73). Monster cannot verbally communicate using the latter; instead, his speech becomes increasingly reconfigured toward gangsta as he submerges deeper into gangbanging. For example, "Fuck you slob-ass muthafuckas, this is ET muthafuckin' G, fool"—where "slob" is a derogatory term for rival Blood gang members, "ET" is Eight Tray (Shakur's own set) and "G" means "Gangsta" (*M*, 133). Philosopher Mikhail Bakhtin notes that words exist in other people's mouths and contexts and serve other people's purposes.[21] Words in language only become "one's own" when "the speaker populates it with his own intentions, his own accent—adapting it to his own semantic and expressive intention."[22] *Monster* appropriates language for gangsta ends and effect far more than the other two narrators, and "owns" language the most. In tune with the extreme nature of the narrative, *Monster* implies that failing to grasp such linguistic developments may result in death.

Tookie does not relate his gangbanging years with the same degree of gangsta diction, though he does explore the problems with such urban dialect. When *Blue Rage* occasionally uses gangsta vernacular, the words are incorporated within quotation marks as if to emphasize that they are now outside of the narrator's formal vocabulary. Critics have noted that the increasing isolation of America's black underclass is not just economic and spatial but also linguistic.[23] *Blue Rage* addresses the ways in which contemporary urban African American youth can be segregated from their white counterparts through language. Having moved from rural Louisiana to South Central, Tookie and his sister are mocked for sounding "proper," meaning "that because our speech patterns were devoid of ghetto vernacular, we were acting 'white.' Being called proper was a euphemism for being an Uncle Tom—the white man's black man" (*R*, 44). The narrator quickly picks up ghetto vocabulary on the streets. His mother responds by sending him to speech etiquette classes; she believes in the view that "white" English is needed for societal success (*R*, 45). Though teased for this instruction, in Williams's children's books the narrator notes why his mother was so determined that he should speak formally: "You need to speak well to do well in school and to get a good job as an adult."[24] That *Blue Rage*'s narrator references his dialect classes emphasizes his acute consciousness of the power of accent and speech. These skills can affect how one is perceived in terms of both class and race.

Black urban English has pervaded contemporary Mexican American youth cultures, too. As the narrator of *Always Running* elucidates, when he and his friends learned to speak English on the streets, it was often "black English" they first tried to master (*AR*, 85). More notably in the memoir, the narrator of *Always Running* learns "Spanglish" informally on the streets. The text often subverts English and Spanish, blending words to create Spanglish, also known linguistically as "calo."[25] The narrator incorporates Spanglish into his narrative to construct his life on the street realistically and, to accurately present his own linguistic experiences as an immigrant. The Spanish in *Always Running* forces the English-speaking reader into an alien world, cleverly recreating the feelings of anxiety that the narrator describes when his family moved to America and he attended school. His incorporation of Spanish into the English narrative also challenges the mainstream attitude of the early 1960s, that Spanish was a private language to be silenced and kept behind closed doors, while English was a public language required to assimilate successfully into American life. The narrative's extensive incorporation of Spanish derides the tradition of presenting Spanish as inferior to white, superior English.

An established ritual in both Mexican and African American gangsta subcultures is the use of personalized gang monikers on the street. The birth name (Scott, Rodriguez, Williams) associated with the parent culture is displaced by a ghetto or barrio persona (Monster, Chin, Tookie). Nicknames represent acceptance and membership into the gang and reassert individual identity within that group. The moniker "Monster" is particularly noteworthy for the way in which it subverts traditional meanings and reproduces power structures, establishing identity by challenging normative values. The gangsta subculture rejects the parental meaning of the word "monster," its negative connotations displaced with a badge of honor. For marginalized youth to rebel against the punitive and unsympathetic mainstream culture and become a criminal, a "monster," is celebrated. Monster explains that once he has been honored with such a moniker, he is expected to "live up to the name" (*M*, 13). Such inventive language offers a means to gain status through the gang and indicates street savvy.

Even if the memoirists have developed street smarts, they show little political or educational self-awareness at this stage. Yet their life experiences on the streets will eventually prove to be formative in their conversions into memoirists. While prison scholars tend to focus on prison itself as the crucial moment of change, cultural critic Robin Kelley contends that Malcolm X's pre-prison years are the most generative and set the scene for his radicalization.[26] Brumble believes "Kody feels that these stories define him, give his measure, and allow us to understand his fame."[27] The street tales are particularly important for the narrator of *Always Running*, considering this is the site at which his conversion predominantly takes place. For the other two narrators, though they are not yet aware of it, the streets will play a decisive role in their conversion. As chapter 3 illustrated, these memoirists earn status through toughness on the streets. But as will now be revealed, they all go on to write memoirs and gain literary status. For two of them, this conversion significantly takes place in prison, suggesting there is a need for a more flexible model of conversion that incorporates Kelley and Brumble, as well as recognizing the importance of the prison.

The streets of LA's ghettos and barrios provide a distinctive informal level of education, with prison providing another, arguably more productive layer of informal education. Prison education is portrayed in *Blue Rage* and *Monster* as replacing a previously defunct school education, supplying much-needed reading and writing skills that enable one to write a book despite the difficult circumstances. In these two memoirs the streets only provide verbal skills, but prison permits development of reading and writing proficiency. As a result of these skills—combined with other contributory factors, such as a political and historical education leading to self-awareness—prison becomes the site at which classic conversion takes place. When Tookie is taken into the LA County Jail on murder charges, he states, "this was the beginning of phase two of my life" (*R*, 206–7). Just as language helps Monster stay alive on the streets, here literacy can potentially help one survive the state.

In being depicted as a site of conversion in *Blue Rage* and *Monster*, the prison becomes a contested space. It is a harsh environment that paradoxically can be a space for mental discipline and education, becoming a site of personal salvation. The narrator of *Monster* boasts that prison is the final "test" in a series that includes juvenile hall, camp, and youth authority (different types of secure detention for delinquent minors), and with each "comes longer, harder time" (*M*, 27). The narrator does refer to the possibility of learning criminal ways from fellow incarcerated outlaws and illustrates that gangbanging is an extensive practice in prison (*M*, 164). But while being the site of ultimate punishment and criminality, it is simultaneously portrayed as an educational space. For Monster, prison plays a pivotal role in his self-education where his reading and writing skills improve. Prison becomes a site of positive learning in which young men can make an autonomous choice to pass their time productively rather than physically fighting. So, perversely, the oppressive state saves the criminal, or provides opportunity for some kind of personal redemption despite the intention of prison.

Earlier prison narratives set the trend for the prison cell as an alternative place of educational retreat. Malcolm X placed prison second to college as a place for learning; Eldridge Cleaver claimed to have been educated by the Californian prison system.[28] The narrator of *Blue Rage* similarly asserts that prison enabled him to study more intensively than if he had attended college with its women, fraternities, and parties: "Where else but in a prison could I have attacked my ignorance by being able to study intensively sometimes as much as fifteen hours a day?" (*R*, 275). The prose of *Blue Rage* regularly flows as if the narrator has memorized a dictionary: "We didn't want to be disenfranchised, dyseducated, disempowered, and destitute" (*R*, 92). Though such words appear from the start of the narrative rather than during his prison days, Tookie makes plain that it was not until he "attended" prison that he discovered the dictionary. Malcolm X was also renowned for memorizing the dictionary, an action that is such an unusually intensive form of study that it exceeds college and school expectations. The narrator engages in a study group with two fellow prisoners, claiming "we needed to learn hundreds and thousands of new words" (*R*, 252). Like Malcolm X, for Tookie these words fulfill a void left by formal education and displace the informal vocabulary learned on the streets.

In addition to this impressive vocabulary, *Blue Rage*'s narrator exhibits his wider circles of study in prison. He introduces his world of "noble" studying by including numerous Latin and French words listed in italics that the reader is unlikely to have previously encountered (*R*, 245). Among numerous examples are "carte blanche," "entente," "soiree," "lex talionis," and "felix culpa" (*R*, 252, 102, 101, 88, 89, 168, 265). By proving his knowledge of Latin, for a long time the international language of science and scholarship throughout Europe but today rarely taught, the narrator is crucially defying the white stereotype of blacks as uneducated animals. He implies that the prison authorities encourage such typecasts of black men as cursed and crude criminals: "as long as I remain imprisoned, I will continue to be challenged to remain a human being and not a beast" (*R*, 294). That he gained an education at all while incarcerated, let alone a far-reaching one, is remarkable. His engagement with rare scholarly subjects such as Latin, as well as specifically black subjects (mainly history and politics), firmly establishes his credentials despite incarceration.

For the narrator of *Monster*, too, foreign languages provide a test of self-education within prison. Both Monster and Tookie chose to study

Swahili, with the latter narrator emphasizing that this was "auto-didac-tic—self-taught" (*R*, 268). Monster's engagement with Swahili forms part of his political and religious conversion to the Nation of Islam. Tookie's decision to learn Swahili was inspired by a wish to recapture a more accurate picture of his black ancestors.[29] He is proud of his stringent dedication to the task, practicing for one hour every day with his neighbor as well as reciting in the yard between his strict exercise routines (*R*, 268). For inmates who failed to complete high school, California prisons offer the chance to undertake the General Educational Development (GED) tests. When passed, the GED proves that a candidate has high school level skills. Yet Swahili is an exclusive subject, not offered at state high schools. The narrators opt for their own education, defying the formal GED by reclaiming rights to their African ancestors' dialect. Mastering these unusual foreign languages (both Swahili and Latin) can be viewed, like writing a book, as a disciplined and impressive educational feat.

Though the narrator of *Monster* is far more extensive in the details of his street education, he contends he could never have been touched by such readings in the street (*M*, 223). In prison the narrator finds a linguistic alternative to his gangsta vernacular and lifestyle. On the streets, guns had previously been the tools of communication: "verbalizing was not an issue. Shoot first" (*M*, 228). Inside prison, he is introduced to "brothers who could kill with words" and words now displace guns (*M*, 228–29). (In an interview in 1994, Rodriguez similarly commented, "Today I fight with words, ideas and poetry."[30]) The violent, cartoonish vocabulary wanes and, upon release, the narrator requests that his friends do not use words such as "nigga" or "Monsta" (*M*, 364). Language and literacy are presented as sufficiently powerful to spark the narrator's prison conversion. He carefully analyzes the effect of words, explicitly addressing their sheer strength and spiritual nature: "I felt the words seeping deeper into me, their power coursing through my body, giving me the strength to push on. I was changing, I felt it" (*M*, 223). In addition to being an informal education institution, prison also becomes a location for personal conversion.

In addition to his linguistic conversion, Monster's evolving political identity is fed by guidance from his mentor Muhammad Abdullah and from the books he is supplied (prison memoirs by Malcolm X and Eldridge Cleaver, among others). The narrator is acutely aware of this, reflecting in the narrative's closing pages, "prison had been where I'd acquired knowledge of self and kind" (*M*, 367). For the state, prison is the ultimate site in which to repress the black man. For the inmate, incarceration facilities can become the perfect place in which to learn about suppression. Once educated, Monster realizes that, having not been "a good black American" all his life, he had been resisting (*M*, 330). But the narrator contends this resistance was "retarded" because it had no political objective (*M*, 330). He vows to change his status as an unconscious resister, and can do so when he later re-enters prison at San Quentin. As a fellow prisoner points out on their entry at the legendary incarceration facility, "this is the house that George Jackson built—you'll read books here, see things here, that are gonna change the way you walk, talk and think. This is the best place for an aspiring young revolutionary. This is repression at its best" (*M*, 341). Literally living through the experiences of others such as Jackson, the narrator supplies evidence to prove the legitimacy of a prison as the ideal place for gaining and enacting political awareness. More narrative space is reserved for the streets but the narrator explicitly denotes his time in prison as the vital spark to his conversion.

Tookie's detailed referencing of prison as a site for education is inextricably linked with his death-row status. He sarcastically notes that death row offered him an escape route out of South Central (*R*, 208). Instead of being confined by the social immobility of the ghetto, he is now trapped in the ultimate prison cell, what prison scholar Brian Jarvis labels "a prison within a prison."[31] Yet, as the narrator stresses on several occasions, death row is constructed for punishment and execution, not reform (*R*, 195, 208, 256, 294). With no option for rehabilitation, death row prisoners are left to reform themselves, with *Blue Rage*'s narrator implying they should convert their "prison cage" into "a study laboratory; a secluded place of challenge to mould an educated mind" (*R*, 245). Empowerment through education provides a means of distancing themselves from violent wrongdoing. Self-education resists the popular death-row image of the unsalvageable, wild animal and retrieves self-respect; as Tookie explains, "writing had a sublime effect on me" (*R*, 272). Of the two gang memoirists who serve time, the narrator of *Blue Rage* in particular highlights prison as a "quasi-university" (*R*, 245).

The concept of prison as the crucial site of transition where the authors gain sufficient self-education to convert from criminal gangbanger is maximized on a structural level. *Blue Rage*'s thirty-eight chapters carry significant titles that chart Tookie's development both as a young black Crip and as an adult Afrocentric male. On the very first page of the foreword, the narrator states: "The two halves of this book represent two extreme phases of my life" (*R*, xiii). He explains that the "Blue Rage" of the memoir's title refers to "a chronicle of my passage down a spiralling path of Crip rage" while "Black Redemption" refers to "the stages of my redemptive awakening" (*R*, xiii). The narrator is signposting the narrative to show the development of his salvation. Chapter headings in *The Autobiography of Malcolm X* similarly chart the narrator's maturity from "Nightmare," through "Satan," "Saved," "Saviour," and "Out."[32] Of note, the chapter "Saved" includes the narrator's growing literacy, thus marking prison as the site of his conversion from illiteracy. In *Monster* the chapters are similarly titled to chart the narrator's logical development from gangbanger to revolutionary, suggesting that he has distinctly matured. The narrator publishes under a Muslim name, plainly not his gangsta name as identified by "a.k.a. Monster." The gangsta's transformation becomes a commercial construct.

Though *Blue Rage*'s narrative structure makes plain the narrator's objective to write a straightforward conversion tale, it can be argued that he took advantage of the genre as a result of his real-life situation. The memoir was released as Williams literally fought for his life on the basis of his conversion. In 2005, as his execution was scheduled for December, Williams appealed to the Governor Arnold Schwarzenegger for clemency. Schwarzenegger became governor in 2003, the year before *Blue Rage* was released, and the narrator reminds the politician that they met briefly on Venice Beach in the 1970s when then-actor Schwarzenegger complemented Tookie on his muscles (*R*, 150). Williams's petition to the governor highlighted his work from prison as an anti-gang activist, his children's books, his status as a prize-winning author, and his several nominations for the Nobel Prize. These included five recommendations for the Peace Prize by a member of the Swiss Parliament and four by academics from the United States and Europe. The most vocal was Professor Phil Gasper, a philosophy expert at Notre Dame de Namur University in California. Williams was also nominated four times for the Nobel Prize for Literature by William Keach, a professor of literature at Brown University. All this was made possible, Williams claims, by his self-education in prison. Williams's lawyers argued he was living proof that human redemption was possible and should be recognized and rewarded. The 1960s prison narrative has been deemed a text with a social function, acting as a vehicle for social change. In Williams's case, the prison conversion narrative has a monumental intention: to help escape death. Though Eldridge Cleaver was only serving a temporary sentence in prison, there is irony in his earlier statement: "That is why I started to write. To save myself."[33]

Blue Rage's narrator thus engages the genre to prove the legitimacy of his full conversion. It is an opportunity for the narrator to construct his reasoning for clemency; books have the potential to be his salvation. In his adult memoir he repeatedly hints at his worth, having "set a standard others could follow, creating a natural transition from criminal to black man of learning" (*R*, 258). He highlights his success as an author (mentioning awards won and nominations received) and points at the value of his narratives, asserting: "The recording of human errors must be a vivid reminder of what to avoid repeating" (*R*, 260). The narrator humbly admits his faults and suggests that he can now correct the mistakes: "Though a role model I could never be, I could act as an African *griot* or Paul Revere, warning youths about what is coming down the crooked path" (*R*, 273). His adopted Swahili name, Ajamu Niamke Kamara, means someone who teaches from experience, and this is stressed in the memoir (*R*, 291–92). His narrative becomes a forum for his right to live and part of his larger crusade for freedom. The conversion framework is used not only to convert the narrator but to convince others of his conversion.

The self-education of Williams, leading to his status as a published author, may have paradoxically led to his death. Williams's *Life in Prison* (1998) was dedicated to a list of black political heroes and activists that he had discovered in prison.[34] These names included George Jackson, Angela Davis, Assata Shakur, Malcolm X, Nelson Mandela, and Geronimo Pratt. They are also cited in the acknowledgments at the end of *Blue Rage* and referenced within the text itself. His roll call of black writers, some of whom have themselves written conversion memoirs, reflects his pedagogical desire to educate others on black history and stir black pride (something he never experienced himself as a youth). *Soledad Brother: The Prison Letters of George Jackson* is often recommended in high school libraries and is continually a favorite for Black History Month. When the governor rejected Williams's final appeal against his pending execution, he controversially singled out Williams's referencing of Jackson, claiming that Jackson's violent past serves as "a significant indicator that Williams is not reformed and that he still sees violence and lawlessness as a legitimate means to address societal problems."[35] Some see irony in the fact that violence should have made Schwarzenegger a fortune as an actor, yet as governor of California he rejected Williams's rebuttal of violence. The power of self-education, the act of writing, and the conversion genre were not enough to save him. His own black memoir and respect for fellow black memoirists incriminated him in the eyes of the governor. Just as Tookie was let down by his formal schooling, he was failed by his autodidactic education and the conversion genre.

Despite referencing periods in the LA County Jail, the narrator of *Always Running* is aware that he was lucky not to receive a harsher punishment. He notes that for many homeboys "the walls would soon taste of San Quentin, Folsom and Soledad" (*AR*, 189). Similar to Monster and Tookie, for the narrator of *Always Running* language springs to life: "words radiated with truth and power—not the words or forms of it, but the feel of it" (*AR*, 168). For him however, the potential power of words is uncovered not in prison but in the "magical hours I spent in the library" (*AR*, 139). The narrator implies that he eluded a prison sentence on the grounds of letters the court received from high school teachers and professors of Chicano studies at California State University (*AR*, 229). He hints at the sheer power of literacy and education; such skills can keep him out of prison. His conversion takes place at an unusual point for the genre (in the library and on the streets rather than in prison).

The structure of *Always Running* is also unlike that of the other two memoirs. The text does not have the straightforward narrative trajectory from gangbanger to memoirist through political consciousness that *Blue Rage* and *Monster* demonstrate. Though the other two narrators slowly build up to the conversion chapters that form clear separate installments of their story, in *Always Running* the criminal and revolutionary years are combined, challenging the expected smooth transition into a new identity. Gangbanging competes with the Chicano movement for the narrator's attention. Despite attempts at rehabilitation, he confesses on more than one occasion that "I was back to the way of the 'hood" (*AR*, 233). Two competing lives are collapsed into one account, with opening chapter quotations from figures such as Antonin Artaud (radical French philosopher) and Nelson Perry (African American revolutionary). These are combined with chapters that commence with citations from a gang member and a barrio boxing coach. Accounts of friends killed in a police chase are followed by assemblies to discuss social revolution. After his arrest for intent to commit murder, his description of prison revolves around poetry; and his attendance at the Chicano Moratorium Against the War results in him being sucked into the criminal justice system. Even the glossary of Spanish terms includes a mixture of barrio terminology and revolutionary expressions.[36] With its conflict between his gang and redeemed, radical identities, such a collapsed account is an unusual way of approaching a conversion narrative.

The experiences of the narrator in *Always Running* are different from those of the other two memoirists, with no prison term to spark his conversion, and the resultant narrative is dissimilar in style. In contrast, the narrators of *Monster* and *Blue Rage* cannot exercise physical freedom but can exploit their time in prison to educate themselves and ultimately undergo their conversions. It is highly significant that the skills needed to write a book are learned within prison specifically. In the case of *Blue Rage* in particular, the narrator negotiates the traditional genre of his memoir with intentions that reach far further than merely educating oneself.

The narrator of *Blue Rage* exploits genre and narrative structure to support his conversion, and further highlights his redemption by situating himself in the role of teacher. The other two narrators likewise construct themselves as instructors, albeit to different degrees of authority. Their pedagogical tone incites trust and respect just as society traditionally expects classroom teachers to be held in esteem. The memoirists demonstrate that they need the respect of mainstream society and literary kudos to various ends, including for personal self-esteem and even to prevent one's execution. Now the narrators present themselves as alternative educators, working outside mainstream mores.

In 1996 Williams wrote a series of children's books, using the unusual theme of street gangs to aid the development of reading skills. *Blue Rage*'s narrator details how he learned to use simple and straightforward vocabulary for the books so they could be appropriately understood and enjoyed (*R*, 272). Each book in the series includes a glossary of terms to aid with pronunciation and understanding, showing how the narrator intentionally facilitates literacy for the reader. For example:

Gangbanger	(GANG-bang-er)	Gang member who uses violence to make other people do what he wants.
Homeboy	(HOME-boi)	Friend or partner.
Weightlifter	(WAYT-lif-ter)	Someone who lifts weights to increase his strength and muscles.[37]

Even for the adult memoir, the narrator consciously discusses his use of language, explaining that he "toned it down, breaking the stereotype of a prisoner being grandiose in his use of language and vocab for the sake of appearing intelligent" (*R*, 245). In author correspondence with Shakur, he deemed *Blue Rage* "remarkable" because "it contained no curse words."[38] The narrator of *Blue Rage* is cognizant of his choice of words, leading by example in his lack of swearing and distancing himself from his gangsta days.

Williams's *Life in Prison* (1998) targeted high school children to discourage them from prison, providing another overt example of the narrator acting as an instructive mentor. Though aimed at an adult audience, *Blue Rage* follows this tutorial pattern and the book is driven by a similarly pedagogical aim. The opening four pages of *Blue Rage* are filled with quotations from young people, former gang members, college teachers, all personally thanking Williams for his inspiration and instruction. In one of these citations, from a juvenile rehabilitation officer, as a direct result of Williams's texts, "dictionaries are going off the shelves faster than I can buy them—more books are borrowed from the library than before" (*R*, opening page). The narrator of *Blue Rage* is thus established as a teacher even before we formally meet him as a narrator and read about the gang exploits for which he is famed. Such citations reflect the intentions of the children's series and *Life in Prison* and set the authoritative and pedagogical tone for *Blue Rage*.

In *Blue Rage*, the regular use of rhetorical questions as well as phrases in bold and Latin words in italics encourage the reader to pause and reflect, suggesting emphasis in the same way a teacher may underscore a point in class (*R*, 32, 74). In the early pages, the reader receives the first of many explanations from the narrator, who clarifies his use of the term "dys-education" (*R*, 23). In line with the societal critique that runs throughout the memoir, the narrator carefully defines societal terms to provide the reader with a full understanding of his analysis. For instance: "What I call the colony—commonly known as the ghetto—is a modern urban version of the plantations on which African slaves lived in America. *Colony* is a more accurate term than ghetto, i.e. a group of people who have been institutionalized in a distinctly separate area" (*R*, 13). Kenneth Mostern's discussion of *The Autobiography of Malcolm X* highlights that its narrator continually "insists on his role as a pedagogue," claiming that "one of X's chief traits throughout is that of the man who aspires to achieve pedagogical authority regardless of his specific social situation."[39] *Blue Rage*'s narrator behaves likewise, exercising his instruction despite being behind bars rather than in front of a blackboard in the classroom.

Monster's narrator imparts facts and figures of the gangsta lifestyle in an explanatory manner and carefully translates the gangsta terms deployed in the 'hood. He reports that "crack dealers employ more people in South

Central than AT&T, IBM, and Xerox combined," and that being in a gang in the 'hood is analogous to growing up in Grosse Pointe, Michigan, and going to college: "everyone does it" (*M*, 70, 138). Though *Blue Rage*'s narrator does occasionally define gangsta terms (words like "cuz," "dozens," "homeboy," and "'hood") the narrative is primarily presented as an encyclopedic knowledge of societal references, particularly those from black history (*R*, 51, 53, 80, 98). By comparison, *Monster* exudes an air of gangsta erudition. The cartoonish, staccato vocabulary of violence speeds up the pace of *Monster*'s narrative (at the possible expense of authenticity, for some readers). But such gangsta explanations bring it back to a controlled, stately manner in which the narrator retains command. Monster holds himself accountable for telling the gangsta story as well as explicating those events.

Monster's narrator is authoritarian, permitting no oppositional reading. Autobiography scholar Laura Marcus contends that such inflexibility is a common characteristic of a conversion narrative.[40] Monster rose rapidly among the command ranks in his gang set; in prison he takes on comparable leadership roles. At first this involves directing the Eight Trays when incarcerated. After the narrator converts to the Nation of Islam, he takes a Muslim name with leadership connotations. The narrator highlights the meaning of Sanyika as "unifier, gatherer of his people" (*M*, 363). The name echoes his forceful narrative personality, telling the reader what to think from the outset, closing down questions and fiercely controlling the reader's approach to the story. "I am a gang expert—period," declares the preface (*M*, xiii). The narrative continues with the narrator dominating the prose: "I propose to take my reader . . . come with me . . . " (*M*, xiii–xv). The closing sentences of the preface give the ultimate command: "Look then, if you dare, at South Central through the eyes of one of its most notorious Ghetto Stars" (*M*, xv). As Marcus explains, the narrator's angle is presented as the only one that can render the past intelligible, because they regularly "control their reception by asserting the supremacy of an enlightened present moment, perspective and consciousness."[41]

The dictatorial technique of *Monster* and *Blue Rage* differs from that of *Always Running*, which promotes a more participatory style of teaching. The numerous Spanish words of *Always Running* are set in italics, differentiating them from their English counterparts as in a language textbook. Despite being aimed at a competitive reading standard, the Spanish reduces the English-speaking reader to an elementary school linguistic pupil. The presence of a lengthy glossary enables the reader to work actively toward an understanding of a sentence in which only the Spanish word or phrase is given. This encourages them to consider the placement of words in a sentence as well as their sounds. (The first time I read this memoir, I found myself unconsciously reading sentences aloud.) The Spanish-English glossary, combined with lyrical metaphors and expressive punctuation marks, ensures the narrative maintains the reader's attention and involvement. The poetic narrative often sounds as if the written word is the product of an effort to re-create a traditional Mexican oral performance. Historically, street poetry in Mexican barrios was composed with performance in mind, as a lack of education in poverty-stricken and rural areas relied on oral transmission and memory.[42] *Always Running*'s narrator cites barrio poets and reveals that he originally wanted to name the memoir "Barrio Expressions," demonstrating his acute awareness of oral, poetic traditions (*AR*, 108). Oral performance relies heavily on interaction with the audience or community, and *Always Running* relies heavily on the reader's willingness to participate.[43]

Regardless of individual teaching styles, teachers are expected to be trustworthy. The narrator of *Blue Rage* openly and honestly offers flaws in his reliability, far more so than the other two narrators, which ironically incites trust in the reader and saves his moral upstanding as a pedagogical role model. For example, he admits to failing a police lie detector test and comments on the problems with his recollection of events, confessing to memory loss as a result of personal drug abuse and being drugged by the authorities in jail (*R*, 83, 212, 215, 223, 230). This chapter is aptly titled "The Missing Years" (*R*, 221). Gang expert Alex Alonso refuses to believe the contents of *Blue Rage*, claiming that PCP (a drug popular with gangbangers in the 1970s) medically caused chronic memory loss.[44] Yet Tookie defiantly uses a discussion of his damaged memory to positive effect in constructing his history. Though the gangsta lifestyle has affected him physiologically, by admitting to being flawed and infallible he works against the expected conventions of the autobiographical genre, constructing himself as a reliable narrator and teacher.

Concepts of memory and remembering have traditionally been encoded within black culture. Black cultural theorist Henry Louis Gates explains this as being due to African Americans having been denied access to their history.[45] Under slavery, with reading and writing banned, immense problems were created: "without a written language—there could be no ordered repetition or memory, and without memory, there could be no history. Without history, there could be no self."[46] The similarities between the institutions of prison and slavery are rife and have been explored in detail by prison scholars. For example, prison authorities remove individual human identity by forcing prisoners to wear identical outfits, comparable to conditions of slavery. It is hence significant that *Blue Rage*'s narrator should embark on a process of improving his memory skills. The narrator criticizes Malcolm X's alphabetical technique of reading the dictionary to remember words. Instead of reading the dictionary cover to cover like a novel, he creates a system of mnemonics, selecting words randomly from both a dictionary and a thesaurus (*R*, 235). With training in mnemonics, the human mind is considered able to perform astounding feats of memory that are impossible for the inborn memory alone. Such an act serves to counterbalance "The Missing Years" and, like the author's learning Swahili, serves as evidence of a supreme educational feat and highlights that issues of memory are of particular significance for African American history.

As modern-day prisoners, the narrators of *Monster* and *Blue Rage* are aware of the parallels with their ancestors' struggles to survive.[47] *Monster* describes San Quentin state prison as a "huge slave ship," and the list of acknowledgments at the back of *Blue Rage* is headed by slave memoirist Frederick Douglass (*M*, 342; *R*, 325). Slave historian Heather Andrea Williams identifies pedagogical importance in slave literacy, arguing that during the Civil War literacy distinguished African American chaplains and soldiers as prestigious leaders who could teach others how to read and help them write letters home.[48] In the postwar South those former slaves who had mastered reading and writing often became teachers themselves of adults and children in formal and informal settings. The narrators of *Monster* and *Blue Rage* similarly become teachers of Swahili to fellow prisoners. Tookie also acts as a mentor when his son Stan is incarcerated, encouraging him to "abandon cryptic gang vernacular for more comprehensible language, coupled with an interest in retaining new vocabulary" (*R*, 313). Stan needs complete literacy to understand the convoluted court documents to fight for his freedom.[49] Literacy had practical applications for slavery that included forging passes to aid escape and reading about abolitionist activities.[50] Following treatment at the hands of a racist judiciary (*Blue Rage*'s narrator believes he received an unfair trial), literacy is essential for understanding complicated legal documents to fight for life and freedom.[51] *Monster* also needs literacy skills to read the "heavy" language in the pamphlets that his mentor gives him in prison (*M*, 215).

Historically, freed slaves embraced literacy as a means of self-determination and upward mobility. For contemporary prisoners as well as slaves, reading and writing has liberal, practical, and (particularly in the case of these memoirs) pedagogical benefits. All three narrators exhibit a desire to teach their readers, revealing a positive slant on their relationship with education. But such productivity is set in tense contrast with their narrative tales of failing schools, gangbanging, and life on the streets. There are clear contradictions and tensions between the narrator as young man and the potentially pedagogic (and authorial) narrative voice. The degree of consistency (or inconsistency) between these voices varies greatly in each of the three memoirs.

To some degree there is a covert and sublimated integrationist ethic working here. One can have status, wealth, and prestige in the ghetto without formal literacy. However, to compete in the larger society of the United States, or even to survive its oppression, one needs conventional language and literacy skills. There is a latent acceptance of the notion of success in life that is implied by mastering the language of the mainstream. This sub-theme about the relationship between literacy and integrationism is implicit in each of the memoirs. As has been divulged, the quest for literacy leads these memoirists to alternative modes of success.

As *Always Running* elucidates, for Mexican American immigrants who have to grasp a foreign dialect, language is a particularly charged terrain: "We needed to obtain victories in language . . . but we were often defeated from the start" (*AR*, 219). Likewise for African Americans who historically have been prohibited from learning to read and write, literacy has been a critical and sensitive point of discussion in their history. Like their slave forefathers, the narrators of *Monster* and *Blue Rage* cannot exercise physical freedom, but their narrators can negotiate genre as a site for individual expression. Language and literacy skills, usually attained through formal education, are presented in all three narratives as essential for acquiring social mobility, identity, and status in mainstream American society. They also provide the means to better understand one's self, history, and community.

Despite the relevance of such themes for black and Mexican culture, they mark a departure from traditional forms of gangsta, potentially steering the content of gangsta in a new direction. As the previous chapter detailed, urban American society has grown increasingly violent over the past three decades, and so too has popular culture. The memoirs juggle consumer appetites for sheer violence with the narrators' concerns for educating themselves. The narrators take relevant subjects for their ethnic and racial cultures, but explore them within a traditionally violent form of popular culture that is not customarily associated with such issues. The need to justify violent acts is an anticipated narrative construct of this genre; the need to explore institutional failings and alternative educations are a more surprising narrative trajectory. This framework builds dramatic tension, leads towards delinquency, and then guides the narrator through their conversion and out of a life of crime.

Though gang memoirs in some ways work outside gangsta norms, they simultaneously align themselves with the genre of contemporary prison literature within which themes of language, literacy, and education are more customary. Like their literary forbears, the narrative climax of *Blue Rage* and *Monster* arrives with the self-education that is archetypically achieved in prison. Despite educational adversity as children and setbacks of incarceration as adults, the memoirists acquire an education sufficient to author a book. Even *Monster*, whose narrative is the most "classically" gangsta, lays importance on his days in prison. And though conversion takes place for the narrator of *Always Running* outside prison, his narrative carries similar weight as evidence of impressive achievement. Like prison memoirs of the 1960s and 1970s, the act of writing and publishing not only represents a significant feat in the face of hardship, but the form of the memoir carries worth. Just as prison memoirists critique the prison system, the memoir is an opportunity for gang members to voice their own experiences of education and speak on behalf of all Mexican and African Americans sharing similarly hostile experiences. Autobiography can be seen as a strategy that helps make gangsta into a serious cultural movement, working against those gangsta rap opponents who had refused to recognize the social and historical importance of the music.

There are clear differences of individual experience among the narrators, but all three memoirs demonstrate tension that stems from being a gang member or a pedagogical narrator. The revealingly diverse balances between this violent past and conscious present are written into the narrative progression of each book. Such friction is particularly noteworthy in *Blue Rage*, whereby the narrator uses his language and literacy skills to command intellectual respect and to construct himself as a learned, pedagogical narrator who can explain his gangsta days in hindsight using critical questions of race and racial bias. The wiser, dictatorial narrative voice distances the narrator from his younger, criminal days. In some ways, these tensions set the memoirs apart from gangsta rap. The memoirists stand out against artists such as Tupac whose success was founded on an increasingly hostile reputation.

Chapter Five

MURDERER, MONSTER, NOVELIST, OR NOBEL NOMINEE?
Press Reception and Media Constructions of Gang Memoirs

Having addressed the contexts of the memoirs, reasons for their emergence, and their textual features, this research now seeks to understand how these popular narratives have been interpreted by commentators. How and why did the media impose discourses on the memoirs? As reception studies scholar Janet Staiger explains in her research on the press reception of films, these theoretical frameworks can be helpful in determining the cultural meanings of a specific text.[1] In 1991 Staiger conducted a study of the media reception of the film *Silence of the Lambs*. She considered how reception studies "illuminates the cultural meanings of texts in specific times and social circumstances to specific viewers, and it attempts to contribute to discussions about the spectorial effects of films by moving beyond text-centered analyses."[2] This chapter takes inspiration from her study, considering the situation of the authors in real life, just as Staiger considers public events taking place around the actors themselves. I will explore critical reviews to see what discursive frames (both progressive and reactionary) they deployed to understand and interpret these texts for readers. The reception of these memoirs gave occasion for critics to enter various charged debates about crime, race, violence, and pedagogy that were taking place at the time of their publication.

The media reception does not demonstrate the same level of sensationalized and moral panic–driven coverage that one might expect, as was imposed both on the proliferation of actual gangs in southern California and on gangsta rap music in the late 1980s and early 1990s. The reception is generally a more sensitive and circumspect interpretation than anticipated, and this chapter offers suggestions as to why. Nonetheless, a great deal of discussion still is framed in terms of authentic street voicing—sometimes at the expense of the consideration of literary attributes, particularly in the case of the two black authors. Chapter 2 raised critical questions of the burden of representation in black cultural studies, and media reception often reproduces that discourse. The need to depict black and Mexican life realistically, as reproduced in the media, will be explored here.

The power of this realist frame imposed on the writing and publicity image of Mexican and African American authors means that when they do publish literature with merit and success, it heightens the conversion narrative. Should the authors fail at that conversion and therefore work against typology, it is all the more newsworthy. The conversion-narrative framework is common in the reception of all three memoirs, combining aspects of their narratives and their life events. Nonetheless, these conversions are configured very differently in the media reception of the three books. Their transformations are presented from street to literary (Rodriguez and *Always Running*), from murderous to lauded conversion to death (Williams and *Blue Rage*) and from murderer to lucrative author and back to prison (Shakur and *Monster*). In the latter case, the downfall of the author leads to cynical questioning of his conversion.

This chapter demonstrates that it is not simply a matter of their discursive construction as authors, but whether, given struggles over the restrictions on publicity of those imprisoned, they are even allowed to be explored discursively at all. The media dissemination of coverage by and about these authors became a struggle. The fact that media reception can potentially become a site of discursive battle is perhaps nowhere clearer than in the case of these authors, facing imprisonment and execution. Their publicity images took on inordinate importance.

I sampled a broad range of newspapers and magazines.[3] Rather predictably given the southern California setting for all three books, I discovered that the *Los Angeles Times* had covered the memoirs more heavily than any other publication.[4] The newspaper is an interesting case study, with its spectacular news coverage of gangs in the late 1980s and later sober and profound analyses of gang memoirs. In addition to other regional LA publications such as the *Los Angeles Weekly* and *Daily News of Los Angeles*, there was a wide mixture of respected national newspapers, including the *New York Times* and *Washington Post*. City newspapers such as

Denver's *Rocky Mountain News* and Minneapolis's *Star Tribune* also generated coverage.

The sample incorporated smaller local California newspapers, including Ontario's *Inland Valley Daily Bulletin*, La Jolla's *Copley Newspaper*, and Riverside's *Press Enterprise*, and the occasional international newspaper such as the London *Times*, Melbourne's *Sunday Age*, and Canada's *Hamilton Spectator*. In all cases reviewers, like news reporters, are constrained by factors including the newspaper's ownership and agenda, as well as its readership expectations and its location. The memoirs predictably featured in publishing trade magazines including the *Kirkus Reviews*, *Publishers Weekly*, *Bookseller*, and the *Horn Book Magazine*. Given the timing of the memoirs in the aftermath of the LA riots they figured, somewhat unsurprisingly, in political and investigative journals such as *Atlantic*, *Nation*, *Newsweek*, and *Progressive*. That the gang memoirs were reviewed in so many different types of publications, not just in LA and even in small newspapers and critical magazines, suggests that these memoirs were taken seriously by a range of editors and readers.

Considering the recurring pattern of sensational and dramatic reporting in traditional news coverage of gangs and gangsta rap, it is significant that these trends are not as visible in the reception of gang memoirs by book reviewers. The chapter will briefly examine the moral panic–style gang coverage that permeated the news and then explore the reception of each memoir. Though *Monster* was published marginally earlier than *Always Running*, much of its press attention came after the initial year of publication, so I will commence with *Always Running*.

The press coverage of contemporary street gangs, which peaked in the late 1980s and early 1990s, tended to demonize gangs. As one former journalist at the *Los Angeles Times* explains in hindsight of his newspaper's coverage, it was "simplistic" and "generally painted a scary scene" in which "thank God we have the cops to protect us."[5] Their coverage was influential in swaying public opinion against gangs. Gang scholar Martin Jankowski offers extensive analysis that addresses the ways in which coverage offered scant evidence to support claims, used generalized comments rather than quoting official statistics, or cited exaggerated statistics for incarceration and homicides.[6] News journalists loved using the term "gang-related" because it generated interest for readers and viewers without reporters having to worry about being accused of impairing the truth. Indeed, any group of people who are involved with crime can technically be termed a "gang" even if they have no street gang affiliation.[7] Gang scholar Malcolm

Klein has regularly voiced apprehension that "media images, which form so many of our views, are usually inconsistent distortions of street gangs," adding "we have to get beyond them."[8]

At the peak of gang-related crime, to some degree the media interest was justified. Despite exaggerated statistics, street gangs were growing fast and murder rates were soaring. Scandalous news stories of gangsta criminality proved to be extremely saleable. In his exploration of the relationship between gangs and the media, Jankowski notes: "the news media are in business not only to disseminate information but also to make a profit . . . the image of gangs provided by most of the news media does accomplish the desired economic goals of creating a general interest in buying a particular newspaper . . ."[9] Jankowski acknowledges the print media does not have the time nor space to include all the news, and that stories therefore must be "interest-generating," usually meaning a story must involve violence and crime and have a sensational, newsworthy spin.[10]

A select few gang journalists established reputations for in-depth, sensitive reporting, including Mike Davis and Jesse Katz.[11] Katz was a Pulitzer Prize–winning journalist who worked for the *Los Angeles Times*: "I felt my mission at the *Times* was to get beyond the fear and hype. I was trying to explore the causes and dynamics, the history and ethics, the rational as much as the irrational aspects of gangbanging."[12] Still, gang violence became part of a wider media and political construct as well as a material fact, in which ghetto violence and behavior fueled a public moral panic. The work of those such as Davis and Katz could not compete with this exposure. For example, the "crack attack" of the late 1980s was manipulated by the media to score votes for politicians and justify urban poverty.[13] As Klein explains, the connection between African Americans and crack was "blown way out of proportion by some zealous police officials . . . and headline-hunting media reports."[14] Media scholars such as Yvonne Jewkes and Joel Best have explored the power a media moral panic can exert over public opinion, as well as the dangers of such coverage.[15] The media rarely consider the reasons why a particular group might behave in a certain way. Gang and crack coverage generally ignored the sociological underpinnings that were supporting and encouraging the growth of the urban ghettos.

Where gang subcultures see themselves as social bandits, mainstream press coverage tends to construct them as antisocial villains.[16] Contemporary cultural studies has been concerned with under- and misrepresentation of marginalized groups; scholars have dedicated much time to studying the mass media, exploring the ways in which the media define dominant discourse, for example presenting groups as deviant. Stuart Hall is fascinated how sociological classifications of "normal" and "deviant" are constructed by the media.[17] Hall's work often explores the sheer power of the media in influencing political, social, and cultural opinion in response to those subcultural practices and subversions that might threaten the state's legitimacy. Hall argues that the politics of this regime of racial representation is "a struggle over meaning which continues and is unfinished."[18] The struggle certainly was played out in the media's treatment of gangsta rap, which was presented as culturally problematic and was aligned with sensationalistic demonizing of black youth culture in general.

Rap arose into a climate of censorship that pervaded contemporary American culture in the 1980s. The social conservatism of this decade, encouraged in part by the Reagan administration, was reflected in the many protest groups worried by violent or sexual imagery and lyrics in various popular forms. Rap music's violence and misogyny became a source of contempt for the Parents' Music Resource Center (PMRC), which was founded in 1985. The PMRC reflected changing notions of censorship and propriety in response to relaxed prohibitions on violence in popular culture (as demonstrated in chapter 3). The organization was aided by the white-dominated media, for whom the controversy over gangsta rap, according to black cultural scholar bell hooks, "makes great spectacle."[19] When realist discourses of urban poverty, violence, police abuse, drug-dealing, and substance abuse were recorded by artists, such evidence of moral decline became fodder for conservative racial condemnation of the ghetto and great news for the media.

In comparison to traditional news reportage, reviews and interviews with the authors are openly subjective. I shall now see how those opinionated articles construct the reception of the memoirs.

For the most part, book reviewers take these gang memoirs seriously. Perhaps as rejoinder to the demonizing construction of gangs in mainstream news reporting, reviews of gang memoirs often emphasize the structural determinants of gang life. In the case of *Always Running*, this involved framing the memoir in terms of sober sociological explanations for violence. At the same time, this memoir often prompted literary comparisons, further legitimizing gangsta memoirs as a serious subject for analysis. Despite the rightward tendencies in social policy in the early 1990s, the discursive frames employed by the reviewers to discuss Rodriguez's autobiography appear to be relatively progressive.

Always Running was released in 1993, toward the end of the intensive media focus on gangs. One of the most disapproving book reviews of either memoir appeared in Denver's *Rocky Mountain News*, a traditionally conservative publication. The journalist blasts *Always Running*'s violent imagery as "unacceptable,"[20] offering a one-sided, dismissive approach that echoes the earlier media panic surrounding gangs: "It's disturbing. It's gruesome. It's sick."[21] The review is bolstered by strategic words such as "engulfed" and "plague," what Joel Best deems a "vocabulary of attrition" designed to intensify hysteria among readers.[22]

The *Rocky Mountain News* review also resembles in its hypocrisy the sensationalist coverage of both crack and gangs. The reviewer slams the memoir, claiming it "strikes too close to home now that the gang plague has engulfed Denver."[23] Yet he is simultaneously happy to reference the narrator stabbing an enemy through the eye with a screwdriver. Just as violence has the potential to sell memoirs and shift newspapers, it can attract attention and stimulate the audiences of book reviewers. But the *Rocky Mountain News* review was an anomaly. The commonality across press coverage was that reviewers surprisingly do not openly employ melodramatic styles. Only two reviews of *Monster* refer to the equally shocking machete incident, in which the gang dismembers an enemy.[24] This avoidance of those violent episodes that might previously have served as fodder for moral panics, suggests that media coverage of actual gangs differs markedly from the coverage of narrative constructions of gang life.

Always Running has generated critical reception that, like the journalism of Jesse Katz, explores the reasoning behind gang proliferation. The memoir encourages reviewers to think in socioeconomic frameworks, provoking discussions of poverty, unemployment, and other factors that contribute to the proliferation of gangs. Reviewers addressed the plight of those living in the barrio. The *San Francisco Chronicle* review opens by asking, "what can be done to avert another riot, stop gang wars, get guns and drugs off the streets, slow a soaring school dropout rate, improve job training . . . ?"[25] Numerous reviews highlighted what the *Kirkus Reviews* deemed the narrative's "ever-present political analysis."[26] They trust and respect the narrator's socioeconomic opinions, encouraging the reader to accept him as an expert on gangs as well as wider society. As the *Progressive* explained: "this is much more than the story of one gang member who got out—the problem, Rodriguez makes clear, is not with the gangs but with the society that creates gangs."[27] As a journal with a leftist perspective the *Progressive*'s attitude was predictable, but similar viewpoints were interspersed throughout newspaper coverage. As summarized by the *San Francisco Chronicle*, Rodriguez "has more to say about urban despair and gang life than many of the more sensational or scholarly studies of the past several years."[28]

The narrator's son, Ramiro, provided many reviewers, including the journalist for the *Rocky Mountain News*, with a smooth connection between the narrator's former life and contemporary frameworks. The story of Ramiro in particular offers a personal, heartfelt slant, which chimed with the progressive agenda of publications like the *Nation*.[29] Even in the most irate review of *Always Running*'s graphic violence, the reviewer in the *Rocky Mountain News* is somewhat appeased: "perhaps the only benefit comes at the conclusion of Rodriguez's book where he realizes his shortcomings as a father . . ."[30]

In addition to the *Kirkus Reviews*, several California newspapers acknowledged that the growth of contemporary gangs can be at least partly attributed to racism.[31] A distinction emerged between the reception in California, with some attempt to understand gangs, and that in publications from outside the state that leaned toward dramatizing LA's gang scene (including Denver's *Rocky Mountain News* and Minneapolis's *Star Tribune*).[32] The California publications frequently explored the historical positioning of the memoir through nostalgic discussions of specifically Mexican experiences in California. Rodriguez's family featured again as reviewers framed the family's migration from Mexico, repeatedly raising themes such as racism that are central to the immigrant experience.[33] For example, the *San Francisco Chronicle* stressed that Rodriguez was two years old when his family moved from Mexico, only to experience extreme overcrowding in rat- and roach-infested apartments and school policies that discriminated against Spanish-speaking children in the barrios of East LA.[34]

Several reviews concentrated on the Chicano movement, which is central to the memoir and an essential component of contemporary Mexican history in California. Fellow Chicano critic Ilan Stavans, writing in the *Nation*, argues that the memoir is a useful tool for helping us understand the Chicano movement and its role in Chicano history.[35] In its discussion of the Chicano movement, *Always Running* pays particular attention to the massively underfunded and ethnically exclusionary schooling that prompted demands for pedagogical change (*AR*, 11, 221, 250). Several reviewers engaged with the concerns of Rodriguez over schooling by acknowledging the two key teachers who steered him away from gang life:

"teachers to the rescue," states the *San Francisco Chronicle* as a sub-heading.[36] Significantly, one of the reviews—written as marketing material to publicize the memoir itself—was written by Jonathan Kozol, a social critic renowned for his books on public education in the United States. Kozol deemed the memoir "urgently and politically explosive—a permanent testament to human courage and transcendence."[37]

While *Always Running* was examined through a sociological framework, reviewers also emphasized literary aspects of the memoir. Numerous reviewers framed meaning in terms of literary merit. The *Washington Post* described the memoir as "hauntingly lyrical," and Kozol claimed the narrative was "richly literary and poetic."[38] The *Nation* likened Rodriguez to Piri Thomas; *Entertainment News* stressed that the memoirist's inspirations were literary greats such as Charles Bukowski and John Fante.[39] Even tabloid newspapers such as the *Daily News of Los Angeles* compared Rodriguez to John Steinbeck.[40] The *New York Times* included *Always Running* on lists of "new and noteworthy paperbacks" and "books for vacation reading," positioning the memoir alongside Michel Foucault, the collected writings of Frank Lloyd Wright, and books on jazz and painting.[41]

Rodriguez's literary standing was further reinforced by a tendency to use fellow literary artists to review *Always Running*. Reviewers included Patricia Holt (a former publisher, cultural critic, and author), Carol Anshaw (novelist), Gregg Barrios (playwright), Ilan Stavans (short story writer and cultural commentator), and Piri Thomas himself.[42] Around 1993 and later, reviewers noted that Rodriguez's name was included on a list of notable Hispanic writers; he was nominated for California poet laureate, and was being honored at literary festivals.[43] Prison scholar H. Bruce Franklin argues that when unknown writers with little formal schooling produce works that are accepted in mainstream critical circles, it offers a progressive challenge to elitist canon formations.[44]

At the center of the narrative construction of these reviews is the conversion narrative from criminal past and violent exploits to esteemed author, with headlines typifying the redemptive and self-reinventing potential of literature. The *Chicago Sun Times* stated, "A poet tells of life with LA gangs," while the magazine *Connexion* declared, "Gang survivor spins experience into literary gold."[45] The act of conversion remains a focal point for much of the reception: "From gang member to storyteller. Former gang member turned author published" (*Cable TV Chicago*).[46] Rodriguez's publicity image continues to be dominated by the concept of literary conversion. In a typical review of his recent novel *Music of the Mill* (2005), the

San Antonio Express labeled Rodriguez a "21st century literary renaissance man: from poet to memoirist and short story writer to children's book author and journalist."[47] There is notably no mention of gangs, suggesting his literary persona had completely displaced his former reputation. Such reception of Rodriguez adds credence to the veracity of *Always Running*'s narrative conversion, which was important as a ten-year-anniversary edition of *Always Running* was released in 2005.[48]

The critical reception of *Always Running* reproduced the structural critique of society that is established in the memoir and explored by the narrator to understand the gangbanging phenomenon. The reviewers gave the narrator credit for his struggles with language and schooling and raised discussions of poverty and discrimination. The narrator simultaneously implies that, as much as he wants youths to read his memoir, he wishes to be classed a serious literary artist worthy of reviews in respected newspapers. The reception, the *Rocky Mountain News* aside, certainly interpreted the memoirist and his memoir as such.

Though they were published in the same year, only one review incorporated both *Always Running* and *Monster*. That was a piece in *Publishers Weekly* that explored the "lively diversity of voices" in the aftermath of the LA riots.[49] *Always Running* is deemed "angry autobiography" (*Kirkus Reviews*), "therapeutic autobiography," and "memorial/testimonial literature" (*Washington Post*).[50] But reviewers in the London *Times* compared it with the memoir of a white LA screenwriter on a journey into heroin addiction, while the *Washington Post* compared it with the memoir of a San Diego police detective.[51] This suggests that *Monster* and *Always Running* were seen as different entities in 1993 and that there was no emerging publication trend of contemporary street gang memoirs identified in the press at that time. (This runs counter to my retrospective identification of this publishing trend, as detailed in chapter 1.) The lack of comparative reviews in the reception of *Always Running* and *Monster* becomes increasingly understandable in view of the diverse frames of reference engaged by reviewers to explore the two memoirs. *Monster*'s reception often linked the author with the site of prison, which has controversially been seen as the "typical" black experience, as explored in chapter 3. While the literary capital of both *Always Running* and its author was often highlighted in its press reception, Shakur's conversion was customarily configured in terms of material transformation.

The press exaltation of *Always Running*'s author in literary terms was in contrast to the reception Shakur received. The only reviewer to refer to Shakur's literary skills was the Pulitzer Prize–winning critic Michiko Kakutani, writing in the *New York Times*, who compared Shakur to Richard Price and Tom Wolfe on aesthetic grounds.[52] However, the dominant press discourse in many publications defined Shakur's achievements in terms of income and number of books sold. The *Atlantic* noted that "the word after the Frankfurt Book Fair was that Monster had received an advance of at least $150,000, with more to come from the paperback sale (Penguin later paid around $60,000) plus future royalties."[53] The *Los Angeles Times* declared it a "successful paperback" on the grounds that the original printing was 100,000 copies in ten languages.[54] The money-spinning potential of the memoir has been openly considered in its reception since its initial publication, including a discussion of its film rights sparking further income and the luxury house that Shakur purchased for his family in Riverside, far away from South Central.[55]

Shakur's lucrative achievements as illustrated in the press reception pointed toward the ghetto entrepreneurialism discourse that played a major role in the success of gangsta rap. He conformed to the gangsta's enterprising initiatives, out to seek financial gain for oneself, often working independently rather than with others.[56] But Shakur did so by replacing drugs or other crime with legal work. By the early 1990s and certainly under the Clinton administration, a lack of viable employment opportunities turned many black youths to involvement in the drug trade, while others were inspired by the success of ghetto entrepreneurs and artists in the rap industry.[57] If black youth could not beat capitalism in their deteriorating living conditions, they could attempt to join it, embracing private entrepreneurship rather than struggling against the system. As cultural scholar S. Craig Watkins explains: "Without a doubt, it is one of the greatest ironies that an enduring and celebrated tradition in American capitalism—entrepreneurship—was largely responsible for transforming hard-core from an underground, peripheral subculture to a mainstream, multi-million dollar enterprise."[58] Watkins contends that the artists themselves were only too aware of these ironies. For some reviewers Shakur's financial gain was constructed in resourceful ghetto enterprise terms; for others the book was an exploitative debasement of the memoir mode. A reporter on CBS's *60 Minutes* cynically noted: "this LA gang leader's grasp of the English language has made him a quarter of a million dollars."[59] Though reviewers appeared to care about the poverty that pervaded *Always Running*, they seemed dismissive of Shakur's wealth-generating achievement.

Monster's press reception explored the divisive issue of gaining financial worth from stereotyped representations of black criminality. An LA-based magazine called *Buzz* would be the site for a furious written dispute between Shakur and a Harvard-educated black waiter called Leonce Gaiter.[60] Gaiter was infuriated that Morgan Entrekin, a white publisher and the original impetus behind *Monster*'s publication, had promoted Shakur as "a primary voice of the black experience."[61] Gaiter raucously retorted: "To me, this is a white man who thinks that a monster who butchers African Americans is a major voice for all African Americans, a white man who thinks of all blacks as less than human, as a murderous sub-species . . ."[62] Though Gaiter would later target Shakur as well, his initial rage was steered at the publishing world. The leftward-looking *Atlantic* was one of a handful of publications to address this problematic question of black male imagery in contemporary popular literature (previously raised in discussions over gangsta rap and violent ghetto films).[63] The reviewer for *Atlantic*, Mark Horowitz, observed that it was "back in fashion" to use gang members of LA as "authentic" voices of the black experience.[64] Nonetheless, he was keenly aware that critics might protest that a brutal murderer cannot be truly representative, an interesting debate that Horowitz exemplified by using quotations from the differences of opinion displayed in *Buzz*.

That Gaiter was initially concerned with the publisher is worthy of note. To some degree he tries to alleviate authors of full responsibility for issues of representation. Gaiter deployed Shakur, his memoir, and the publisher to fit his own wider opinions concerning black exploitation by the white establishment. Gaiter voiced his fury with this "white media establishment incapable of concealing its innate racism."[65] Similarly, the white corporate owners of capitalist mainstream music labels were attacked by cultural critics like bell hooks for generating huge amounts of income through marketing black criminality.[66]

When the respected and popular Minneapolis *Star Tribune* purchased the rights to publish a three-part installment of *Monster* in 1993, the newspaper sparked discursive battles over black representation and experience similar to those in *Buzz* and *Atlantic*.[67] The story spurred several readers to write letters complaining bitterly that the newspaper was glamorizing gangs. They wanted stories that displayed positive actions by African Americans, requesting coverage "of the good things minorities do."[68] Likewise, a feature on Shakur in the *Oregonian* compelled an unhappy reader to express disdain that "the large amount of space and the attractive picture you gave of Scott were disappointing."[69] The reader continued, "his evil deeds are glossed over, and he is made out to be some sort of hero. I am sure there are many people who are much more worthy of the space and could be an inspiration to us all."[70]

The *Star Tribune*, as in the *Atlantic*, revealed that the interpretive problems posed by the memoir presented two, clear-cut opposing viewpoints. Several readers in the *Star Tribune* concurrently praised the newspaper's audacity for showing that "we need to know what goes on in these people's lives."[71] The final word from Lou Gelfand, the official reader's representative for the newspaper, sided with them: "The gang world is messy and cruel, and a good paper doesn't look the other way. We should know as much as possible about the issues and people shaping our community. If you don't think gangs affect the quality of life in the Twin Cities, your news intake is limited to football scores and the consumer price index."[72] It seems that the attitude of Gelfand (as well as the newspaper itself, in choosing to publish a controversial installment) reflected the fascination with the ghetto that gripped sociologists and citizens alike in the aftermath of the 1992 LA uprisings. Gelfand was stressing the "realness" of the newspaper in illustrating what life was really like "out there," rather than just a "fascination" with the subject to which Horowitz referred.

The *Atlantic*, the *Star Tribune*, and the *Oregonian* all highlighted the burden to represent black reality. As Quinn demonstrates in her study of gangsta rap, this effort has been transformed into a black, working-class ghettocentric image. The St. Ides beer commercials of the late 1980s, featuring rappers in the ghetto, were broadcast on MTV and other channels that tended to exclude the poor and penetrate the suburbs, so such endorsements were selling "ghetto authenticity" to largely white suburbia.[73] Readers of the three publications were inadvertently referencing one of the most conspicuous and ubiquitous of the discursive frames imposed by white society in post–civil rights era America.

Black cultural studies discourses of authenticity have been tackled by contemporary scholars such as Todd Boyd, who have explored further the scholarly work around black representation significantly forged by Stuart Hall. Boyd considers the burden routinely placed on black artists to fight against limiting or damaging black representations. In his exploration of blackness as a commodity, Boyd is pleased that the mass media, especially Hollywood, has allowed room for minorities. Even so, he worries that it is problematically the "excessive" and "damaging" images of black men that still dominate.[74] He acknowledges that these violent cinematic tales of the gangsta are often much-needed, sophisticated commentary that would otherwise get no exposure. But like the readers of the *Star Tribune* and the *Oregonian*, he contends that they should be supported by "similarly poignant stories about other aspects of black life" to ensure the reader is not merely receiving one-sided stereotypes.[75]

As illustrated in chapter 2, Hall argued that simplistic representational debates were no longer adequate. According to Hall, binaries such as "high and low; resistance versus incorporation; authentic versus inauthentic; experiential versus formal" are a "crude and reductionist" way of establishing meaning and representing race.[76] Of most importance for this book is the authentic-versus-inauthentic dynamic. All three memoirs invoke the powerful discourse of the authentic voicing of the street and therefore conversion. This discourse is further imposed on them in their media reception—except that, as demonstrated by certain readers in the *Star Tribune* and the *Oregonian*, the media flips this binary and deems Monster an inauthentic, co-opted voice of the streets.

Such readings still work within the simplistic, binary logic that came under critical attack from Hall. Rodriguez attempts to work against traditional criminal stereotyping by emphasizing the formal and aesthetic value of his work, but the media reproduce this binary reversal by endorsing his literary merits. The media again surrender to overly simplistic frames by asking if these texts-and their authors-are "good or bad"? It could be argued that Gaiter similarly succumbs to these one-dimensional agendas by replacing the black criminal with its polar opposite, not merely educated but Harvard-educated: "*This* is the voice of the black experience."[77]

While Entrekin, Shakur, the *Oregonian*, and the *Star Tribune* were being accused of misrepresenting the black experience, some of the more privileged publications voiced their respect for *Monster* and its author. The *Atlantic* and the *New York Times* aligned the author with empowering black historical figures such as prison memoirists Eldridge Cleaver and Malcolm X.[78] Horowitz referred to early promotional material that described the memoir as "the most remarkable and important book of the black experience since Eldridge Cleaver's *Soul On Ice* and George Jackson's *Soledad Brother*."[79] Kakutani drew parallels between Cleaver and Shakur, referring to them admiringly as "Mr. Cleaver" and "Mr. Shakur."[80] She cited the "fierce, liberating power" of both narratives and stressed that both authors "went to school in jail."[81] These reviews firmly positioned *Monster* within an established genre of esteemed prison literature. Rather than viewing the narrative as reproducing stereotypes of blackness, the memoir was seen as cause for celebration for subjugated people. The narrative was presented as an achievement and symbol of victory under oppressive circumstances. Kakutani attempted to counter the marginalized representations of black criminality or "otherness."

The presence of Kakutani prompts me to draw brief attention to the gender of reviewers. When gathering the press reception of the memoirs I anticipated a plethora of male reviewers who had been assigned gang memoirs, because the public generally view gangs and gangsta culture as a masculine entity. I was surprised that there was no favoritism toward male critics.[82] Instead, female reviewers are often picked for their literary standing (Holt and Anshaw for their reviews of *Always Running*) or their reputation as a book reviewer (Kakutani). Assigning *Monster*'s review to Kakutani indicates more about the status of the memoir as an anticipated bestseller and a highly literate and skilled book than it does about the gendered relationships surrounding gangsta. This reinforces the notion that such memoirs were seen primarily as books, rather than as gangsta subjects or part of a wider gangsta culture.

Kakutani aside, almost all the reviews of *Monster* deployed prison themes (though not necessarily prison authors) as frames for discussion. Prison literature is often deemed intriguing reading because, as prison scholar H. Bruce Franklin explains, "The criminal narrator is sharply marked off from the readers."[83] Such authors are usually addressing a distinct "respectable reading public" with no direct experience of prison.[84] Kakutani, Horowitz, and several other reviewers interpreted *Monster* as an accurate and important account, privileging this black voice that bore no relation to their own experiences as journalists. Reviewers were intrigued by the memoir because of the difficult circumstances under which it was written. As Melbourne's *Sunday Age* noted, it is "not exactly a literary life."[85] The reviewer for CBS News sarcastically commented, "He won't be making the rounds of the talk shows or book parties."[86] Reviewers repeatedly noted intricate details of the memoir's production, including the facts that Shakur wrote using a prison-issue pencil and spent most days in solitary confinement.[87] They capitalized on this fascination with life inside prison by often interviewing Shakur. The *Los Angeles Weekly*, the *Oregonian*, and the *Nation*, among others, interviewed Shakur and quoted extensively from those conversations.[88] By comparison, none of the original book reviews of *Always Running* interviewed Rodriguez, despite the fact that he was more accessible than Shakur. Shakur's comparative inaccessibility appeared to make him a more sensational subject to interview.

Unlike Rodriguez, whose violent past was eventually airbrushed from his literary persona, Shakur's authorial status did not displace his reputation as a criminal in the reception of his memoir. Instead, *Monster's* reviews demonstrated the incompatibility between the criminal/prison on one hand and the author/literature on the other. Such tensions were demonstrated by numerous headlines and excerpts, including "A killer, a thug, a warrior and a thief. He is also the newest toast of the literary world" (opening lines of article in Florida's *Sarasota Herald-Tribune*) and "Inmate author made out as hero" (headline in the *Oregonian*).[89] Such reviews pointed toward the exceptional and surprising standing of Shakur as a successful author, by contrast implying that his status as a prisoner was conventional. The reviewers thus subtly and controversially highlighted the site of prison as the "normal" black experience. This tense relationship can also be witnessed in much coverage of *Blue Rage*.

The prison conversion narrative traditionally concludes with the transformation of the narrator into a fully rehabilitated alternative persona. However, the narrative trajectory from gangbanger to memoirist through political conversion remained problematic in *Monster*. Following his release from prison, instead of exuding characteristics of redemption and reformation, the narrator accepted $2,000 in drug money from fellow Eight Trays (*M*, 363–65). In the epilogue the narrator admits that he beat a crack dealer who refused to stop selling drugs outside his home (*M*, 379). To punish the dealer Monster "confiscates" his van and brazenly reveals that he received a seven-year sentence. Yet the narrator unashamedly states, "I make no excuses for this, and I have no regrets" (*M*, 379).[90] It appears that author Sanyika Shakur remains eclipsed by narrator Monster Kody. By suggesting that he cannot push aside his gangsta identity, the narrator eludes the conventions of the genre.

The reception of Shakur was the inversion of that for Rodriguez: Shakur reverted from author back to street gang criminal. Numerous articles considered the actual life of the memoirist outside the narrative. Kakutani in the *New York Times* was the only reviewer to stress her belief in Shakur's redemption by using his Islamic name.[91] Most reviews called him by his gang moniker or birth name and several addressed his release from prison post-publication and his subsequent re-imprisonment for breaking the terms of his parole.[92] Numerous publications pointed toward the emptiness of the conversion narrative and its author. Though offering evidence of this incomplete conversion, they did not attempt to explore reasons. As the headline read in the *Los Angeles Times*, "Monster goes from best-selling list to most wanted list."[93] The sequence of the opening sentences in the *Daily News of Los Angeles* and Riverside's *Press Enterprise* are to similar effect: "Best-selling novelist and notorious former Crips gang member . . ." and "Author faces parole problem."[94]

By the very nature of its autobiographical genre, Shakur's book was supposed to be a true testament of his life. His conversion was committed to print, an unchangeable format. Reviewers judged it necessary to show that the author had betrayed his audience and by the nature of his actions rendered his own text bogus. Ensuing coverage positioned the memoir in view of his re-arrests (four up to 2004; he was re-arrested in November 2007 and is currently in Pelican Bay State Prison), questioning whether "true-life" conversion has occurred. For instance, *Newsweek* referred sarcastically to Shakur's "supposed transformational autobiography," while the *Los Angeles Times* noted he had only "seemingly turned himself around."[95] Though Susan Faludi's piece in the alternative *Los Angeles Weekly* was favorable overall, she quoted Shakur's brother, who acknowledged: "he's back in jail. He doesn't walk the walk."[96] The *Free Lance-Star* noted that when Shakur was first re-arrested he remarked that he wanted to go back to prison "to write some more."[97] This comment blurs the boundary between the unmitigated criminal and the convincing, converted memoirist, illustrating the difficulty for reviewers to make clear assumptions about the author. Press coverage of real-life events since publication has affected how the memoir is interpreted, with critics at pains to point out how Shakur's latest incarcerations undermine the logic of the narrative as a conversion tale.

Shakur's notoriety became a barrier to his promotional work as an author. Several articles documented the state of California's attempt to prevent media glamorization of criminals.[98] As a result of a new law in 1995, Shakur was prohibited from conducting press interviews. In several articles Shakur was cited alongside Charles Manson as examples of prisoners who should be banned from interview privileges. But bad publicity, even censorship, can often be good publicity. For Shakur, his re-arrests and the 1995 ban ensured his name and his memoir sustained popularity in the printed press and the public mind.

Shakur's re-arrests and the 1995 ban were in line with the proclivity for strict punishments that infused 1980s and 1990s American society, as detailed in chapter 1. His lack of conversion and return to prison point toward the failure of harsh penal policies in the rehabilitation of criminals. Reviewers have tended not to consider this error, revealing a blind spot in their coverage. Staiger contends that, when conducting reception stud-ies, "the range of readings is considered not only by what seems possible at that moment but also by what the readings did not consider. That is, the structuring absences are important as well."[99] Where the reception of *Always Running* explored sociological themes, *Monster*'s critics tended not to reference the Reagan-Bush era and its punitive attitude toward crimi-nality and punishment. The reception of *Monster* picked up on sociologi-cal themes of the prison but did not link them to his re-imprisonments in the 1990s, nor specifically discuss punitive penal policies. There is an argu-ment that the nature of Monster's crimes was sufficient to warrant prison time in any era. The reviewers' acceptance of these intense punishments as normal means they never challenge the effectiveness of the penal system. It would take the publication of *Blue Rage* and Williams's protracted battle to overturn his death penalty conviction to crystallize media discourses of punishment, conversion, and justice.

Faludi, interviewing Shakur for the *Los Angeles Weekly*, also demon-strated some unexpected frameworks for reception. Though gangs were being demonized by the mainstream print press, she suggested Shakur was paradoxically exploiting the extensive media coverage of gangs and its embellished tone. Most gang scholars have focused on the negative impli-cations of the media. However, gang scholar Jankowski considers how a gang member might manipulate the media to benefit their gang by qui-etly assisting in the recruitment of new members, advertising for business, and sending threatening messages to other gangs.[100] This unconventional concept is supported by *Monster*'s narrator, who suggests his gang rev-eled in any media attention: "the set was enjoying tremendous coverage by the media" (*M*, 115). Faludi was alone in pointing out Monster's manipula-tion of the situation and raising discussions surrounding the media. Faludi knew Shakur was using the news media to his own ends, and she explored these unconventional possibilities between gang violence and media rep-resentations. Shakur informed Faludi in this interview: "Getting media coverage is the shit! If the media knows about you, damn, that's the top. We don't recognize ourselves unless we're recognized on the news."[101] Fal-udi's approach was extremely progressive considering that cultural studies of such texts (Brumble, Tal, Ek) have avoided media representations of gangs and press reception of gang memoirs.

Like Faludi, some other reviewers made interesting moves in their recep-tion in view of traditional panic-fueled gang coverage. Several reviews of *Monster* took advantage of the attention-grabbing word "Monster" in their headlines.[102] Yet the reviewers avoided the criticized gang-member-as-monster school of journalism by carefully not being the ones to label him a "monster."[103] Numerous reviews cited the tale of how the narrator acquired his moniker.[104] The reviewers could satisfy the innate human fascination for bloody and vicious stories, their own and those of the readers. Simultaneously, they were excused because their sensational reviews derived from the autobiographical material. Rather like the memoirists themselves, who use narrative distance to license the recapitulation of violent stories of youth, journalists used the memoirs to warrant the reproduction of titillating stories.

In *Monster*'s case, the narrator's treatment of the media suggests he actively sought celebrity status and thrived on media interest. The reviews satisfied his quest for attention, albeit for being re-arrested outside the narrative in "real life." Though *Monster* (as chapter 3 revealed) has the weakest social critique of the three memoirs, it still illustrates significant police and prison abuse. In this period of penal law and order, the reviewers did not explore this analysis. Instead they looked toward the author's re-arrest, offering him no sympathy for the rightward tendencies in social policies, nor considering the potential failures of that harsh penal system. That *Monster*'s reviews were written with the least sociological or analytical depth, and *Always Running* the most, is consistent with the broad findings of this research. While *Always Running* was located in more progressive frameworks, *Monster*'s reception in many ways worked in the opposite direction, reproducing the biases, censoring activities, and discursive binds that one might expect. There is some evidence to suggest that reviewers supported the sustained demonization of ghetto youth through their reception of the memoir.

In many ways the press reception of *Blue Rage* was similar to that for *Monster*. In both cases, the authors were rarely compared to literary icons. Like Shakur before him, much emphasis was placed on Williams's incarcerated status. Like both Rodriguez and Shakur, the reviewers paid an inordinate amount of attention to the writer of a memoir constructed as an unmediated voicing of violent black masculinity. But the reception of Williams and his work was also rather unusual. The coverage of Williams's execution in 2005 blurred the line between editorials and traditional news reporting; he and his texts appeared in the hard news as well as the opinions section. News journalists and book reviewers referenced his dual image as a hardened death row killer and a reformed and respectable children's author. This study will therefore include discussions of the original version of *Blue Rage* (2004) as well as the posthumous edition (2007). It is also relevant to consider coverage of his series of seven children's books (1996) and the young adult reader's *Life in Prison* (originally 1998, republished 2005).

By the time *Blue Rage* was published in 2004, California's legislative attempt to ban media/prisoner interviews had been quashed. The press reception indicated Williams wrote for newspapers and journals, met with journalists, and conducted youth conferences for peace by satellite from his prison cell. For example, Hugo Martin for the *Los Angeles Times* interviewed Williams over the telephone while television personality Rita Cosby questioned him live for the *Big Story* on Fox News.[105] Executions are newsworthy public spectacles in themselves (and have been since medieval times), particularly when the accused is a Nobel Peace Prize–nominated author. Publicity is crucial for anti–death penalty crusades and Williams actively engaged the media for his own cause, developing a complex and contradictory relationship with the media.

Williams's books became guideposts as journalists entered the sinister world of prison and death row. Death penalty stories in the media are usually presented from the victim's perspective in order to make them more dramatic and newsworthy.[106] A sample paragraph of this style of copy, an article in the *Buckeye Review*, described the distressed state of the stepmother of one of the murder victims in Williams's case, cited the relative's statement about achieving closure and "justice," and gave the full names and ages of all four victims.[107] The article, which Williams provoked as a consequence of his conversion into author, was part of a rebalancing of previous media trends by presenting the viewpoint of the death row perpetrator. In particular, the publication of *Life in Prison* provided the media with tales of the prisoner's immediate experience of death row. With *Always Running* and *Monster* the reviewers were not speaking from personal experiences of gangs and prison. In Williams's case, however, there was so much material flowing to the press that even those journalists who did not interview the condemned nor obtain a media pass for the execution event itself felt they knew his story intimately. By the publication of *Blue Rage*, particularly the posthumous edition, discussions surrounding the memoir had a notably personal touch.

In news coverage of serial killers, the brutal actions of the perpetrator are often fused with exhaustive detail of the murderer's life story, which contributes to an understanding of what they have done. Celebrity studies scholar David Schmid argues that serial killers are initially famous in the media for what they do, yet they become further known as a result of public fascination in their life history.[108] Williams similarly was famed for his Crips associations, which involved accusations of shooting four victims in a robbery. He then fed the media by providing them with a ready-made memoir to add to the public understanding of his actions. Those who wished to understand how Williams landed on death row quoted directly and extensively from *Blue Rage* as proof of the life that thrust him toward murder. Such reviewers included two gang "experts" who—though gang scholars are surprisingly underused in reviews of any of these memoirs— refracted the experiences detailed in *Blue Rage* through an understanding of gang culture: gang sociologist Lewis Yablonsky and gang biographer Celeste Fremon, who both, writing for the *Los Angeles Times*, suggested no evidence is more powerful than the words of Williams himself.[109]

One of the dominant frameworks for discussion in the media coverage before Williams's execution was whether literature could literally save a life. Notwithstanding his five Nobel nominations, one ultimate measure of literary success for Williams was played out through the life/death debate surrounding his pending execution. Just as the reception surrounding *Monster* displayed tensions between the narrator's concurrent roles as criminal and author, this friction is carried to extremes where Williams's body of work is concerned. As chapter 4 illustrated, his books have the power to lead to his downfall (his dedication to George Jackson justified Schwarzenegger's refusal of clemency), though the press reception repeatedly insinuated that literature had the power to save him. Almost every review made some reference to Williams as both author and death row inmate, and carried a heightened sense of urgency with dramatic and thrilling headlines. The *Los Angeles Times* asked, "Can a series of children's books that decry violence bring [him] redemption?" and the *Montreal Gazette* stated he "writes children's books while on death row. Is it enough to win him clemency?"[110] A sarcastic headline on a book-reviewing website, "how to play the legal system in seven simple books," still suggested the immense potential power of authorship.[111]

A clear discursive battle was playing out in the media reception, and Williams was fully aware of the side that carried deadly possibilities. In *Blue Rage* Williams braced himself for the media-fueled celebratory "circus atmosphere" he expected to accompany his Nobel nominations (*R*, 303). He simultaneously anticipated members of the media would "flip their script and undercut the nomination" (*R*, 303). Professor Phil Gasper (who nominated Williams for the Nobel Prize) and other respected professionals voiced their support. By contrast many reviews emphasized Williams's status as "murderer" and focused on the violent nature of his crimes, promoting a pro-death stance. The *Montreal Gazette* opened an article by describing the crime scene photographs from the murders Williams was accused of committing, "the bloody torso—the blasted left side of [her] face—mangled left arm—spilling abdomen . . ."[112]

Book reviews tend to be more serious and intellectual in nature than general news and do not have the same degree of power to sell newspapers. Yet this type of reception suggests book reviewers are still acutely conscious of the market in contemporary American culture for representations of violence and even death. In the same way that those reviewers who used the word "Monster" in the titles of reviews of *Monster*, reviewers of *Blue Rage* can be seen as either genuinely concerned about gangs and Williams's plight or exploiting prurient interest in their readers to sell more copy.

Despite the temptation to lapse simplistically into pro/anti-death penalty debates or employ the expected literary/criminal frameworks, the press reception involving Williams's work invoked wider terms of reference for discussion, such as geographical dimensions. One of the early reviews of *Always Running* in the *Washington Post*, entitled "West Coast Stories," opened by stating, "Books are often our only guideposts when we are strangers in a strange land," pointing to the reviewer's physical and psychological distance from LA and his lack of understanding of the city with its gang culture.[113] The disdainful review of *Always Running* in the *Rocky Mountain News* also differentiated between Denver and "the mean streets of LA."[114] Nearly all the reviewers of *Blue Rage* and journalists covering Williams used headlines or opening sentences to locate their pieces in the geographical landscape of California, specifically LA or even South Central: "Black California . . ." (*Jet*), "In South LA . . ." (*Los Angeles Times*), "California redeemer . . ." (*Montreal Gazette*), "California murders Tookie Williams" (*Counterpunch*).[115] Geography is a major determinant of Williams's fate: his memoir blames the despair of South Central for leading him into gangs, and he now relies on the state for exoneration.

The huge amount of media coverage to which the *Los Angeles Times* contributed, combined with the unusual circumstances, created Williams (the memoirist) as a public persona and catapulted him into stardom. A media spokesperson for the LAPD disdainfully commented in an interview, "the case of Tookie became a huge cause célèbre."[116] The *Los Angeles Times* published an open letter from Sergeant Wes McBride of the LA

Sheriff's Department to the Nobel Prize Committee, requesting that Williams's nomination be dismissed: "We should never elevate gang members to statesmen."[117] But those reviewers and journalists who voiced disgust that a condemned murderer could be nominated for a Nobel Prize were in turn helping manufacture and sustain Williams's public persona (perhaps even generating more support in favor of his cause). The irony of McBride's comment is manifest. Schmid, who explores the way serial killers are elevated to celebrity status, is only too aware that murderers are famous for their monstrous actions, yet are "made legible by the same media spotlight that creates media celebrity."[118] Some paradox, then: those same journalists who wanted Williams put to death were fanning the flames of stardom.

The press response to *Monster* also included discussions of the author's fame and celebrity status. As a result of Leon Bing's *Do or Die*, Shakur had already acquired a certain level of public recognition.[119] Words such as "legendary" and "celebrity" were used regularly throughout reviews of *Monster*, interchanging his gang eminence as an "Original Gangster" with media-fueled celebrity status. Statements such as "Monster Kody is now a media darling" and headlines such as "Glamour in the 'hood" reflected a shift from ghetto notoriety to mainstream popularity.[120] Shakur was even featured in *People*, a magazine known for its celebrity gossip.[121] He championed the strategy of marketing through ill repute—Faludi noted that Shakur signed autographs when he was arrested post-publication for breaking the terms of his parole.[122] Writing about contemporary stardom, cultural studies scholar Richard Dyer explains that consumption and success are "the key notes" of the image of stardom but simultaneously argues that it would be wrong "to ignore elements that run counter to this. Through the star system, failures of the dream are also represented."[123] Reviews such as the one in *Newsweek* insinuated that the tenets of celebrity culture demand manhood fashioned on glamor, not responsibility.[124] The thin line between criminal and celebrity, notoriety and popularity, are the target of much criticism from reviewers in the context of *Monster* as well as *Blue Rage*.

Williams's celebrity persona was bolstered not only by the attention of the media but by the adoption of his cause by well-known celebrities. High profile figures such as Hollywood actors (Jamie Foxx, Danny Glover, Martin Sheen, Tom Cruise), controversial gangsta rappers (Snoop Dogg), activists (Angela Davis, Bianca Jagger), and politicians (Jesse Jackson) entered the battle over his future, propelling him further into celebrity status, far exceeding Shakur or Rodriguez. The presence of celebrities made book reviews and press coverage more attractive to those who had never heard of Williams before or were uneasy about his death row status.[125] Several newspapers referenced the celebrity supporters of Williams; the *Los Angeles Times* claimed the last time "stars of glitz, gore and glamour" had gathered was for the murder trial of O. J. Simpson.[126]

Constructed public personas are not solely the province of media coverage: publishing houses also exert influence over the image of authors in the public eye. Publishing houses, in choosing to publish such works, have themselves come under fire in the press. A review in the *Horn Book Magazine*, a trade periodical, criticized the publisher involved with Williams's series of children's books for "selling these books based on a reputation. He's making Tookie Williams just as important as the control of the books."[127] The specific motivation to publish a violent memoir or be associated with a notorious author certainly lays the publisher open to particular interest. Rapper Tupac's controversial producer Suge Knight was aware of the lucrative possibilities of thug associations and reputedly was willing to work with Tupac only when the rap star's criminal reputation grew. Williams's experience reveals similarities in the publishing industry, as *Blue Rage* struggled to find a publisher who was not solely interested in "blood, gore, and ghetto vernacular" (*R*, 273). This suggests Gaiter's concerns as displayed in *Buzz* were ongoing and not limited to the early 1990s. Another trade magazine, *Bookseller*, reported that independent publisher Milo Books (who released the British version of *Blue Rage*) had called on Britain's book trade to sign a petition opposing Williams's execution.[128] Both Milo and *Bookseller* made their faith in Williams clear, thus encouraging fellow publishers to do the same.[129] Reviews of Williams's works referred to his publishers much more frequently and discussed them in far greater depth than did those for *Monster* or *Always Running*.

After Schwarzenegger made his decision to execute Williams, Simon & Schuster bought the rights to a posthumous rerelease of *Blue Rage*, anticipating that, like many celebrities before him, Williams would become more famous in death. The limited number of reviews of the new edition demonstrate that press reception of the same work can change and evolve. Staiger maintains that one of the variables that media reception scholars should address is whether there are "changes over time."[130] Just as subsequent events in Shakur's life began to intrude on his memoir, the reviews of 2007's *Blue Rage* showed that real life outran the work and changed the perception of the book. The immediacy and urgency characterizing headlines when the book was originally published (in lieu of the pending execution) were displaced, as was the focus on literature as a redemptive tool. For the first time Williams was compared to other prominent and inspirational black authors Claude Browne and Eldridge Cleaver by the *Los Angeles Times* and the *Kirkus Reviews*.[131]

The alignment of Williams, after he died, with such writers demonstrates that death has the power to alter how we approach an author, in this case tending to hold them in higher esteem. Reviewers now paid prominent attention to the death of the author, as with the *Kirkus Reviews* headline: "Autobiography of the former gang leader and prison activist, executed in 2005."[132] The term "executed" carries weighty implications, reinforced by Celeste Fremon's comment in the *Los Angeles Times:* "although we're all accustomed to reading works by long-dead authors, when the writer has died by government order, it cannot help but give one's reading experience an unnervingly weird spin."[133] Williams's death was ironically to become the biggest publicity event of all the three autobiographies, as reflected in much of his press reception. The *New York Daily News* stated grimly that "the best thing that has happened to Stanley (Tookie) Williams's writing career may be his impending execution," citing booksellers who cannot keep his titles in stock.[134] Like rappers Tupac and Biggie Smalls, he achieved enormous sales posthumously. The headline in the *Daily News* read, "Drama sells his books."[135] Despite his works being unable to save him from execution, the *San Francisco Chronicle* noted that the death of Williams produced a huge surge in his book sales. The newspaper cited that sales of *Life in Prison* increased from 1,000 to 3,500 copies a month in the months before his death.[136]

There is some degree of reciprocity between gang memoirs and media coverage of street gangs, with memoirists using the opportunity to critique the treatment of gangs in the printed press (*M*, 279, 284; *AR*, 6, 249). This is particularly noteworthy in *Blue Rage*, whose narrator used the narrative opportunity to deflect impending *Rocky*-style (that is, scathing) responses to his memoir and to himself as a former gang member. Indeed, the author of the *Rocky Mountain News*'s review of *Always Running* found parts of the book "too disturbing to ever accept" and could not understand how gang authors could be congratulated for their books.[137] The narrator of *Blue Rage* acknowledges the "curiosity" of the mainstream media and is fully aware of frequent commentary on his "sincerity and intelligence" while "stick[ing] daggers into my back to appease the gods of 'balanced' journalism" (*R*, 291). In one final retort he spoke back to the media by citing a "spurious" article in the *Los Angeles Times* in 2003, in which he claimed he was "targeted for a literary public lynching" (*R*, 319). The memoirist is acutely aware of the extensive power of the media and prepares the reader for book reviews to succumb to traditional gang coverage. Yet despite his concerns, the reviewers appear to reflect a calmer and more progressive attitude than one might expect toward the subject of street gang memoirs.

Why this more perceptive and careful interpretation? Perhaps it can be attributed to the memoir form itself. As seen in chapters 3 and 4, memoirs are highly mediated texts and several steps removed from actual gang activity. Unlike gangsta rap, reading is an introspective, lone activity that is deemed less socially harmful than the visceral and often communal pleasures of music. Yet, as demonstrated in chapter 1, these books can potentially be seen as part of a wider gangsta movement. Notably absent from the reception of these memoirs are comparisons with gangsta rap or ghetto films of the late 1980s and early 1990s. I was surprised that hip hop magazines such as *Vibe* and *The Source*, read by many dedicated fans of hip hop and gangsta music, did not review *Monster* (though *Vibe* would later cover details of Williams's execution alongside rapper Snoop Dogg's anti–death penalty protests). Perhaps the typical gangsta rap fan is not immediately drawn to gang memoirs, implying that different forms (music versus book) appeal to divergent audiences. This can be read as supporting evidence that gang memoirs are not always deemed by reviewers to be part of a wider body of gangsta culture.

Despite the cycle of contemporary gang memoirs following hot on the heels of gangsta rap, the authors have been taken seriously while their musical counterparts were being subjected to intense criticism and often dismissed as "potboiler" artists. Discussions of censorship are present in the reception of the memoirs, particularly for *Always Running* (though surprisingly for sexual imagery rather than violence, as will be discussed in chapter 6), but not at the level of panicked discussion surrounding rap, stimulated by the PMRC, that was played out in the media. Book reviewers respect the form of the memoir and take their task seriously, even when the content is a morally controversial and formerly sensational topic in the press. Rodriguez and his narrative are elevated to the literary canon; the other two memoirists, despite their criminal inclinations, are lauded by these reviewers for becoming published authors.

Given the autobiographical form and their heightened life journeys, the memoirists themselves rather than the memoirs unsurprisingly were often the primary subject under review. In her studies of films, Staiger proves that extra-textual events are important to consider in the light of the media reception of texts.[138] The compelling extra-textual attempts at conversion of all three authors were central to the critical reception. The lauded career of Rodriguez as gang member turned celebrated author, the trials and subsequent re-arrests of Shakur after the publication of *Monster*, and, most riveting of all, the ultimate execution of Williams, all form major topics for reviewers. Despite a gap of fourteen years between the initial release of *Monster* and the latest publication of *Blue Rage*, my analysis revealed that the memoirs were, in broad terms, similarly received. The reception is irrespective of type. However, in 1993 and from 2004 onwards, the LA publications do seem to lay the two African American memoirs open to particular amounts of coverage.

Chapter Six

QUICK READS FOR RELUCTANT READERS
Consuming Gang Memoirs

Though "exclusive" reading practices of journalists and reviewers are vital when considering the production of meaning of these memoirs, of equal significance are "everyday" readers. As chapter 1 detailed, the readership of these texts is very broad. The readers I will primarily focus on in this chapter are low-income, LA-based, at-risk youth. In some ways they are typical of the wider readership, for young people certainly comprise one of the key markets of these books. Simultaneously, the specific social situation of these readers renders them an exceptional rather than representative group of readers. These marginalized youths are far from the white American, European, and Australian audiences (both youth and adults) who consume the books in significant numbers, contributing greatly to their commercial success. The subjects in this chapter also include LA-based teachers, librarians, and former gang members; but the focus will remain on the schoolchildren. The best means of accessing these subjects—except the former gangbangers—was through schools, and that is where I conducted most of my research. Going into schools and libraries resonated with the educational themes that I have been exploring throughout the book.

The importance of exploring reader responses, in addition to textual analyses of the memoirs, has been chronicled in earlier chapters, but is worth reiterating. Cultural scholars may produce sophisticated and specialist readings in which they learn and impart much about the structure and meaning of a text. Yet, in many ways their readings sit in a cultural vacuum with little understanding of the tangible uses of that text. Textual analyses can be greatly enriched by considering the ways in which different audiences derive their meaning from a text as well as exploring what individual readers may do with a text. As cultural scholar Christine Gledhill explains, "to the critical enterprise, ethnographic work contributes knowledge of the network of cultural relations and interactions in which texts are caught and which help shape their possibilities, suggesting what they are capable of generating for different social audiences."[1] While my fieldwork was far from scientific or exhaustive, it was far more than merely anecdotal. It allowed me to explore the social circulation of these popular-cultural texts to a much greater degree than primarily text-based scholarly studies.

Within this book there are three forceful reasons why such research into the interpretive communities of gang memoirs works with young, underprivileged readers.[2] First, these memoirs give voice to the underrepresented lives of these groups. Indeed, they have considerable identificatory potential. As pop-cultural sites for the production and circulation of black and Latino youth identities, the memoirs must be taken seriously, for they elicited very real identification. Second, the act of reading them is itself educational, and these texts are self-consciously seen to encourage reading and literacy. Third, they have potentially dangerous or harmful effects (the glorification of gangs and violence). The narrative tension between violence and gang episodes versus education and conversion permeates this research. That tension is now negotiated in this chapter by readers themselves. Themes of identity, pedagogy, and violence provide a clear rationale for the choice of readers considered here; there is a great deal at stake in the reading of these texts by such young people.

I intend to explore this reading group predominantly composed of LA-based schoolchildren to see how they draw meaning from the texts, and what those meanings tell us about the everyday circulation of the memoirs. What do these books mean to those schoolchildren in California? What issues and themes raised by the memoirs attracted the attention of those young people? Alongside the students' viewpoints, it is necessary to consider how teachers and librarians interact with such memoirs. The narrators all point toward the failure of the LAUSD, so I wanted to go to those very schools and interview teachers and librarians as further readers in real-life contexts. The majority of the students confirmed that they used the library, though some more frequently than others. It is therefore significant to consider how the memoirs were classified and disseminated in school libraries. The perspective of these adults warrants consideration because their views influence the reading expectations and experiences of students in subtle but far-reaching ways, affecting how the young people construe the memoirs. How do these additional members of the interpretive communities influence the reading experience of the students?

One librarian with whom I spoke classified such books in her library under the heading "Quick Reads for Reluctant Readers." She explained that gang memoirs are placed in this section because they are extremely popular, even with unenthusiastic students, on account of "their sex, drug and violent content." This phrase, "Quick Reads for Reluctant Readers" can be used to signify many of the key issues that will be raised in this chapter. The memoirists themselves were once young reluctant readers who struggled to learn to read and write, a pattern often being repeated by schoolchildren. There is some irony that, despite presenting themselves as warriors partaking in a war (as detailed in chapter 3), they are not even adults. As Monster surmises, "That's all we were; children" (*M*, 111). Discussions of schooling in the memoirs highlight the youthfulness of the narrators at the peak of their gangbanging careers. There are parallels between the themes of the memoirs and autobiographical experiences of authors on one hand (as have been explored in earlier chapters) and young readers on the other (as shall be seen herewith). There are unusually close connections between the two in terms of moving and growing from invisibility to visibility and from voicelessness/powerlessness to literacy/conversion.

This chapter will commence by explaining its methodologies. It is then divided into three themes that emerged from the fieldwork: the politics of representation; violence and anti-violence; and pedagogy, literacy, and the conversion narrative. All three texts were well known, but *Always Running* is the most famous and most taught, and I will focus in like manner on Rodriguez's memoir. The chapter will end with closing comments on the popularity of this text.

Most of this fieldwork took place in community environments like the classroom, with educators present. There were two primary types of fieldwork: responses to prior readings of the texts (within the classroom context or outside) and responses to textual passages that I circulated. In both cases questions were loosely framed within themes of violence, pedagogy, identity, and language, or discussions were encouraged to move in these directions. The materials gathered have been prioritized and edited to present a typical sample of opinions and reading practices of the memoirs by young people and educators in LA.

In December 2006 I visited three senior high schools in the LAUSD, two in a predominantly Mexican area of East LA and one in a traditionally

African American westside neighborhood. The schools will be referenced in this chapter as A, B, and C respectively. All three were of low socio-economic status, a factor judged by the LAUSD according to the number of students who qualify for free lunches. I interviewed teachers and librarians at all three schools. At A and B I conducted informal group discussions with five classes of approximately thirty students, and at C with fifteen students in the class. Teachers were present in all the classes; students varied in age from fourteen to nineteen. Even if students had not read these memoirs, we had general conversations about such books as I passed around copies of the adult memoirs as well as Williams's *Life in Prison* and his series of children's books.

In January 2008 I spent time at two more high schools with similarly low-income demographics, one in East LA (D) and one in South LA (E), again conducting individual interviews with teachers and librarians.[3] From varying groups in 2006 and 2008, forty-five completed student questionnaires concerning the memoirs were received; these form the basis for some of the analysis in this chapter. All of the teachers I interviewed taught English and all were female apart from the teacher at school B.

None of the English teachers had ever used *Monster* or *Blue Rage* in a classroom context, but all except at school E had taught *Always Running* as a course text. One library held nine copies of *Always Running*, two copies of *Monster*, and one each of *Blue Rage* and *Life in Prison*. This pattern was common, though the numbers varied slightly. Another library in a school of a similar size held twenty copies of *Always Running* (twelve in English, eight in Spanish), two of *Monster*, and one of *Life in Prison*. According to the forty-five questionnaires, at least twenty-eight students had read *Always Running* (though more had heard of it or read it in part); five had read *Monster* and four *Life in Prison*. None of those who completed questionnaires had read *Blue Rage*, though many had heard of it. Most of the high school libraries did not carry the series of children's books by Williams aimed at elementary ages, partly because they are aimed at younger readers, but also because the books are difficult to access with their limited print run).

Building on lessons learned in 2006 about organizing questions and extracting applicable information from students, at school D in 2008 I conducted focus groups with two different classes in which students were presented with paragraphs of text from the three autobiographies. I followed the approach taken by cultural scholar Joke Hermes, who tackles reader responses using detective fiction. For written texts she concludes:

"audience-led re-reading of popular texts, it seems to me, is the most sensible way forward."[4] Hermes contends it is only with "reader-made maps in hand that we can navigate and come to be in a position from which we can evaluate popular culture's layered meanings and determine what it has to offer society as a whole."[5] I led two classes of approximately thirty students each, one consisting of seniors (seventeen to eighteen years old) and one of tenth graders (fourteen to fifteen years old). The paragraphs of text were chosen for being particularly compelling, crystallizing key themes of the memoirs, and demonstrating stylistic traits of each memoir. The extracts were presented anonymously to the groups. These text-centered analyses provided rich material for investigation of all three memoirs.

At school E, the teacher arranged for me to conduct an in-depth discussion with three African American girls, all aged fourteen. One astutely commented that hardcore gang members are unlikely to attend school and that these books will not reach particularly at-risk young people that way. Only peripheral gang members or those with loose gang affiliations, those with family members in gangs or those who live in gang-ridden areas, are likely to come across such memoirs at school. A probation officer whom I interviewed reiterated this point, explaining that gang members on probation will attend special delinquency schools and not mainstream LAUSD institutions. I sought to interview former gang members outside the schools—with questions similar to those I asked in the classrooms—to see if they imparted any particularly contrasting views on the memoirs. One was an African American who was gangbanging during Shakur's heyday of the early to mid-1980s; the other four were Mexican American.[6] Of the Mexican Americans, one had reached the peak of his gang career in the late 1980s and was in his mid-thirties; the other three were aged eighteen to twenty. All had served jail or prison time and had reformed within the past two years (2004–6).

This fieldwork was far from scientific or strictly methodical, and I acknowledge there may be several criticisms pertaining to this.[7] When considering limitations it is important to note that pupil responses are influenced by context. I was not necessarily receiving the full story of the readers' responses to these texts but instead a mediated version. It is difficult to rely on their lack of engagement with violent passages, for they were no doubt delivering to some extent what they thought I and the teachers wanted. The context of debate (schools) surely influenced a lack of discussion of the pleasures and investments in violence. Put simply, the potential investment of young readers in violent themes was not something that was easy to access or prove. The reader expectations and the context of reading/responding influence the schoolchildren's answers. Teachers and myself to some degree inevitably police responses, so the interpretive community has frames of reference within which to structure their responses.

Place-based identity emerged as fundamental to student interest in the memoirs, particularly the textual focus groups at school D. Belonging to neighborhoods with street gangs within South LA and particularly East LA were central themes. Recognizing one's own locale provided rich materials, and pupils' sheer excitement and pride of having their surroundings represented in the texts was clear. At various points in this book I have specifically referenced LA as the site of the narrators' violent urban childhoods, what Monster deems "a concrete jungle of poverty and rage" (*M*, 111). Now the readers demonstrate the importance of visibility for themselves as marginalized peoples and their locales. The notion of marginalized people finding their voice/visibility works on two levels: as a key theme of the text itself, and as a focal theme during the reading experiences of those texts by local youth.

The narrators themselves direct readers toward reading the narratives as grounded in a specific place, particularly within *Monster* and *Always Running*. These two memoirs reference "LA" in their subtitles. Within *Always Running* such LA-centricity is highlighted by the narrator for its class-based geographical mappings. Ownership of property and controlling land in the United States has historically been associated with personal autonomy and freedom, as reflected in *Always Running*. In the two areas where the narrator's family live, East LA and Watts, Mexican Americans are denied access to public spaces, sometimes informally by white residents and sometimes formally by order of the LASD (*AR*, 35). The Rio Grande is described as being "only the first of countless barriers set in our path" (*AR*, 19). Such themes of boundaries and restrictions for Mexicans in LA are repeated throughout the narrative: "we never stopped crossing borders" (*AR*, 19). As a result, Mexican Americans are forced into poverty-stricken enclaves within the city with overcrowding and inadequate facilities. Within *Monster*, the city is presented as being inextricably linked with gangs in which competition for territory is of utmost importance. "Fuck street signs," states the narrator; "Walls [gang graffiti] will tell you where you are" (*M*, 169).

The importance of students' identification with LA was illustrated by the two groups at school D who read the paragraphs of text. Participants were highly concerned with the geographical location of the stories, with references to East LA and LA remaining prevalent throughout our conversations. When I asked the students if they felt the language of each paragraph was easy or difficult to understand, someone immediately pointed to the extract from *Always Running* and claimed, "this matches our language." When asked to highlight certain words, numerous students chorused "South Gate," "Lynwood," and "Huntingdon Park." Such geographical allegiances were vital in gaining popularity for this extract over the paragraphs from *Monster* and *Blue Rage*. Several students underlined the words "discarded market carts and tore-up sofas," with one student writing "Yup, so true, you see them everywhere here." Simple, authentic images of the barrio provided a heightened level of realism that was effective in gaining student recognition in addition to more specific geographical descriptions.

I was led to question whether such responses were specific to youths within LA. In some ways the generic investment people have in disinvested locales can be deemed authentic, as demonstrated by gangsta rap. Skirmishes over turf have played a central role in gang wars since the inception of contemporary street gangs. Realistic place-bound imagery and discussions of locale formed a crucial characteristic of West coast gangsta rap, with groups like NWA boasting album titles such as "Straight Outta Compton."[8] For many consumers of the music, including white suburban audiences and book reviewers like those referenced in the previous chapter, their fascination was fueled by a lack of knowledge of life in the ghetto. They recognized names like Compton, Inglewood, and Watts from crime sprees on the news and wanted to know more about the "otherworldliness" of this environment. Just as that interest is sparked by lack of firsthand knowledge, the intrigue for students in LA is invigorated by their strong identification with the memoirs' settings and their familiarity of life in the barrios and ghettos. If I had interviewed non-LA-based readers of these memoirs, they would also respond to the place poetics, just as did consumers of rap.

In many ways there was a notable importance attached to identifying with *Always Running* as a Latino experience. When I spoke in private with the Latino teacher from school A, she held up the book and stressed that even the words on the cover of *Always Running*—"La Vida Loca"—"tells you what it is about before you read it, it's an immediate connection. It's an immediate identifier, there's a few of them in Spanish." In other words the phrase relates to a specific culture (Mexican American) but also to a precise aspect of that culture (cholos and gangs). The subtitle is then combined with "LA" to give a specific context. Later in my interview with the same teacher (A), she reiterated: "I can't stress enough how much what Rodriguez goes through is Latino and that automatically connects with them, even before they start reading." This makes the reading experience for the young LA-based Latino very private, something unavailable to the mainstream non-LA-based white consumer.

The teacher at school C felt strongly that her students identified explicitly with *Always Running* rather than *Monster* or *Blue Rage* because of the culture. Though her institution is located in a traditionally African American westside neighborhood, she highlighted that today approximately 80 percent of the students were Latino. On the forty-five questionnaires (of which some respondents were from school C), four identified themselves as African American, one as Afro-Latin, and the remaining forty were all Latino. The teacher explained: "Rodriguez talks about the transition period [from Mexico to LA] which a lot of my students are in at the moment." For her students there was extensive identification with the text despite the readers not being located in East LA or Watts like the narrator. She cited a real-life example: "I have one student reading *Always Running* whose English is a very poor written standard. And yet here she is wanting to find out what certain words mean and she's really excited about it whereas she isn't normally." The young people for whom this memoir is inextricably linked to Mexican social reality become emotionally involved and attentive.

The teacher from school A contended that her students identify with the narrator of *Always Running* as a Mexican, in LA, and explicitly at school. The teacher from D explained that 60 percent of their students will never graduate and attributed this steep dropout rate to language problems because they have to learn English first, and so fall behind in class. While she acknowledged that *Always Running* is "a little dated" because schools today are more inclusive and teachers behave more appropriately than detailed in the memoir, she still maintained that "a lot of my kids identify with this renowned bestselling author going to class and not having an idea what was going on." When I asked the teachers how they would introduce *Always Running* to a class, none of them mentioned gangs. Instead, they all described a memoir that illustrates a Mexican boy in LA who is essentially out of place (reinforced by the police), unwanted (at school), and ultimately disposable. The teachers at school C and D were particularly emphatic that the young people's own experiences growing up lead them to understand the book and enjoy it. The teacher from school D informed the students that Rodriguez's wife had attended that very institution, which created a notable murmur. She argued that even if Rodriguez's experiences are extreme, they are present to a lesser degree in contemporary American schools and in life in general.

The importance of place and identity in reader responses was also raised in text-based discussions of *Monster*. Two students named *Monster* as their preference, one because "I live in that neighborhood—I am bussed in here [to school D]." Thus, geographical alliances may be applicable across all three memoirs for a range of young people. In this case they aligned themselves most with *Always Running* because their school was located in the same area as the narrative itself. Their familiarity with the environments presented in the memoirs became a strong means of directly connecting themselves with the text, even in the case of *Monster*. This led me to quiz the Latino teacher from school E as to which of the three memoirs she thought might be most likely to appeal to her students in South LA. She believed Williams's texts and *Monster* would unarguably attract more African Americans in these neighborhoods on the basis that place-based identification intrigues young people. Yet the use of "BLOOM, BLOOM!" in the *Monster* extract led one young person to comment that such words were not in the dictionary, and another to note that this text was "the most simplistic" and the "most screenplay-like." These students interpreted *Monster* along fictional lines, deeming it less realistic in style and therefore less attractive for most than *Always Running*. There is some irony that some students accessed their own neighborhoods through a "screenplay-like" text.

Cultural scholars like Greg Dimitriadis have argued that, when conducting audience analysis of a text, it is crucial to address which scenes people focus on.[9] Dimitriadis contends that specific scenes of a hip hop film may reveal much about how his subjects (African American young men) construct, sustain, and maintain notions of identity, grounded within an urban community. When this question about popular scenes was posed to the teacher at school C with regard to teaching *Always Running*, she immediately referred to the incident in which the narrator and his friend trespass to play basketball on county property, ignoring the warning sign posted by the LASD (*AR*, 35–37). During a police chase with racial epithets, the friend slips from a roof and dies. Several other students from school D who had read the memoir in full alluded to this episode without prompting. Similar to her colleague at school A, school C's teacher linked this scene to the students' own life experiences as Latino. She argued that they identify with this scene because "they all have stories like that—being harassed by the police, just wanting someplace safe to play, suffering racism. They can identify with that kind of racism."

The teacher from school C stressed that young people decode the memoir in ways that are related to their social and cultural circumstances. She was herself white and emphasized this notion of affinity through association by arguing:

> They want to read it because they really identify with it. They call me just the white girl from Iowa! I can't identify with it—I remember reading *Always Running* and saying "Oh come on this doesn't really happen!" But after talking to these kids and to Rodriguez himself you realize it does. For the same reason I might read Willa Cather because I can identify with the prairie element, they want to read *Always Running*.

Reading the memoirs and class-based discussions of the texts opened up spaces for young people to consider the social conditions of their own lives. In triggering appraisals and even critiques, the texts are potentially politically mobilizing. The importance of identity for these young, socially vulnerable people was manifest.

These readers responded to and identified with simple, authentic images of the barrio, and yet they also reacted to the heightened notoriety vested in place names. Street gangs were presented as a commonplace feature of everyday life in LA, as demonstrated by comments from students at all five schools. Discussion surrounding the memoirs gave rise to many personal stories about gangs in their neighborhood. As one of the three African American girls at school E confirmed, "in South LA, it's all you see—gang-banging." All three cited family members or neighborhood friends who were in gangs, and one girl had been mistakenly shot in a drive-by gang shooting. Though they did criticize the criminal nature of gangs, I was surprised how sympathetic these young girls were. One contended: "the government makes the gangs in my neighborhood, but the government ain't doing anything to stop those gangs." Their comments suggest that their relationship to street gangs is through realistic, lived experiences in an environment that is beyond their control. This complacency in the presence of gangs in their neighborhoods suggests that any publicity of place-based imagery is good exposure on some level. Thus there are two competing types of place recognition and identification at work here.

The young people's debates surrounding gangs engendered both pride and ambivalence. In general they were aware that the presence of gangs may be interpreted as evidence of deteriorating and dangerous neighborhoods. Asked how they thought the news media view street gangs, they responded with answers such as "like they are horrible," "as bad, dangerous, causing all the problems," "exaggerates it," and "more violent than they really are."[10] These comments are consistent with critiques of the media presented in all three memoirs. Readers interpreted the memoirs as offering a counter-reading to mainstream media representations of gangs and their neighborhoods. They were conscious that their neighborhoods had the potential to be criticized for being dangerous, as well as drab and poor. Simultaneously they were aware that the presence of gangs prompted notoriety, marking their neighborhoods as sensationalized and newsworthy. The readers expressed resistance to the sensationalizing of their 'hoods, but also some seemed to infer that even negative publicity is visibility. It is a perverse sense of pride that can be similarly witnessed in gangsta rap.

Feeling represented generated excitement among these students, who oftentimes felt they lived largely invisible lives—and this excitement was encouraged by teachers, despite the negative reputations of their neighborhoods. At school D the teacher was keen to tell me in private about "the pride that comes from this neighborhood—yes it's a ghetto, but they are proud to say they came from here." The teacher, who is herself Mexican American, encouraged a level of emotional attachment among the students at school D because of *Always Running*'s context. She explained to one group that Chicano literature is not exclusively from LA, citing also Texas, Arizona, and New Mexico. Therefore, "Rodriguez is very unique in what he has done and we should be proud of him." When she initially introduced me to the students, she stated, "Isn't it amazing that this woman wants to come from the other side of the world to study *our* literature in East LA?" One student raised an episode in *Always Running* in which Mexican Americans claim a small section of "beach" along the river, naming it "Marrano [filthy] Beach" (*AR*, 62). Despite the sewage and rubbish, the narrator highlights that it was "ours." Just as the narrator seeks positive undertones in the face of poverty, discrimination and segregation, so did the teacher enthusiastically encourage the young people's pride in the barrio. These students had already demonstrated awareness of their neighborhood's faults; the teacher now sought to balance any place-centered insecurities by exuding honor and dignity at being a member of that locality. This serves to demonstrate that the ambivalent response to these at times sensational, at times realistic depictions of their neighborhoods was not limited to students but also incorporated their teachers.

In discussions of neighborhood gangs, the young people became an authoritative and knowledgeable voice on the subject. Educator Allen Carey-Webb has experimented with using alternative or unusual texts in the classroom as a means of understanding youth violence. His class in inner-city Detroit read and discussed *Monster* at length, though his findings were summarized in a short paragraph as part of his essay "Youth and Violence: Topics for the Classroom." Carey-Webb noted that students comprehended the narrator's actions in ways "that the adults didn't know, understand or appreciate."[11] The perspectives of the students with whom I conversed were similarly fueled by their firsthand experiences of growing up in the ghettos and barrios of LA. At school D, a young person casually commented: "Where I live we have a drive-by at least once a month—so my six-year-old brother who is reading *Always Running* knows the score." At school B, the teacher asked the class to explain to me "what has been going on 'round here in this neighborhood," positioning them as experts on these environments. One student responded, "there has been a lot of shooting up parties recently. There has been a lot of racial tension. One of the girls from this school, her boyfriend got shot because he was black." Such gang violence was treated not with surprise but with a degree of banality. On some level they were disputing book reviewers, cited in the previous chapter, who deem the memoirs unrealistic and exaggerated accounts. Instead, they themselves were empowered as authentic sources of knowledge on the subject for both the teachers and me.

The memoirs have been criticized for promoting the gangsta lifestyle as glamorous, potentially triggering excitement and fascination among young people. Gang scholar Malcolm Klein voices concern that school students may "want to be a part of that [gang] fantasy. It's exciting. This is a world where John Wayne exists after all."[12] The students that I met, even the youngest ones, did not see the memoirs' representations of gangs as titillating. They drew experiential connections between the texts and the larger social world of gangs. And yet, in talking about neighborhoods they were careful to distance themselves from the gangs. Students repeatedly reproduced discourses of responsibility and self-determination (say "no" to gangs), discrediting the gangsta allure of the memoirs as posited by Klein and also literary scholar David Brumble. The young people appeared self-consciously to draw a boundary between themselves and the street. They were underscoring the difference in behavior of those young people on the street from that of their own and their classroom peers. The subjects therefore challenge assumptions and stereotypes about the juvenile, inappropriate, and possibly criminal behavior of marginalized young people (particularly men), suggesting that Klein to some degree underestimates the critical reading strategies of young people.

Though these books are marketed as contemporary street gang memoirs (as detailed in chapter 1), they were seen by students as being about more than "just gangs." In the paragraph of text extracted from *Monster* and distributed at school D, the narrator shouts "Gangsta!" before shooting someone. Despite the use of this word, the young people did not point solely to street gangs as the dominant subject of the memoir. When asked what they felt the overriding themes of the entire text might be, they responded simultaneously, "bangers," "Watts," and "racism." When the same question was posed to the students with regard to the extract from *Always Running*, the answer was similar. They felt the text revolved around "cholos," "bangers," *and* "stereotypes," "racism," "greasers," and "Los Angeles." For these young people, the gang element was not the dominant theme of such literature but instead part of a larger fabric of interwoven everyday themes and issues. The students' personal awareness, actual experiences, and particularly their readings of the memoirs suggest that Klein and other critics of the memoirs are wrong to assume that young people will automatically be drawn to gangsta imagery first and foremost.

The politics of recognition elicited by these memoirs are complex. The books can be interpreted as not being specific to LA, because arguably any community, any group of people can relish visibility (for example, an upper-class schoolchild in Northern England presumably would be equally excited to read a memoir where they recognized their surroundings!). It was not surprising that these readers took great pleasure in the sound of their own neighborhood or craved a degree of recognition. Alternatively, the memoirs can be read as exclusive to LA because of their gang element. This offers a different kind of investment, which stresses the ambivalence of recognition. It is rewarding to be recognized, and yet the gangs and poverty prompt an element of shaming and notoriety that ironically challenges the original investments in the texts. Given that territorialism is so key to gang culture, it is not surprising that location should be a big part of the memoirs, or a significant factor in their appeal to readers who are often equally invested in (or confined to) particular locales.

Chapter 3 of this book addressed the ways in which contemporary popular culture has grown increasingly violent, as well as the controversial issue of possible violent effects of such popular texts. This chapter now addresses the actual consumers who have been subjects of concern in discussions of pop culture potentially provoking aggressive behavior. The young people seemed to understand and reproduce teachers' concerns that these were potentially dangerous books. To some degree the students seemed to be performing appropriately for the concerned adults, which could explain the young people's surprising lack of engagement with the violent imagery in the memoirs. Students and teachers alike rejected sensationalized, violent frameworks for interpreting such memoirs, constructing them as important books that should be taken seriously.

The responses from these readers suggest that LA-based young people do not identify with violence in the same way that the narrators identify with heroes of the mainstream American culture of violence in the memoirs. When on trial for murder, Monster boasts that he will be acquitted in court, predicting he will be deemed merely another child corrupted by the aggression and brutality he watches on television programs like *Mission: Impossible* and *Rat Patrol* (*M*, 41). Cultural scholar Robin Means Coleman conducted an audience study with a convicted criminal, Caryon, an African American young man who was incarcerated for conducting copycat killings based on a scene from the ghetto action film *Menace II Society*.[13] The study explored how he opted for "thug life identification" because it was closer to his own lived experiences.[14] Narratives that addressed "the real" were important to Caryon as well as the children in classrooms. The genre of violent ghetto-centric films was attractive for Caryon because such texts acknowledged his social and subject position.[15] The behavior of Monster and Caryon is confirmed by historian Carl Husemoller Nightingale's *History of Poor Black Children and Their American Dreams*, which argues that heavy viewers of television are more likely to use guns and be involved with crime, especially among African American young men.[16]

Perhaps there is something different about the form of a book rather than film or television; for these young people claimed they would not glorify the violence as presented in the memoirs. On several occasions in group discussions, students suggested that at-risk youth might be more negatively influenced by ghetto films than gangsta memoirs. There is certainly a valid argument that memoirs are less visceral and spectacle driven. In private, the teacher from school D confirmed that the students would be insulted if I asked them if they were swayed by violence in a memoir: "they will laugh at you. They will be like, why? It's just a book. Do you think we're stupid or something? They recognize the difference." She recognized that reading is itself educational, equipping young people with a basic social skill not furnished by watching films or listening to music. The pedagogic argument surrounding these memoirs rests not merely on content but also form; books by definition are more pedagogical.

When I distributed the paragraphs of text at school D, very few students pointed out the violent imagery, such as the narrator of *Monster* shooting rival gangbangers or the narrator of *Blue Rage* assaulting someone in prison. While several students claimed their favorite text was the latter, only one of these was fascinated by the boastful discussion of violence. Instead, they based their preference on the *Blue Rage* extract being "more educating," "about study and education," and "it sounds like someone who is trying to get by . . ." Several students were impressed by the author's use of the word "hyperbolized," suggesting it made him sound more intelligent and educated. Two students preferred the paragraph from *Monster;* one of these based his preference on the neighborhood affiliation detailed in the text. The other said his favoritism stemmed from the humor: "the irony— he shoots somebody then goes home to watch comedy." This student explained *The Benny Hill Show* to the others. His interest in the paragraph was not grounded in the shooting or the gang wars, but in the amusement of the narrator's paradoxical behavior. As with the earlier student who compared *Monster* to a film ("screenplay-like"), this suggests that these readers interpret *Monster* as far from authentic street reportage.

The four Mexican American former gang members more frequently referenced the violent and gangsta themes of the books. Nonetheless, they still believed the importance of literacy outweighed any impending danger; one stated, "It's better for kids to read about gangs than not read at all," while another was adamant that "whatever book you read is good 'cause reading is good and books have knowledge." Three of these young men underscored the need for a responsible adult (whether parent or teacher) to help guide students to understand that text. One spoke of his young son and avowed, "I would need to be there to explain that just because this man wrote a book it doesn't mean what he did was right." Similarly, the former African American gang member contended that these memoirs should be taught under tightly monitored circumstances. He deemed them potentially dangerous books and argued for the need to have a conscious adult present to guide the young person through the text and take out appropriate meanings. The reading environment is always integral, supporting the notion that the texts themselves have no predetermined or intrinsic meanings. As this chapter shall later reveal, teachers also regularly acknowledged the importance of their role as mediators in which the reading environment is central.

Rodriguez and Shakur are aware of the importance of the setting in guiding a young reader in their production of meaning. In the actual reading of such memoirs, a young person in many ways is being guided by an older, wiser, experienced mentor or teacher (the narrator), reproducing the narrative logic of the memoirs: young gangbanger versus older narrator. In an interview with Rodriguez he contended that "these are hardcore and intense books" on account of the violence.[17] He declared that "younger readers" may require the actual presence of teachers or parents to guide them. Similar to Rodriguez's line of thought, Shakur believes that "to use *Monster* in the classroom one has to be careful. Careful that is, that students read it all the way through."[18] His rationale is that the first half of the book is "very very violent and . . . irresponsible to the extreme." Therefore the student must continue to the second half where "politics begins to take centre stage." He was adamant that the educator "has to be on point" to steer the student in an appropriate direction.

It became apparent that Rodriguez himself visits schools and even individuals where necessary, pointing out the social significance of his memoir. As illustrated, for young readers the gangsta content of *Always Running* tends to take second place to issues surrounding Mexican experiences of LA. However, the teacher at school B admitted he had used the accessibility of Rodriguez to help "save" students in extreme cases of criminal behavior. In the class discussion at school B, the teacher informed the group about a student he had taught in the past at a school in Watts, a special needs student who was "into tagging and gangs and needed a lot of work from us teachers to keep him out of juvy." The teacher had given the young man *Always Running* and even managed to get Rodriguez "to email him and tell him he was being stupid." Current students then wanted to know if the young man was still alive, to which the teacher replied positively. The teacher implied that Rodriguez's direct contact had saved the student's life.

In this case, text and author are unusually engaged in the actual lives of young people. In another story, the same teacher from school B explained to me privately that he had taught a student who was the first family member not to be a gangbanger and was struggling to resist the lure of the gang. The teacher gave him a copy of *Always Running* to read: "it made him feel good and made him feel like he was doing the right thing." The teacher also secured the student some "one-on-one" time with Rodriguez to ensure this young person remained on the right path, though he admitted this was unusual and saved for "desperate" cases, as Rodriguez is busy. The teacher extended his use of the memoir to incorporate not just literary, but therapeutic dimensions.

Though the students acknowledged this remedial potential of the memoirs, the one area in which their outlook varied was Williams's series of anti-gang texts aimed at elementary school children. For the most part the young people were unified in their reactions to, and opinions of, violence in the adult memoirs. Toward the end of the textual group sessions, I passed around two of the children's texts for observation. In both groups they sparked heated discussions; the students split into two clear sides.[19] One side vehemently argued that "we should use the elementary books because they show what you are not supposed to do. Because we are always told what we are supposed to be but we should also show them the other side and say what they are not supposed to be." Along these lines, Williams's series was praised for "showing the reality rather than the kids' books that have a nice, happy ending." Similarly, the three African American girls at school E recounted a class in which they had read Williams's *Life in Prison*, also aimed at an audience younger than the adult memoirs. They were adamant that the text had truly dissuaded their fellow students (particularly the young men) from the notion that violent crimes leading to prison sentences carry any status. The teacher at this school was resolute that "Tookie is the real teacher" who "can do more good than two hundred regular teachers put together."

On the other side, Williams was, perhaps surprisingly, treated as a problematic figure by students. Approximately half of the two focus groups at school D were disappointed with their fellow students' reactions as they felt it was easy to be brainwashed at such a young elementary age. (Working in large groups carries the benefit that students question and challenge one another, essentially probing deeper without input from myself or the teacher.) This side contended that the books might make children more interested in gangs and violence. One student expressed extreme unease at Williams's glossary of words, saying that "if you teach an elementary child to say HOMEBOYS, this will encourage them to speak in this manner and therefore encourage gang affiliation when they are too young to know any better." For the students, issues of violence within gang literature are age-specific as well as being inextricably linked with real life. Another student stated that *Always Running* still needs to be taught to younger schoolchildren because the narrator himself was "only young when he did lots of those things." But the schoolchildren in this group agreed there should be a cutoff age when teaching such memoirs, concluding that readers need to be at least thirteen years old before they are offered access to such violent books.

The polarized opinions of these young people toward Williams's series of children's books can, on occasion, be informed by adult attitudes from outside the classroom. Teachers and librarians understand that students regularly identify with memoirs like *Always Running* and therefore encourage their usage, but such progressive outlooks are susceptible to the educational censorship system of "challenging." School boards, prompted by parental challenges, have the power to withdraw texts from libraries and classrooms. One librarian and two teachers informed me that *Always Running* had been the repeated target of challenging. According to the American Library Association (ALA), *Always Running* took eighty-ninth place on their list of the hundred most challenged books of 1990–99.[20] In Kalamazoo, Michigan, Rodriguez was invited to speak at a high school in 1997, but upon parental request was banned from taking a copy of the memoir with him. *Always Running*'s challenges are more frequently based on its sexually explicit content than its representations of violence.

Such censorship activities, in which sex is privileged over graphic gangsta aggression, suggest that sexual imagery is deemed a more dangerous presence.[21] Moreover, sex seems to be more alluring than violence for young readers. The teacher from school C said of the sexual imagery in *Always Running*, "That's the part that a lot of the students like! They can tell you what page it is on!" When the Parental Music Resource Center (PMRC) was originally founded in 1985, it was over concerns about a lyric by the artist Prince detailing masturbation.[22] When the PMRC released the "Filthy Fifteen" list of songs they found most objectionable, nine were included for their sexual language. Similar attitudes pervaded Hollywood; a running joke in the early 1990s was that if the cinematic ratings board "saw a nipple it's R, unless it's cut off, in which case it's only violence, and it's a PG."[23] It is perhaps curious that in this overall climate of censorship, sex seems to be more proscribed than violence. There is some irony that the (arguably more) extreme violence of *Monster* has been ignored by parents and school boards.[24] The challenging of *Always Running* thus reflected key societal anxieties over sex.

The librarian and teachers were aware that a climate of censorship pervades contemporary America. Their determination to continue to use *Always Running* despite such conservative feeling reflects their general attitudes of encouraging reading at any cost. As one librarian summarized, "My job is to promote reading and I do believe people read more if they want to read it." They advocated such gang memoirs even if there was a risk of sparking parental complaints. The librarians and teachers can play on gossip about "sexy images" that spread among young people. On the questionnaires, when the young people were asked if they had heard of or read the books, it was usually detailed as being "school-related" or "word of mouth." Just as PMRC warning labels on music CDs prompted an increase in sales, young people are drawn to books that have been challenged, making the memoirs even more popular.

Three teachers spoke of objections they had received for teaching *Always Running*. One had since received instructions from her principal that she was only allowed to teach it to ages sixteen and under if she requested parental consent. Another teacher had received a complaint from a parent who found the book on the family kitchen table, but was excused when the teacher explained the memoir. When I asked how she justified her use of *Always Running* to these angry parents, she replied: "I say that it's one of the most popular books with students, especially in California. I would say our library has several copies and even excerpts of the book have been used on standardized tests we have had. In one of our textbooks there is a poem by Rodriguez. So he's one of the authors who have been accepted into the multicultural canon. I would point out that fact." The teachers still teach the book and encourage its usage, which indicates the progressive nature of the staff of the LAUSD in East LA and South Central. Even twenty years after the PMRC was formed and over fifteen years since the publication of these memoirs, these books—particularly *Always Running*—have considerable staying power in educational environments.

In the classroom there were roughly equal numbers of male and female students, and the books were eagerly consumed by both. Of those who had read any part of the memoirs, no girls or boys raised concerns about the representation of women or sex. In discussions of violence in chapter 3 of this book, the attitude displayed by the narrators figured gangsta as a "man thang." Chapter 5 then revealed that gangsta culture is not necessarily viewed in such terms by others, employing equal numbers of male and female reviewers, if not more female. Within the classroom, the earlier conversations about neighborhood gangs illustrated that the students were aware that gangs tend to be male-dominated. Though many knew of people who were in gangs, they only spoke of male gangbangers (for example, in the shooting incident described at school B, or in the discussions among the three girls at school E) with females referenced only peripherally as girlfriends of gang members. They were thus echoing the representations of gender within the memoirs themselves.

Just as gangsta rap has more female listeners than might be expected, the readers of these books were not necessarily dominated by men.[25] The audience studies by Dimitriadis and Coleman involved only male consumers of gangsta texts and, for these subjects, their interpretations of the media texts raised themes of masculinity. Dimitriadis was not surprised that "the black gun-toting gangster" was attractive for young marginalized men.[26] Yet in the classrooms I visited, both sexes were vocal in their replies and contributed equally to discussions of these gang memoirs. Instead of identifying with Rodriguez's tales as a male experience, girls and boys alike related to the narrator's experiences as a Mexican young person growing up in LA. At school C, the teacher told the tale of one young woman who had never read a book in its entirety, nor shown any interest in English class, until she was introduced to *Always Running*. The teacher explained that the girl constantly pestered her with questions about the memoir and about Rodriguez himself. This serves to remind us that female affinity with the text and its author can be just as strong as male equivalents.

When I raised questions surrounding violence, both male and female students tended to reproduce a strong moral discourse. This parallels the moral overview of the narrative voice in the memoirs. Students rejected violent frameworks for discussion, noting that it was clear what the "right path" was, even if it is not followed. These classroom conversations once again stressed the memoirs' unusually vital role in young people's lives.

In the classroom, these books provide students with an alternative hero, embedded not in gangsta violence but in their real-life experiences as marginalized young people in the ghetto and barrio. They are particularly engaged by the conversion element of the narratives and the transitions in the narrators' lives, encouraged by teachers and librarians. Once again there are clear parallels between narrative developments and themes in the memoirs and the experiences of these readers. The strong educational theme in the memoirs and the topics of developing consciousness (leading to conversion and transforming identity) and literacy are then reflected in the lives of readers. Equally, the educational and preventative uses of the texts as reading tools and historical aides mirror the narrators' arguments that, to some degree, a valid schooling and educational background could have "saved" them from their criminal tendencies.

In discussions with the teachers from schools A, B, and C about the practicalities of teaching *Always Running*, it became plain that they use the memoir for literacy and also for historical instruction among younger age groups. Dimitriadis voices concern that "this postmodern generation is without any history," arguing for engagement with popular culture forms to ensure history reaches young people. He considers whether films like *Panther* (about the Black Panthers) or rap lyrics that discuss Malcolm X should become part of school curricula.[27] The teacher from A expressed similar sentiments, stating that she specifically incorporates a historical angle when teaching *Always Running*.[28] She was worried that the Chicano movement is "not so real" anymore for these students. She believed it was imperative to address such issues, particularly considering their location in East LA: "it's like living in Birmingham, Alabama and not knowing what went on in the civil rights movement." Teachers at A and C explained that students are not taught the Chicano movement in history lessons until the eleventh grade and that therefore, when it is reached in *Always Running*, it should be explored among young readers.

The teachers regularly demonstrated their willingness to incorporate alternative texts into the classroom for historical and political lessons, despite possible opposition. At school B, when the teacher was deliberating on the historical importance of *Always Running*, he steered the group conversation toward Tupac. He explained to the students that he had taught the rapper's "poetry" on various occasions because Tupac's high school journals were "very political and not just about thug life, with in-depth references to the history of the Black Panthers and South Africa's apartheid." On one occasion the teacher had been verbally attacked by a colleague: "he said I had blood on my blackboard—he said that by teaching Tupac in class I was glorifying gangs—he said I was complicit in that because I was one of the people making Tupac into a hero." The students were angered by this evocative phrase, and nobody dissented when one young person seemingly spoke for the entire class: "Tupac was not just a poet, he was also opening people's eyes to what goes on and should therefore be used in schools." The importance of Tupac was that he could forge links between ghetto life and historically relevant subjects for young people. The presence of Tupac in the classroom supports the notion that these schools have a surprisingly progressive and open-minded agenda. Their approach stands in sharp contrast to the repressive policing and more punitive and censorial trends in American society mapped elsewhere in this book.

A student from school E noted: "A gangbanger won't talk about Shakespeare in class. But if you talk about Tupac he will be the first one with his hand up and will get involved."[29] Though the allure of *Always Running* among students was partially grounded in experiences as Latinos in East LA, most of the teachers noted the popularity of Tupac among their Latino students. Teachers argued that students "really identify with him" despite his being African American, because of his one-parent family and his upbringing in poverty. As the teacher from school A explained, he is "idolized in this neighborhood even though he's black because people tried to suppress him and that adds more to his allure." Tupac's lyrics, poetry, and journals became more popular as motivational teaching tools because of his celebrity status. Another student justified this: "Whenever you study Tupac or Biggie Smalls, it's always interesting and exciting for us kids because you already know something about it."[30] The students unanimously agreed with the teacher's attitude, which suggests that replacing monolithic and homogenous curriculum with texts more relevant in terms of ethnicity, geography, and subject results in increased motivation and interest from students.[31]

Students were encouraged to view Tupac's work as having political and historical connotations; similarly, the teachers pointed students to read the memoirs in certain frames. Despite discussions incorporating Tupac, students and teachers did not envisage these memoirs as part of a wider body of gangsta culture (which may include gangsta rap and ghetto films). In discussions of genre, the teachers contended that they did not interpret such works as being specifically about gangs. Nor did they believe that such contemporary gang memoirs had a relationship to prison literature of the 1960s. When the teacher at school C mentioned that Rodriguez had spoken at her institution on several occasions, I asked how she introduced him, as a "former gang member" or a "novelist"? Her response was that he was a "novelist, a poet, and an author who has been accepted into the multicultural canon," with no mention of gangs.

The reading practices of students, as an interpretive community, are strongly informed by their teachers. In terms of pupil responses being influenced by context, I have already noted that we are receiving a mediated version of the youths' response to violence. The second means by which they are influenced is teachers "policing" or mediating student responses to the texts. It was noticeable that these adults directed students toward ethical and salutary components of the books, rather than reading them as gang tracts. For example, the teacher at school C encouraged her students to "read him like a role model instead of just wanting to dwell on the gang part—they see this guy, he came from the streets, lived in neighborhoods that I lived in, he figured out what he wanted to do and now he's successful with a successful business." Likewise, the teacher from school A encouraged students to look toward the conversion aspect of the memoirs, asserting that the three autobiographies should be regarded as "progressive literature" whereby the author "goes through hell and comes out on top." For the most part, students believed in the importance of reading at any cost, even if the content of a text might be troubling. The adults agreed but felt that the young people needed to be directed toward the conversion angle of the memoirs.

With teachers highlighting the transformation of the narrator of *Always Running*, the young people in turn asserted the memoir was written as an example of what path not to take. When I questioned students about possible motivations for writing the books, not a single reader referred to monetary or profit incentives. The schoolchildren remained convinced that the authors wanted to warn other young people of the dangers of street life and criminality, keeping discussion of rationales within moral frameworks. The students did not believe the memoirs had been written for white Western audiences from outside the ghetto. While this suggests the naivety of students, I would argue that it in part stems from the teachers' input, pushing students toward the view of the memoirs as conversion narratives. Hence the young people contended that Rodriguez was writing for "young people, former gang members, even people who are still in gangs," "teenagers with gangs and ethnicities," "young people who might make a wrong choice," "for those they hurt and those in violence," "people who are currently the age the authors were when the events in the book happened," and "young people who have considered becoming gang members." Though *Always Running* was marketed to a wide-ranging target audience, the students incorporated those readers (at-risk youth) who become a target in the sense that Rodriguez is intentionally trying to reach out to them.

The librarians play a similar role in encouraging student interpretation of the texts and are in turn strongly influenced by their own sources. The first librarian with whom I spoke set a pattern that was applicable to most other institutions. She refused to classify books in her collection under "gang literature" or "prison literature" (because "to do so would stereotype the whole idea") and would regularly use terms like "Young Adult Literature," "African American popular fiction," or "Quick Reads for

Reluctant Readers," all of which capture student attention. She explained that to choose books for her collection, she relied heavily on the *School Library Journal*, the *Young Adult Library Services Association Journal* (a division of the ALA) and the *Voice of Youth Advocates*.[32] She was particularly enthused about the latter, explaining: "is really teen centered and they have a graphic novel section every other month and I get a lot of my reviews from there because they are really in touch with teens and are getting the hottest books." She said she would often be swayed by award-winning books and sometimes asked students to sit with her when she makes orders to "pick out the good ones." The presence of these memoirs in school libraries thus reveals awareness of the books in pedagogical circles outside the school environment and also reinforces their popularity among young people. The librarians themselves are influenced by these seemingly progressive sources.

The profiles and presence of the authors themselves can further inform the reading responses of the schoolchildren. The extensive popularity of *Always Running* can be attributed in part to Rodriguez's accessibility. Being available for talks in LA is surely one of the reasons *Always Running* has continued to maintain its profile among young people as well as the general population. The memoirist frequently volunteers to speak at schools, prisons, and other non-profit and anti-gang organizations across LA, as well as speaking at literary and other fee-paying events nationwide. Rodriguez had made at least one appearance at all the schools I visited (at school E the teacher believed Rodriguez had visited but could not confirm this). Just as the media reception in chapter 5 addressed the memoirists in addition to the memoirs, so too do school readers want to know more about Rodriguez. During the two focus groups at school D, the teacher informed the students she was friends with Rodriguez (having come into regular contact with him during her teaching career) and that they might meet him when they studied *Always Running* in class with her next year. The young people were impressed that their teacher knew him, confirming that they held published authors in high esteem ("Wow, do you really know him Miss?").

This teacher stressed to the class that Rodriguez "is still here," describing his "much loved" book-store/coffeeshop in the San Fernando Valley where he now lives. He established the business because he was worried there were limited places for young people to frequent in that area. Thus the teacher was emphasizing the reformed aspect of the memoir, supported by the fact its converted author is "very real and very living." Unarguably, the narrator's conversion from gangbanger to reformed criminal and anti-gang activist was seen as laudable by teachers and librarians. Rodriguez's visits to schools provide material evidence of his successful conversion (his conversion literally coming full circle). Teachers have capitalized on this, using the author as an example of literary greatness while simultaneously a role model who "managed to come through the worst and get out." Two teachers explained that students often want to ask Rodriguez about the conversion of his son Ramiro, to whom the book is dedicated. The first chapter of the memoir, detailing Ramiro's troubles in the gangsta lifestyle, prompts student enquiries: "Did he make it out of the gang?" "Is he ok now?" The memoirist's heartfelt plea to Ramiro touched a chord with these students, and teachers confirmed they would get excited at being able to ask Rodriguez personally about his son.

The real-life situation of Williams also affected demand for his books in schools and prompted discussion around the memoirist himself. The teacher from school C confirmed that his case was extremely well publicized. On the questionnaires, over half the young people vividly remembered Williams's coverage on the news. This teacher explained that Williams's pending execution prompted empathetic class discussions among her students. She contended that because there was a chance he might be pardoned, her students wanted to help—"Can we write a letter? Will that help?" She explained that around the time of the execution in 2005, Williams's books had been constantly borrowed from the library, which corresponds with the post-execution surge in book sales detailed in chapter 5. She contended "kids want to read what is closest to them," referencing the fact that Williams had come from a similar neighborhood and that the controversial debate surrounding his life/death was omnipresent at that time. There is evidence that the real-life context of the memoirist did have some bearing on the consumption of his books.

The same teacher acknowledged that shortly after Williams's execution, his books were no longer popular, a fact confirmed at other schools. As teacher C clarified, "when they realized 'oh and he died,' they moved on." She argued that "because Tookie is dead, now we just have words left," implying that books without relevant memoirists are not as fascinating for young people. When the research paragraphs were distributed at school D, one student suggested that Williams's narrative was "the most autobiographical in tone—it sounded like he wanted to leave a legacy," before discovering that the author was deceased. But the conversion of the author has to be viable to inspire schoolchildren. The teacher at school

D commented that students now viewed his memoir as being "about the death penalty" rather than about conversion. For the students, Williams's life was ultimately entwined in gangsta (he died for gang-related reasons), so he has not proven his distancing from gangsta or his full conversion in ways that Rodriguez can, and therefore cannot provide the same inspirational example. While the murders of gangsta rappers Tupac and Biggie Smalls were a marketing boom for their music, it also increased young people's emotional investment in the artists. Yet the execution of Williams did not similarly increase the schoolchildren's long-term investment in his texts, mainly because conversion was denied. By comparison, the young people believed that the murders of Tupac and Biggie had cruelly denied the artists the opportunity to enjoy their life of conversion after escaping the ghetto.

The lack of complete conversion of Williams and Shakur renders them less compelling for young people. Shakur has spent much time since 1993 in prison and is currently incarcerated, making his conversion unconvincing. Quite a few students had not heard of Shakur or *Monster*, partly because of his inaccessibility. Similarly, Williams's execution was seen to alienate young people. Even his anti-gang books for younger children, which might have had a ready place in schools, were largely interpreted through his controversial public image. This serves as evidence that the power of conversion in these memoirs is taken extremely seriously, not only by teachers and librarians, but also by the children (who presumably aspire to better lives). This links in with arguments forged in the previous chapter, whereby book reviewers noted that Shakur's situation (prisoner) was the inversion of Rodriguez (converted). Yet while the press reception was fascinated by the emptiness of Shakur's conversion and his re-incarceration and life in prison, young people were not interested. While the execution of Williams prompted book reviewers to hold the author in even higher esteem, for the schoolchildren his execution rendered their fascination as redundant because it served to prove his lack of conversion.

In all three memoirs the narrators are disillusioned and frustrated by their schooling experiences at the hands of the LAUSD. Each narrative highlights individual experiences, but all point to the failure of the LAUSD, as depicted in chapter 4 of this book. Yet in my brief exposure to these schools, I did not witness similar faults. My reader response work shows a clear impression of success of the LAUSD, to some degree undermining the memoirs' social critiques. My experience of schools suggests that they are progressive places in their policies toward teaching these books. From this angle, there is no parallel between the texts' themes or tales and the experiences of actual readers.

This book has argued for consistency between the three memoirs in terms of a coherently emerging genre, but this chapter reminds us of the need simultaneously to recognize points of difference between them. This is particularly relevant with regard to the narrative structure of *Always Running*. Here it is pertinent to make use of Gilles Deleuze and Félix Guattari's notion of "deterritorialization."[33] Though initially applied by the two philosophers to explore state machine structures of control, discussions of deterritorialization can be used to allude to the practice of removing a cultural background or social and political frames of reference from an initial, native set of relations. Thus, rigid hierarchical contexts and fixed identities are destroyed.

There are clear disparities between *Always Running* on one hand and *Monster* and *Blue Rage* on the other. This is evidently an ethnic difference to some degree. Chapter 4 addressed the advantages and distinctions of the narrator of *Always Running* being bilingual, as well as possible distinctions in the street/schooling experience and expression between Latino barrio and black ghetto in the history of LA. Moreover, the narrator of *Always Running* did not achieve self-education within the prison system as the other two narrators did. But *Always Running*'s dissimilarity is furthermore a formal distinction in which one may need to take care not to confuse this style with that of the other two memoirs.

Always Running does not fully conform to the teleological formula of *Monster* and *Blue Rage*. It is not entirely consistent with the "I was lost and now I'm found" pattern of progression from fallen past to redeemed present. The suggestion is that *Always Running* manages to preserve the criminal *and* revolutionary personas as coexisting. The narrator is almost a "schizo-subject" whose "deterritorialized" writing is non-hierarchical, with no single overarching narrative prevailing. While this difference was addressed in chapter 4, it warrants referencing in terms of reader reception. If earlier prison memoirs modeled reform as an ethical process re-enacted through autodidactic effort, what should be made of *Always Running*'s approach? The narrator defies the pattern; structure and style do not demonize the past in the name of a better future. Perhaps this can help us understand why *Always Running* has the most appeal to schoolchildren and has lasting power.

Indeed, it could be argued that *Always Running*'s version of events does not reinforce the past (childhood) as merely confused or wasted and the present (adulthood) as enlightened. Instead it gives one's upbringing and developmental years agency (precisely as a place of contradictory possibilities) and is arguably less patronizing to the younger reader as a result. Young readers of both genders may find their age and experience presented in a more sensitive manner than gang memoirs which adhere to the conventional conversion structure. One could argue that the narrative enacts deterritorialization by producing precisely a "minor literature" that accounts for minors and that avoids or critiques the tropes and conventions by which the gang experience tends to be co-opted. For instance, the narrator challenges the macho tenets of the contemporary street gang memoir with popular effect. As the teacher from school A simply stated, "When I first taught *Always Running*, the kids went insane."

Engagement with contemporary pop-culture texts, including gangsta, as sites for discussion encourages further questions about race, place, class, youth, and gender. Such studies into reader responses of these memoirs carry further implications in terms of educational impact. Various critics have begun to consider the pedagogical possibilities of pop culture and examined the ways in which it might enrich the American high school curriculum, even if the subject of those texts is controversial. Carey-Webb argues for the need to incorporate memoirs like *Always Running* and *Monster* in high school syllabi alongside the civil rights movement and rap music. Rather than hiding ashamedly from urban youth violence, he suggests we should explicitly address it in the classroom: "I am convinced that by reading relevant literature, especially contemporary biography and autobiography, by examining film, essay and even music lyrics, and perhaps, above all, by listening to our own students' words in discussion and writing all of us can come to better understand and better address the violence in our lives and in our country."[34] His comment encapsulates the attitude of the teachers and librarians at the schools visited during this study. If these institutions offer a representative picture of schools in East LA and South Central, then it appears to be an exciting time to be a young person submersed in the LAUSD. The LAUSD has become significantly more progressive, in stark contrast to the negative depiction of LA's schools in all three memoirs. I did not envisage the extent of the forward-looking and cutting-edge stance of the contemporary schooling system.

In Dimitriadis's audience study, he contends that reception practices— "how young people picked up and responded to these hip hop texts"—were "unpredictable."[35] Joke Hermes also references a "Plenitude of Reading Possibilities," on the premise that reader responses are regularly accompanied by a wide variety of interpretations.[36] Audience studies often support the notion that texts are polysemic, whereby messages may be encoded one way by the director or author and decoded in another by the viewer or reader. In this study I did not foresee that the texts, aside from the series of children's books by Williams, would be decoded along similar lines by all students in ways that the memoirists encoded them.

Although this chapter has concentrated on *Always Running*, I wish to emphasize that *Monster* and *Blue Rage*, when read, were also extremely popular among the young people. As the teacher at school C indicated, "I used to have a couple of copies of *Monster* in my classroom and they have both disappeared. So I know the kids love it and read it." Yet *Always Running* is unarguably the most widely read by these young people, the most extensively taught, and the most frequently stocked in school libraries, and has greater longevity than its counterparts. The teacher from school C wryly observed that *Always Running* "is the most oft stolen book from our library—the kids take it 'cause they love it so much." This chapter provided rationale for this favouritism, stemming from the students' extensive identification with *Always Running*, forging a relationship with the actual social conditions of reception, and respecting the narrative's arguably less condescending tone (established through its structure). This is despite *Always Running* having the most dated context of the three memoirs. Popularity has been reinforced over the years by the author's availability on the LA speaking circuit. The scope of *Always Running* is seen by educators as more broad-based than just concerning ghetto materials, incorporating historical and therapeutic angles for classroom discussions.

Like the previous chapter, among the young people there was a significant amount of reader engagement with some of the authors themselves, particularly with Rodriguez because of his accessibility and Williams because of his unusual circumstances. I was surprised that students were not more intrigued by the re-incarceration of Shakur. This may serve as an example of how students and adults deem it their own duty to read and interpret the memoirs responsibly. The previous chapter suggested that authors and even publishers were to be held accountable but, within pedagogical environments, readers themselves stepped up to the challenge of conscientious responsibility. These readers rejected susceptibility toward violence and remained grounded within the positive potential of the memoirs.

CONCLUSIONS
Still Running

The relationship between violence and pedagogy is the central theme under scrutiny in this study of gang memoirs. The books incorporate aggressive imagery and are commercially profitable partly because of the gangsta propensity for violence. But these memoirs have demonstrated that gangsta violence is not their only appeal. The books are equally, if not more, concerned with themes of conversion. While the violent component centers on short-term gratuitous pleasure, the conversion is a pedagogical aspect that relates to discipline, forbearance, and long-term goals. The fundamental power of these memoirs lies in their compelling combination of violence *and* conversion. These two constituent elements run parallel and in many ways service one another. It is fascinating that the memoirists integrate both, foreseeing that violence alone would not capture nor satisfy audiences. Even Monster, arguably the most aggressive of the three narrators, attempts to rationalize his behavior and learn from his mistakes. The tension between violence and pedagogy is often reflected in the narrative conflict between young gangbanger and wiser, redeemed man. It is this very friction that renders contemporary street gang memoirs so intriguing.

As chapter 6 revealed, the schoolchildren's modes of engagement with the texts extended well beyond the violent episodes. The young people looked toward the ways the memoirists were acting in culturalist (humanist) traditions, in which individual effort can shape history. They were captivated by the authors' commitment to agency through acts of redemption and conversion, self-education, and writing. They were enthralled by the narrators' abilities to shape their own lives, an achievement made even more powerful because they were rising from poverty. The all-important sense of authenticity in the texts stems from both the element of abjection and the angle of aspiration. This is ultimately illustrated by Rodriguez establishing a successful business and Williams a publishing house. Even though Shakur returned to prison, his brother keenly observed: "I'm thrilled [he] wrote that book and that it was a major success. Because it was the one moment in his life when he could say he had succeeded. A book, you have it for life. A book is *knowledge*."[1] Through emphasizing the conversion tract and their redeemed selves, the memoirists undermine well-worn structuralist stereotypes of criminal gang members and death row prisoners, an observation further demonstrated by the reader responses in LA schools.

The typically American characteristics that pervade these memoirs help to explain their popularity. Writing in 1993, cultural historian Michael Kammen addressed some of the polarized views of American exceptionalism (both repudiating and reaffirming the concept) that had been brought to light in intellectual debates since the early 1970s.[2] Over the past two decades, debates in American cultural studies have increasingly tended to de-emphasize notions of exceptionalism. By 2005 scholars like Shelley Fisher Fishkin were contending that transnational perspectives would eliminate attitudes of American intellectual, cultural, and political superiority.[3] But these memoirs make a case for, at least partially, rehabilitating notions of exceptionalism. The tension and interdependence between violence and conversion in the memoirs is aptly captured by historian Richard Slotkin's famed *Regeneration through Violence*.[4] Like the colonial story explored by Slotkin, regeneration through violence is particularly American.

This project in some ways offers a variation on Slotkin's account. The classic American experience is preoccupied with the violence angle, but these gang memoirs are equally concerned with the story of rebirth and renewal. With regard to regeneration, this book has mapped notions of self-invention and empowerment in polyglot America. There is cultural opportunity in writing gang memoirs, insofar as they potentially provide upward mobility out of the ghetto. But just as there are possibilities, there are difficulties in maintaining that advancement, illustrated both within the memoirs and in some of the reception surrounding the publicity images of their authors. To rise from poverty to success is deeply American and gripping, as is regeneration through violence. These narratives, with their immigrant story/slave history as explicit and implicit back-stories, demonstrate the difficulties and opportunities of growing up in multicultural America. Thus the memoirs exude quintessentially American dimensions, capturing both the nightmare and the dream of America.

Another focus of this book is to stress the politicized dimensions of the memoirs in historical contexts. These gang memoirs offer an extensive critique of the dominant culture and are in many ways profoundly political. The narrators use their negative experiences to positive effect as narrative trajectories. They deploy their narratives to construct identity and empower themselves in a society in which state abuse, racism, and the failure of education are rampant. The memoirs become narratives of resistance, mobilizing and raising the consciousness of young people in their anti-police vitriol or assessment of the state's attitude to punishment.

All three gang memoirs take inspiration from the genre of prison literature of the 1960s and early 1970s, books that were deemed to be heavily political. It is no coincidence that autobiographical writings from prisoners such as Malcolm X, Eldridge Cleaver, and George Jackson flourished when the politics of identity were being tackled by black civil rights (as well as Chicano, Native Indian, feminist, and other movements). Like their earlier prison counterparts, contemporary street gang memoirs become a celebration of the ability to write under subjugation and overcome seemingly insurmountable odds (like incarceration) in order to publish. The narratives crystallize and act as representative of the age-old struggle of the marginalized subject gaining autonomy through writing, in an environment where identity has been quashed.

Nonetheless, there are variances in the styles and attitudes of the three narrators, partly prompted by the slightly different time periods of their narratives. *Always Running*'s discussion of the LA riots in its epilogue highlights the narrator's concern for gangs, but is part of a wider concern with "the economic and political underpinnings of poverty in this country" (*AR*, 247). Rodriguez attempts to make sense of the belligerence displayed in the 1992 unrest, sustaining notions of Chicano protest culture and collective political rage that he experienced years earlier. *Monster* indicates the slightly later positioning of the narrator, when the social situation for gang members was at its lowest. Monster, like his earlier prison forbearers, uses the narrative to construct a sense of his black masculine identity. But the cartoonish vocabulary and aggressive rhetoric that permeates through to the final pages, suggests that the narrator's desire to tell a story is linked with his wish to achieve economic success in an era that, socially and politically, was vastly different from preceding decades. Different aesthetics in the texts themselves result in different politics. Monster conforms to the gangsta's every-man-for-himself attitude that thrived in the post–civil rights era. Shakur contends that *Blue Rage* can be seen as a "forerunner" to *Monster*, suggesting that Williams's memoir provides that "'53 to '79 sense of South Central" while his own text provides the "'75 to '90 sense of banging."[5] Even Rodriguez admits *Always Running* and *Monster* are "two different writing styles, two different kinds of book," in part because "Shakur was coming out of prison of the 1980s, that was a very different kind of era."[6]

The interdisciplinary methods that underlie this project are inspired by the books themselves.[7] The memoirs are important social and political accounts about real-life issues. Simultaneously, the readership that becomes invested in this life writing allows the authors to make money and gain a public profile. They are thus socially embedded books, a fact that lends itself to an interdisciplinary approach in which the readers are to be taken seriously. In particular, the memoirs elicited very strong identification among their young LA-based readers, who engage with and invest in the narratives, a feature that invites academic attention. My encounters within the LAUSD suggest there is a need for future research into how and why such true-life tales of transformation are so popular among these marginalized young people.

As chapters 5 and 6 revealed, real-life incidents can affect the reading of these memoirs, further justifying the need for an interdisciplinary methodology. The primary example is Williams's execution, which highlights the conflicting debates about contemporary street gang memoirs (violent and melodramatic or pedagogic and preventative). The paradox at the core of these narratives is highlighted by Williams's simultaneous status as a death row inmate and Nobel Peace Prize nominee. The execution of Williams during the course of this study must be acknowledged; such events can affect the reading of these memoirs and underscores how they are socially relevant. Would a stay of execution have influenced my own textual readings and conclusions? This life/death situation demonstrates how the memoirs have material consequences that are very profound. Hence there is a need to pay attention to how the readers, witnessing these actual events, interpret these "killer books."

The research illustrates that the production of gangsta popular culture is the result of complicated sociological, commercial, and cultural processes. The recording of these developments, culminating in memoirs, was previously under-documented and is one of the major contributions of this study to scholarly work on gangsta. Despite *Monster* and *Always Running* both being released in 1993, only one historian draws parallels between them.[8] Likewise, I only unearthed one book review that refers to the two together.[9] Until April 2009, Shakur had not even read *Always Running*.[10] In spite of Monster and Tookie referencing one another in their memoirs, no press reception or critical work has forged substantial links between the two. Such a shortage of association in both scholarly studies and media reception of the memoirs suggests that such texts are still viewed individually rather than as a body of gang literature.

But this book argues that these memoirs, more than being examples of gangsta culture, stand as a genre in their own right, as reinforced by continuing literary trends. Further contemporary street gang memoirs have been released in 2010–11 (including those by Sonia Rodriguez and Ice-T); Terrell Wright is at work on a second volume of autobiography.[11] Rodriguez's second memoir was released in October 2011, entitled *It Calls You Back: An Odyssey Through Love, Addiction, Revolutions and Healing*.[12] The book deals with his son Ramiro's incarceration, among other topics. Shakur is currently working on further memoirs from his prison cell.[13] Before his death Williams, together with Barbara Becnel, wrote at least five additional autobiographical narratives that will be published over the next seven years.[14] This serves as evidence that first-person accounts of the gang and the ghetto continue to be riveting and potentially lucrative. Publishing deals act as an indicator of marketability.

That Rodriguez's new text additionally addresses his gang youth work and his writing assignments suggests that publishers are becoming increasingly aware of the lure of the redemptive part of the life story. And the very fact that one of these forthcoming memoirs is by a Latino author is important. The tendency to study gangsta as black renders Mexicans understudied in contemporary pop culture. There is an urgent need (which this book begins to address) to consider the role of Mexican Americans (and indeed other Latinos) in the culture itself and in the operations of cultural power. Chapter 6 brought into view vast numbers of underrepresented young Mexican Americans.

The call for memoirs, for true-life testament committed to print, shows no signs of abating in spite of certain hindrances. In 2006 Colton Simpson's memoir *Inside the Crips* was cited as evidence against him in a trial. Although the book detailed crimes that had taken place over a decade earlier, the prosecutor persuaded the judge that the 2005 publication was relevant to the current case because it showed behavioral patterns. He was found guilty and sentenced to life in prison. Simpson's agent voiced disgust that "The most positive thing he's done for himself—his book— is being used to destroy him."[15] Her statement returns to the tensions between violence and pedagogy that are a fundamental concern of this project. Simpson's case suggests the incredible power of language and writing as a means of achieving redemption—yet those positive forces could not triumph over the repercussions from his earlier violent behavior. Like Williams's execution, Simpson's situation illustrates how these books penetrate real life. The social reality is that such memoirs have material consequences; the implications and power of their words should not be underestimated.

As mapped elsewhere in this book, the publication of *Monster* exemplified fears that, where African American authors were concerned, white corporate publishers were solely interested in "misery memoirs" involving blood, drugs, and ghetto life. These arguments were brought to the forefront again in 2008 by the publication of Margaret B. Jones's memoir, *Love and Consequences*.[16] Though the narrator was half white and half Native American, her tales growing up in a foster family in South Central and becoming a drug dealer for notorious black neighborhood gangs meant that the narrative was regularly classified by reviewers as another gang/ghetto memoir.[17] Respected reviewer Michiko Kakutani praised the book and it received other critical acclaim—until Jones was exposed as a white university graduate who had grown up in affluent suburbia. The *Los Angeles Times* deemed her a "literary fraud," reporting that her readers felt betrayed and angry that they were inspired by her courage, as were "the residents of South LA, whose real stories, and real pain, were appropriated and repackaged for the purpose of selling books."[18] The memoir serves as proof that this literary trend continues to be commercially viable, attracting publishers. But the revelation of Jones's true identity sparked extensive criticism of the publishing industry for pursuing lucrative criminal tales and overlooking facts in the process.[19]

Where do these scandals lead us in the study of gang memoirs? The examples of Simpson and Jones illustrate how such texts provide materials for interesting and often problematic scholarly debate, as has been demonstrated throughout this project. The continuing publication of such controversial memoirs suggests we can expect further complex discussion over their cultural and representational politics. For instance, in exploring such topics, it is too simplistic to assume that black criminal stereotypes are being deployed solely to fill the pockets of white corporate publishers, as exemplified by black-owned Triple Crown Publications.

Several novels have been released since 2001 documenting African American street life, including familiar themes of gangbanging, drug hustling, and the search for economic stability and social recognition. Such books were frequently released by Triple Crown, a publishing house established by Vickie Stringer, whose first novel was written while serving a seven-year prison sentence for drug dealing.[20] On her release Stringer established the business, determined to publish both her own work and others, as well as to create legal employment opportunities for others in the process. The desire to tell her story is inextricably linked with a need to secure economic success. Stringer's accomplishments highlight the notion that "blackness"—or "Mexican-ness"— needs to be examined as a commodity in more multifaceted terms than assuming it is beneficial only to white capitalists. Triple Crown continues to release numerous novels (three in May 2011 alone), indicating the 'hoods are still a relevant and interesting subject for literature.[21] This book participates in critical moves toward the creative empowerment of minorities. Triple Crown certainly confirms the possibility of black agency and autonomy through entrepreneurial activity.

So what is the relevance of this continuing penchant for gang memoirs and ghetto fiction in the climate of contemporary America? *Monster* and *Always Running* significantly were released in the chaotic aftermath of the 1992 LA riots, a time when urban young black and Mexican men were faring badly in society. This book argues that the cultural and racial identities of the narrators are shaped by historically specific conditions and that such memoirs reveal a great deal about urban American society in the 1960s, 1970s, and especially 1980s, and early 1990s. But do they still hold relevance in a cultural, social, and political landscape of 2011 far removed from 1993?

I would contend that these memoirs and the genre they continue to be a part of are still highly significant. My fieldwork in schools in 2006 and 2008 demonstrated that the texts continue to resonate with readers. Even in 2011 the themes explored in these gang memoirs are extremely relevant. In President Obama's America there is still plenty of poverty and violence, particularly among Mexican and African American communities. For example, statistics show that prison rates are still soaring. From 2000 to 2006 prison populations grew by 2.8 percent; by 2008, for the first time in the nation's history, more than one in a hundred American adults were behind bars.[22]

In 2008, of the country's 2,323,000 prisoners, 316,229 were under the jurisdiction of the California Department for Corrections and Rehabilitation, in which incarceration rates are even higher for ethnic minorities.[23] In California in 2008, 26 percent of prisoners were white, 29.1 percent black, and 39 percent Latino. Latinos were twice and African Americans six times as likely as whites to receive a prison sentence.[24] That there are so many black and Mexican men in prison today means that marginalized young men trying to express themselves through prison memoirs is still compelling and contributes to the continuation of this production trend.

California state corrections spending has increased fivefold since 1994 and Governor Schwarzenegger ploughed more funds into prisons ($13 billion annually) than higher education until he left office in January 2011.[25] A 2009 report revealing state rankings of education spending per student situated California fifth from the bottom of the table.[26] That education is underfunded and that priorities lie with incarceration shows these memoirs still offer forceful themes. Perhaps the weakened economy, floundering since 2008, will add fuel to the fire of the illegal drugs market, once again prompting the growth of gangs and providing material for memoirs. California unemployment rose to a record 11.5 percent in May 2009 (only four states had higher unemployment rates).[27] According to a 2009 report by the Justice Department's National Gang Intelligence Center, the national gang population is up 200,000 since 2005, now compromising one million members, who are believed responsible for up to 80 percent of crimes in communities nationwide.[28] I predict these three memoirs will therefore continue to hold cultural relevance and maintain an afterlife. Their authentic tales with anti-establishment and deindustrialized social commentary document a slice of life that still speaks to a wide range of audiences in 2011.

The themes of self-improvement, aspiration, education, and empowerment of minorities are very much captured by Barack Obama's own biographical story that he himself has recounted and constructed through memoir.[29] There are suggestive and fruitful parallels to be drawn between the president's bestselling, frank coming-of-age memoir and the books that have been explored in this study. Obama has learned about unequal power relations from the ground level and demonstrates a hard-won experience that comes to inform value frameworks and attitudes. His memoir moreover regularly returns to charged issues of identity politics, renewal, redemption, and creating status for the marginalized. Like gang memoirists, Obama can fight for recognition with language and the written word.

The hope in his autobiographical story captures the best of America—the possibility for rebirth that, as this book contends, is one of the key marketable and meaningful features of these gang memoirs.

Born in 1961, only two years earlier than Shakur, Obama's liberal yet structural critique is consistent with the more politicized views of the two older memoirists. Williams and Rodriguez were born in 1953 and 1954 respectively. Unlike Monster's more lumpen worldview, Obama's attitudes toward healthcare, education, immigration, and cultural sensitivities suggest he is a product of the 1960s' more radical moment. His second book, which discusses the need for inclusive and compassionate politics, explicitly addresses this: "I've always felt a curious relationship to the sixties. In a sense, I'm a pure product of that era . . ."[30] Yet interestingly, Obama and Monster grew up in the same America. In 1983, as Monster was fully immersed in the Eight-Trays, Obama was becoming a community organizer, disgusted with the White House "where Reagan and his minions were carrying on their dirty deeds" and convinced that change needed to be effected at the grass-roots level.[31] As Monster was becoming familiar with the jails and prisons of LA and California, Obama was volunteering to help black youths on the streets in Chicago. Obama's exploration of the social problems in America led him to significantly different conclusions from those of Monster, more aligned with the ideologies of Rodriguez and Williams.

Obama has already inspired schoolchildren and celebrities alike. The "Obama effect" is expected to encourage both black and Mexican youth to fare better in schools and make strides in their education. In 2009, gangsta rapper and entrepreneur Jay-Z observed: "Obama represents so much hope for blacks and Latinos. The hope he represents is bigger than any of the huge problems he could possibly correct—When you have positive role models, you can change your life for the better. The day Obama got elected, the gangsta became less relevant."[32] Jay-Z's comment again draws our attention back to the tension between gangsta violence and pedagogy. If one opts for education, it provides less reason for choosing gangsta as a way of life.

Indeed, I was surprised that the gangsta figure to which Jay-Z alludes was not as important in this research as I originally anticipated. In closing, I wish to underscore once more the importance of the conversion factor. The title of chapter 4 of this book ultimately encapsulates the dialectic of violent physical action and pedagogical, redemptive language. The LA-based young people that I met were incredibly enthusiastic about the role-model potential of these authors. They were not being ironic or cynical, but were simply captured by the rhetoric of "doing the right thing." The memoirists work on a similar level, destroying the concept that gang memoirs are preoccupied with the gangsta, alternatively stressing notions of redemption and reform. This echoes Obama's ideology as Jay-Z highlights, where black and Mexican youth are now potentially less alienated and marginalized. In Obama's America, we will be seeing more brothers who can kill with words.

NOTES

Note on the sources: where articles were accessed via LexisNexis, page numbers, and names of authors were not always supplied.

Introduction

1. Sanyika Shakur, *Monster: The Autobiography of an LA Gang Member* (New York: Penguin, 1994). The original hardback edition of *Monster* was released in 1993 by Atlantic. All notes reference the 1994 paperback Penguin edition unless otherwise indicated.

2. Michiko Kakutani, "Illuminating Gang Life in LA: It's Raw," *New York Times*, 23 July 1993: C27.

3. Sheriff Le Baca of the LA Sheriff Department commented in 2007 that "LA county and city is, unfortunately, the gang capital of America." See Jill Serjeant, "Little glamour in LA, gang capital of America," *Reuters*, 8 February 2007. Memoirist Luis J. Rodriguez also refers to LA as the "gang capital of America." See Rodriguez's *Always Running: La Vida Loca - Gang Days in LA* (New York: Touchstone, 1994): 4. The original hardback edition of *Always Running* was released in 1993 by Curbstone. All notes reference the 1994 Touchstone paperback edition unless otherwise indicated.

4. For instance, journalist Leon Bing wrote numerous articles on street gang life that often included interviews with gang members. Examples of her work include: "Reflections of a Gangbanger," *Harper's*, August 1988: 26–28; "When You're a Crip (or a Blood)," *Harper's*, March 1989: 51–59; "The Talk of the Town," *New Yorker*, 19 July 1993: 25–26; "In the Brutal World of LA's Toughest Gangs," *Time*, 16 March 1992: 12–16. Such auto/biographical collections incorporate several accounts of gang members. These texts include Leon Bing, *Do Or Die: For the First Time, Members of America's Most Notorious Gangs—The Crips and The Bloods—Speak For Themselves* (New York: Harper Collins, 1991); Celeste Fremon, *G-Dog and the Homeboys: Father Greg Boyle and the Gangs of East LA* (Albuquerque: University of New Mexico Press, 1995); Yusuf Jah and Shah'Keyah, *Uprising: Crips and Bloods Tell the Story of America's*

Youth Caught in the Crossfire (New York: Touchstone, 1997); Gini Sykes, *8 Ball Chicks: A Year in the Violent World of Girl Gangsters* (New York: Doubleday, 1997).

5. Consult the "book club" section of www.streetgangs.com. For example: Nathan McCall, *Makes Me Wanna Holler: A Young Black Man in America* (New York: Random House, 1994); Geoffrey Canada, *Fist Stick Gun Knife* (Boston: Beacon Press, 1996); Mona Ruiz with Geoff Boucher, *Two Badges: The Lives of Mona Ruiz* (Houston: Arte Publico, 1997); Snoop Dogg with Davin Seay, *Tha Doggfather: The Times, Trials and Hardcore Truths of Snoop Dogg* (New York: William Morrow, 1999); Bill Lee, *Chinese Playground: A Memoir* (San Francisco: Rhapsody, 1999).

6. Susan Faludi, *Stiffed: The Betrayal of the American Man* (London: Chatto & Windus, 1999): 472; Shakur, *T.H.U.G. L.I.F.E.* (New York: Grove/Atlantic, 2008), opening cover sleeve.

7. Written correspondence by the author with a representative (anonymity requested) from Simon & Schuster who bought the rights to subsequent editions. In an author interview with Rodriguez in January 2008, he said he had been informed that his memoir still sold 25,000 copies annually and that he had been told by a librarian that it was supposedly the most checked-out and the most stolen book in the LA public library system. (Simon & Schuster do not release sales figures to the public and the LA public library system helpdesk could not formally confirm this fact.)

8. Written correspondence by author with a representative from Simon & Schuster.

9. Stanley "Tookie" Williams, *Redemption: From Original Gangster to Nobel Prize Nominee* (Preston, UK: Milo, 2004): 272. This is the British edition; it was published in the United States as *Blue Rage, Black Redemption: A Memoir* (Pleasant Hill, CA: Damamli, 2004). All notes reference the British edition unless otherwise indicated.

10. It was reported that from 1993 to 2003, in LA alone 10,000 youths had died in gang-related deaths. See Claudia Durst Johnson, *Youth Gangs in Literature* (Westport, CT: Greenwood, 2004): xvi.

11. Williams with Barbara Becnel, *Tookie Speaks Out Against Gang Violence Series* (New York: Rosen, 1996).

12. Heidi Benson, "The Execution of Stanley Tookie Williams: Execution Brought Interest in Williams' Anti-gang Writings, a Surge in Sales," *San Francisco Chronicle*, 14 December 2005: A12.

13. For example, see Robin Kelley's *Race Rebels: Culture, Politics and the Black Working Class* (New York: Free Press, 1994): 183.

14. Eithne Quinn, *Nuthin' But a "G" Thang: The Culture and Commerce of Gangsta Rap* (New York: Columbia University Press, 2005): 11.

15. Biography of Public Enemy on "Hip Online" hiponline.com/music-artists/public-enemy/. Ice Cube cited in Kelley, *Race Rebels*: 190.

16. Todd Boyd, *Am I Black Enough for You? Popular Culture from the 'hood and Beyond* (Bloomington: Indiana University Press, 1997): 104.

17. Author interview with a high school librarian in California, January 2008.

18. Malcolm Little with Alex Haley, *The Autobiography of Malcolm X* (London: Penguin, 1965); George Jackson, *Soledad Brother: The Prison Letters of George Jackson* (London: Jonathan Cape, 1970); James Carr, *Bad: The Autobiography of James Carr* (London: Pelagian, 1975).

19. Kevin Starr, *Coast of Dreams: A History of Contemporary California* (London: Allen Lane, 2005): 78–79, 87–89; David Wyatt, *Five Fires: Race, Catastrophe and the Shaping of California* (Oxford, UK: Oxford University Press, 1999): 232–36; Victor Valle and Rodolfo Torres, *Latino Metropolis* (Minneapolis: University of Minnesota Press, 2000): 159–61. Further examples of historical studies that reference Rodriguez include Garth Cartwright, *More Miles Than Money: Journeys Through American Music* (London: Serpent's Tail, 2009); Alex Moreno Areyan (ed.), *Mexican Americans in Los Angeles* (Mount Pleasant, SC: Arcadia, 2010); Mark Schiesel & Mark Dose (eds.), *City of Promise: Race and Historical Change in Los Angeles* (Claremont, CA: Regina Books, 2006).

20. Starr, *Coast of Dreams*: 78.

21. Wyatt, *Five Fires*: 232.

22. Starr, *Coast of Dreams*: 74–96.

23. I acknowledge that historians are likely to be guarded or selective in their reliance on these memoirs as sources of "truth" in a literal sense.

24. Examples include Lonnie Athens, "Dominance, Ghettos and Violent Crime," *Sociological Quarterly* 39, no. 4 (Autumn 1998): 673–91; Vern Baxter and A. V. Margavio, "Honor, Status, and Aggression in Economic Exchange," *Sociological Theory* 18, no. 3 (November 2000): 399–416; Dinesh D'Souza, *The End of Racism* (New York: Free Press, 1995): 261–62, 506–7; Matthew Lee, "Concentrated Poverty, Race and Homicide," *Sociological Quarterly* 41, no. 2 (21 April 2005): 189–206; Rufus Schatzberg and Robert Kelly, *African American Organized Crime: A Social History* (New Brunswick: Rutgers University Press, 1997): 189, 238.

25. Examples include Martin Guevara Urbina, "Latinos/as in the Criminal and Juvenile Justice Systems," *Critical Criminology* 15, no. 1 (March 2007): 41–99.

26. Lewis Yablonsky, *Gangsters: Fifty Years of Madness, Drugs and Death on the Streets of America* (New York: New York University Press, 1998): 16, 43, 61–64, 118–19.

27. James Diego Vigil, *A Rainbow of Gangs* (Austin: University of Texas Press, 2002): 23, 82; Malcolm Klein, *The American Street Gang: Its Nature, Prevalence and Control* (Oxford, UK: Oxford University Press, 1995): 8.

28. Author interview with Klein, December 2006.

29. Durst Johnson, *Youth Gangs in Literature*: 167–84.

30. Allen Carey-Webb, "Youth Violence and the Language Arts: a Topic for the Classroom," *English Journal* 84, no. 5 (September 1995): 29–37.

31. Examples include Antonia Darder, "Latino Youth: Pedagogy, Praxis, And Policy," *Latino Studies* 4, no. 3 (2006): 302–4; Susan Roberta Katz, "Teaching in Tensions: Latino Immigrant Youth, Their Teachers, and the Structures of Schooling," *Teachers College Record* 100, no. 4 (Summer 1999): 809–40; J. Singer and R. Shagoury, "Stirring Up Justice: Adolescents Reading, Writing, and Changing the World," *Journal of Adolescent and Adult Literacy* 49, no. 4 (December 2005): 318–39. *Monster* is also briefly referenced in John Allen, "Literature, Lives and Teachers," *Pedagogy: Critical Approaches to Teaching Literature, Language, Composition and Culture* 3, no. 2 (2003): 304–11.

32. David Brumble, "The Gangbanger Autobiography of Monster and Warrior Literature," in *American Literary History* 12, nos. 1 and 2 (Spring/Summer 2000): 158–86.

33. Brumble, "Stanley 'Tookie' Williams, Gangbanger Autobiography, and Warrior Tribes," *Journal of American Studies* 44, no. 1 (February 2010): 155–70 (157).

34. Tim Libretti, "Is there a Working Class in US Literature? Race, Ethnicity and the Proletarian Literary Tradition," *Radical Teacher (Working Class Studies)*, no. 46 (Spring 1995): 22–26.

35. Paula Moya, "This Is Not Your Country! Nation and Belonging in Latina/o Literature," *American Literary History* 17, no. 1 (Spring 2005): 183–95.

36. Ibid.: 184. The critical text explored by Moya that makes brief references to *Always Running* is Monica Brown's *Gang Nation: Delinquent Citizens in Puerto Rican, Chicano and Chicana Narratives* (Minneapolis: University of Minnesota Press, 2002).

37. Vincent Perez, "'Running' and Resistance: Nihilism and Cultural Memory in Chicano Urban Narratives," *MELUS* 25, no. 2 (Summer 2000): 133–46; Amaia Ibarraran Bigalondo, "Wolves, Sheep and *Vatos Locos*: Reflections of Gang Activity in Chicano Literature," *Journal of English Studies*, no. 4 (2003–4): 107–13.

38. Boyd, *Am I Black Enough for You?*: 64–65, 73; Auli Ek, *Race and Masculinity in Contemporary American Prison Narratives* (New York: Routledge, 2005): 53–55, 68, 70, 95, 100–105; Kali Tal, "From Panther to Monster: Black Popular Culture Representations of Resistance from the Black Panther Movement of the 1960s to *Boyz N The Hood*," in Elaine Richardson and Ronald Jackson (eds.), *African American Rhetoric(s): Interdisciplinary Perspectives* (Carbondale: Southern Illinois University Press, 2004): 37–58.

39. Boyd, *Am I Black Enough for You?*: 64.

40. Deepak Narang Sawhney, "Palimpsest: Towards a Minor Literature in Monstrosity," in Keith Ansell-Pearson (ed.), *Deleuze and Philosophy: The Difference Engineer* (London: Routledge, 1997): 130–46.

41. Tricia Rose, "Black Texts/Black Contexts," in Gina Dent (ed.), *Black Popular Culture* (Seattle: Bay Press, 1992): 223–27 (223).

42. Kelley, *Yo' Mama's Disfunktional! Fighting the Culture Wars in Urban America* (Boston: Beacon, 1998); Quinn, *Nuthin' But a "G" Thang*; Tricia Rose, *Black Noise: Rap Music and Black Culture in Contemporary America* (Hanover: University of New England Press, 1994); Boyd, *Am I Black Enough for You?*; S. Craig Watkins, *Representing: Hip Hop Culture and the Production of Black Cinema* (Chicago: University of Chicago Press, 1998).

43. Janice Radway, "Reading *Reading the Romance*," reprinted in John Storey (ed.), *Cultural Theory and Popular Culture: A Reader*, 2nd ed. (London: Prentice Hall, 1994): 292–309 (296).

44. Ibid.: 295.

45. Greg Dimitriadis, *Performing Identity, Performing Culture: Hip Hop as Text, Pedagogy and Lived Practice* (New York: Peter Lang, 2001) and *Friendships, Cliques and Gangs: Young Black Men Coming of Age in Urban America* (New York: Teachers College, 2003); Robin Means Coleman (ed.), *Say It Loud! African American Audience, Media and Identity* (New York: Routledge, 2002).

46. My fieldwork also included interviews with various other sources to discern their views on the memoirs. These included gang scholars Malcolm Klein and James Diego Vigil; prison scholar and anti–death penalty activist Angela Davis; Sergeant Wes McBride formerly of the LASD; Lieutenant Paul Vernon, a spokesperson for the LAPD Media Relations Unit; probation officer Mary Ridgway; anti-gang activist Father Greg

Boyle; gang expert Alex Alonso; former *Los Angeles Times* journalist Jesse Katz. These interviews will be cited at various points throughout the research.

47. Author interviews with Rodriguez, December 2006 and January 2008; written interview by the author with Becnel in November 2008, and author correspondence with Shakur in 2008–9.

48. Ruben Martinez, "Perspective: The Mother's Eye" zonezero.com/exposiciones/fotografos/rodriguez/rubenmtz.html.

49. Williams with Barbara Becnel, *Tookie Speaks Out Series*; Williams, *Life in Prison* (New York: Morrow, 1998). It should be noted that Rodriguez also released a children's book in 1999. In author correspondence with Rodriguez in July 2011 he explained that he had been partly inspired by Williams: "Williams's children's books did serve to challenge me to do something similar, although I was also challenged by the fact there were no reality-based children's books in schools. Then Children's Book Press offered me a chance to do this children's book on gangs, so I decided to try." See Luis J. Rodriguez, *It Doesn't Have To Be This Way: A Barrio Story* (San Francisco: Children's Book Press, 1999).

50. Laura Marcus, *Auto/biographical Discourses: Theory, Criticism, Practice* (Manchester, UK: Manchester University Press, 1994): 3.

51. I do acknowledge that some critics would read this differently. For example, David Brumble contends: "Sanyika Shakur is writing; the change of name marks his passage from gangbanger to reformer. The book *remembers* Monster Kody—but it is written from the perspective of Shakur." See Brumble, "The Gangbanger Autobiography of Monster and Warrior Literature," in *American Literary History* 12, nos. 1 and 2 (Spring/Summer 2000): 158–86 (178).

52. Mieke Bal, *Narratology: Introduction to the Theory of the Narrative* (Toronto: University of Toronto Press, 1985): 119. I appreciate that this brief explanation does not take into consideration the full potential of narratological entities including the "implied author," which, according to Bal, is "the result of the investigation of the meaning of a text, and not the source of that meaning." The implied author thus stands removed from both the real author and the narrative agent. See Bal, *Narratology*, 120.

53. Maya Angelou, *I Know Why the Caged Bird Sings* (New York: Bantam, 1983).

Chapter One

1. Sanyika Shakur, *Monster: The Autobiography of an LA Gang Member* (New York: Penguin, 1994); Luis J. Rodriguez, *Always Running—La Vida Loca: Gang Days in LA* (New York: Touchstone, 1994): 4.

2. Stanley "Tookie" Williams, *Redemption: From Original Gangster to Nobel Prize Nominee* (Preston, UK: Milo, 2004).

3. In terms of gang scholarship, Frederick Thrasher became the original gang theorist with his study of Irish immigrants in Chicago during the 1920s. Since Thrasher's work, the growth in size and criminality of the street gang, particularly since the birth of the Crips, has provoked much academic attention from those such as Malcolm Klein, dubbed "the dean of gang researchers." Sociologists, psychiatrists, psychologists,

and criminologists have deployed a multiplicity of methods (ethnographies, interviews, questionnaires) to understand the features and structures of these gangs.

4. For Mexican American gang history, see James Diego Vigil, *Barrio Gangs: Street Life and Identity in Southern California* (Austin: University of Texas Press, 1988), and his essay "Community Dynamics and the Rise of Street Gangs," in Marcelo Suarez-Orozco and Mariela Paez (eds.), *Latinos: Remaking America* (Berkeley: University of California Press, 2002): 97–109.

5. Claudia Durst Johnson, *Youth Gangs in Literature* (Westport, CT: Greenwood, 2004): 176.

6. Donald Bakeer, *Crips: The Story of the LA Street Gang from 1972–1985* (Los Angeles: Precocious Publishing, 1987): 28.

7. Yusuf Jah and Sister Shah'Keyah, *Uprising: Crips and Bloods Tell the Story of America's Youth in the Crossfire* (New York: Touchstone, 1997): 329. In a different twist on this story, Klein argues that some members of the small, localized gangs that were already established at the time (such as the Gladiators and the Slausons) actually left their gangs to join the Black Panthers and Ron Karenga's organization US. Interview with Klein conducted by the author, December 2006.

8. Joao Costa Vargas, *Catching Hell in the City of Angels: Life and Meanings of Blackness in South Central LA* (Minneapolis: University of Minnesota Press, 2006): 180.

9. Mike Davis, *City of Quartz* (London: Verso, 1990): 298.

10. Rufus Schatzberg and Robert Kelly, *African Americans Organized Crime: A Social History* (New Brunswick: Rutgers University Press, 1997): 197.

11. The new afterword to James Carr's *Bad: The Autobiography of James Carr* (London: Pelagian, 1995): 209. *Bad* was originally released in 1975. It says the afterword was "Completed June 1993" but the only clue to authorship is the addresses for "News From Everywhere" and "BM Blob." Presumably it was a collaborative exercise from Pelagian Press.

12. George Tindall and David Shi, *America: A Narrative History* (New York: Norton, 1993): 954.

13. Alphonso Pinkney, *The Myth of Black Progress* (Cambridge, UK: Cambridge University Press, 1984): 74.

14. James Blackwell, *The Black Community: Diversity and Unity* (New York: Harper & Row, 1985): 76.

15. George H. W. Bush, "Inaugural Address," 20 January 1989. See www.national center.org/BushInaugural.html.

16. Tindall and Shi, *America*: 992.

17. Ibid.

18. Ibid.: 976.

19. Ibid.: 998.

20. Ibid.: 976.

21. Stephen Levitt and Stephen Dubner, *Freakonomics* (London: Penguin, 2006): 103.

22. Durst Johnson, *Youth Gangs in Literature*: xxiii.

23. Mark Horowitz, "In Search of Monster," *Atlantic*, no. 272 (December 1993): 28–37.

24. See www.lapdonline.org.

25. See Alonso's website www.streetgangs.com, an excellent resource for information on contemporary street gangs.

26. Ibid.

27. This included for example, the Reagan Administration's Anti-Drug Act in 1986, which was expanded in 1988. Mike Davis, "War in the Streets," *New Statesman*, 11 November 1988: 28.

28. Ibid.

29. Ibid.

30. The American Civil Rights Union, "Reagan on Gun Control and Self-Defence," www.theacru.org/blog/2007/04/reagan_on_gun_control_and_selfdefense/.

31. Angela Davis, *Are Prisons Obsolete?* (New York: Seven Stories, 2003): 12–13.

32. Tindall and Shi, *America*: 976.

33. Vargas, *Catching Hell in the City of Angels*: 14.

34. Lee Stacy (ed.), *Mexico and the US* (New York: Marshall Cavendish, 2003): 667.

35. Thomas P. Bonczar and Allen J. Beck, "Lifetime Likelihood of going to State or Federal Prison," Bureau of Justice Statistics Special Report (March 1997), http://bjs.ojp.usdoj.gov/content/pub/pdf/Llgsfp.pdf.

36. As Klein explains: "I spent many hours watching gang members animatedly discussing events—past events, rumored events, proposed new events—and emotionally feeding off these as much as they might re-enact an Arnold Schwarzenegger or Clint Eastwood movie. They rehearsed and relived the battles, embellishing them with little concern for reality." Klein, *The American Street Gang: Its Nature, Prevalence and Control* (Oxford, UK: Oxford University Press, 1995): 78.

37. *Redemption*'s narrator refers to "bullology" as "braggadocio about women, sex, money, drugs and war." See Williams, *Redemption*: 236. When *Monster*'s narrator reminisces about his early years as a young gangbanger, he visits Williams's house to hear original gang stories from the iconic Crip: "He was a magnificent storyteller. For hours at a time he'd give us blow-by-blow rundowns . . ." See Shakur, *Monster*: 246.

38. Eithne Quinn, *Nuthin' But a "G" Thang: The Culture and Commerce of Gangsta Rap* (New York: Columbia University Press, 2005): 54.

39. Joan Moore, "Bearing the Burden: How Incarceration Policies Weaken Inner-City Communities," in Vera Institute of Justice, *The Unintended Consequences of Incarceration* (conference papers, 1996): 73–75.

40. What Vigil calls "Spanglish." See Vigil, "Community Dynamics" in Suarez-Orozco and Paez (eds.), *Latinos*: 103.

41. As Klein states, "It's not 'I am Carlos' but 'I am Maravilla' or 'I am a Crip' that boosts the gang member's self-esteem." See Klein, *American Street Gang*: 27, 45, 60, 200.

42. Robin Kelley, *Race Rebels: Culture, Politics and the Black Working Class* (New York: Free Press, 1994): 163.

43. Dick Hebdige, *Subcultures: The Meaning of Style* (London: Routledge, 1979): 131; Ken Gelder and Sarah Thornton (eds.), *The Subcultures Reader* (London: Routledge, 1997): 85.

44. Hebdige as quoted in Quinn's *Nuthin' But a "G" Thang*: 53.

45. Kelley, *Yo' Mama's Disfunktional! Fighting the Culture Wars in Urban America* (Boston: Beacon Press, 1998): 45.

46. Klein, *American Street Gang*: 205.

47. Ibid.; Klein, *Chasing After Street Gangs: A Forty Year Journey* (Upper Saddle River, NJ: Pearson Prentice Hall, 2007): 49.

48. Author interview with Klein, January 2008.

49. Martin Jankowski, *Islands in the Street: Gangs and American Urban Society* (Berkeley: University of California Press, 1992): 229.

50. Ibid.: 302.

51. Norman Mailer as quoted in Quinn, *Nuthin' But a "G" Thang*: 85.

52. Kevin Starr, *Coast of Dreams: A History of Contemporary California* (London: Allen Lane, 2005): 87. See also Stacey Patton, "The Rap on Whites Who Try to Act Black," *Washington Post*, 16 March 2008.

53. Quinn, *Nuthin' But a "G" Thang*: 32.

54. Ibid.: 10. Quinn explains that by the early 1990s, audience statistics showing a 65 percent white market share for hardcore rap were being reported. See Ibid.: 82–83.

55. NWA, *Niggaz4life* (Ruthless/Priority, 1991). Quinn, *Nuthin' But a "G" Thang*: 8.

56. Boyd, *Am I Black Enough for You?*: 91.

57. Shakur, *Monster*: vii.

58. *Colors* (Dennis Hopper, 1988).

59. Boyd, *Am I Black Enough for You?*: 88.

60. *New Jack City* (Mario Van Peebles, 1991). See Jonathan Munby, "From Gangsta to Gangster: The Hood Film's Criminal Allegiance with Hollywood," in James Chapman, Mark Glancy and Sue Harper (eds.), *The New Film History* (New York: Palgrave, 2007): 166–79 (169).

61. Ibid.: 171.

62. Note that Olmos is Mexican American and Anders is white; the rest are African American. Boyd argues that the three films most relevant to understanding gangsta culture are *Boyz N The Hood, Menace II Society*, and *American Me*. See Boyd's *Am I Black Enough for You?*: 92.

63. Bakeer, *Crips*.

64. See donaldbakeer.com/book_sc.html.

65. S. Craig Watkins, *Representing: Hip Hop Culture and the Production of Black Cinema* (Chicago: University of Chicago Press, 1998).

66. Boyd, *Am I Black Enough for You?*: 10–11.

67. Cornel West as quoted in Andrew Milner and Jeff Browitt, *Contemporary Cultural Theory*, 3rd ed. (London: Routledge, 2002): 157.

68. Horowitz, "In Search of Monster": 28–37.

69. Jankowski, *Islands in the Street*: 290.

70. Boyd, *Am I Black Enough for You?*: 91. Quinn also details, "It is hard to overstate the influence of Iceberg Slim's literature on black male urban culture." See Quinn, *Nuthin' But a "G" Thang*: 121.

71. Ice-T with Douglas Century, *Ice: A Memoir of Gangster Life and Redemption* (New York: One World, 2011): 40. See also Jonathan Munby's *Under a Bad Sign: Criminal Self-Representation in African American Popular Culture* (Chicago: University of Chicago Press, 2011), which explores Goines, Slim, and Himes at length.

72. Iceberg Slim, *Pimp: The Story of My Life* (Los Angeles: Holloway House, 1969); Donald Goines, *Whoreson: The Story of a Ghetto Pimp* (Los Angeles: Holloway House, 1972).

73. Both texts are regularly described as "autobiographical novels." For example, see the introduction by Irvine Welsh to the 2009 Canongate Books edition of *Pimp*; and, the Goines entry in William L. Andrews, Frances Smith Foster, and Trudier Harris (eds.), *The Concise Oxford Companion to African American Literature* (Oxford, UK: Oxford University Press, 2001): 171.

74. Chester Himes, *White Man's Justice, Black Man's Grief* (Los Angeles: Holloway House, 1973).

75. The series of Harlem Detective novels by Chester Himes comprised nine texts, including *The Real Cool Killers* (New York: Avon, 1959) and *Cotton Comes to Harlem* (New York: G. P. Putnam's Sons, 1965).

76. Chester Himes, *The Quality of Hurt* (London: Michael Joseph, 1973) and *My Life of Absurdity* (Garden City, NY: Doubleday, 1976).

77. Throughout most of the 1960s Himes's crime fiction was published by G.P. Putnam's and Dell Paperback. He had a very small readership in the United States until the late 1960s, after which he was published mainly by Doubleday.

78. Holloway used the term "black experience novels" specifically with regards to Goines. See Andrews, Foster, and Harris (eds.), *Concise Oxford Companion*: 171.

79. In December 2006 and January 2008 I visited several high school libraries, nearly all held books by Goines and Slim in their collections.

80. Author interview with a high school librarian in California, December 2006.

81. Ibid.

82. David Ansen and Spike Lee, "The Battle for Malcolm X," *Newsweek*, 26 August 1991.

83. For example, Ice Cube's "When Will They Shoot?" and "Wicked," both of which appear on his album *The Predator* (Priority/EMI, 1992). See also Quinn, *Nuthin' But a "G" Thang*: 175.

84. Shakur, *Monster*: 219; George Jackson, *Soledad Brother: The Prison Letters of George Jackson* (London: Jonathan Cape, 1970).

85. Williams, *Redemption*: 252.

86. Rodriguez, *Always Running*: 50; Piri Thomas, *Down These Mean Streets* (1967; rprt. New York: Vintage, 1997).

87. See www.publishingtrends.com for further information. Also see *Book Industry Trends 1993: Covering the Years 1987–1997* (New York: Book Industry Study Group, 1993), prepared by the Statistical Service Center.

88. *Book Industry Trends 1993*: 14.

89. Ibid.

90. Tom Weyr, "Marketing America's Psychos," *Publishers Weekly* 240, no. 15 (12 April 1993): 38–41.

91. Ibid.

92. Author interview with Alonso, December 2006. See www.streetgangs.com/books.

93. Quinn, *Nuthin' But a "G" Thang*: 42, 65.

94. Author interview with Rodriguez, January 2008.

95. Ibid.

96. Margo Nash, "Once Upon a Time," *New York Times*, 18 September 2005.

97. For further information on Latino hip hop, see Brian Cross, *It's Not About a Salary: Rap, Race and Resistance in LA* (London/New York: Verso, 1993): 193.

98. Kid Frost's moniker was rumored to be inspired by Ice-T and the two artists were rapping partners early in their careers. See Ice-T, *Ice: A Memoir*: 94.

99. Beatrice Griffith, *American Me* (Boston: Houghton Mifflin, 1948): 32.

100. For instance, gang statistics published by the LAPD in December 1993 suggest the presence of 35,865 Latino gang members compared to 21,944 African Americans. See www.lapdonline.org/assets/crime_statistics/gang_stats/1993_97_ gang_stats/93_12_sum.htm.

101. Author interview with Rodriguez, January 2008.

102. Both California and Latino historians, as well as black cultural critics, have stressed how Latino culture is vital to understanding LA's lower classes. See Boyd, *Am I Black Enough for You?*: 94. For wider discussions of Latinos in LA, see Starr, *Coast of Dreams*, David Wyatt, *Five Fires: Race, Catastrophe and the Shaping of California* (Oxford, UK: Oxford University Press, 1999), and Victor Valle and Rodolfo Torres, *Latino Metropolis* (Minneapolis: University of Minnesota Press, 2000).

103. Author interview with Rodriguez, January 2008.

104. Rodriguez, *Always Running*: 247.

105. For scholarly criticism on the media coverage of the riots, see Valle and Torres, *Latino Metropolis*: 45–60; Darnell Hunt, *Screening the LA Riots: Race, Seeing, and Resistance* (Cambridge, UK: Cambridge University Press, 1997); Robert Gooding-Williams (ed.), *Reading Rodney King: Reading Urban Uprising* (New York: Routledge, 1993).

106. Michael Coffey and Lisa Kendall, "In Aftermath of LA Riots, a Lively Diversity of Voices," *Publishers Weekly* 239, no. 55 (28 December 1992): 24.

107. Ibid.

108. Susan Faludi, "Ghetto Star," *Los Angeles Weekly*, 6 October 1999.

109. Author interview with Rodriguez, December 2006.

110. Leon Bing, *Do or Die: For the First Time, Members of America's Most Notorious Gangs—The Crips and The Bloods—Speak for Themselves* (New York: Harper Collins, 1991).

111. For examples of Leon Bing's articles, see endnote 4 to the Introduction.

112. Shakur, *Monster*: viii.

113. Ibid. In author interviews, December 2006, several interviewees identified Leon Bing's *Do or Die* as the initial impetus behind Shakur's foray into the publishing world and raised Bing's name without prompting as an opening portal to *Monster*. These included gang scholar Diego Vigil, probation officer Mary Ridgway, publisher Alex Alonso, and Sergeant Wes McBride, formerly of the LASD gang unit.

114. Author correspondence with Shakur in 2008–9.

115. Amy Wallace, "The Monster Deal," *Sunday Age* (Melbourne), 25 April 1993: 6.

116. Author correspondence with Shakur in 2008–9.

117. Faludi, *Stiffed: The Betrayal of the American Man* (London: Chatto & Windus, 1999): 482.

118. Horowitz, "In Search of Monster": 28–37.

119. Robert Lusetich, "Monster with Attitude," *Weekend Australian*, 1 June 1996.

120. Wallace, "The Monster Deal": 6.

121. Horowitz, "In Search of Monster": 28–37.

122. Jerry Palmer, *Potboilers: Methods, Concepts and Case Studies in Popular Fiction* (London: Routledge, 1991): 115.

123. Author correspondence with Shakur in 2008–9.

124. Faludi, *Stiffed*: 482.

125. Horowitz, "In Search of Monster": 28–37.

126. Williams with Barbara Becnel, *Tookie Speaks Out Series* (New York: Rosen, 1996). Aided by Becnel, in 1997 Williams established "Tookie's corner," an internet education program as part of the Institute for the Prevention of Youth Violence. See www.tookie.com.

127. Williams, *Life in Prison* (New York: Morrow, 1998).

128. Written author interview with Becnel, November 2008.

129. Ibid.

130. Ibid.

131. At a talk at a college in London in July 2010, Becnel explained that they had experienced similar problems when seeking a publisher for the children's series: "A representative from the New York publishing world said that if these are books for poor black kids, then how will they be able to afford to buy the books? The representative said that Stanley should write violence and profanity until he was established as a writer, then he can go back and try and children's books. Stanley simply said no, he said we weren't that desperate."

132. All profits from *Blue Rage* were ploughed by Damamli into LA–based community projects with dedicated help from Becnel. See www.damamli.com and www.tookie.com. In 2008, Damamli rereleased the children's series with an updated post-execution introduction by Becnel, and a closing page entitled "Remembering the Author." This updated version won the 2008 Prevention for a Safer Society Award for Literature from the National Council on Crime and Delinquency.

133. Author interview with Klein, December 2006.

134. Author interview with Alonso, December 2006.

135. Author interview with Rodriguez, December 2006.

136. Written author interview with Becnel, November 2008.

137. Munby, *Under a Bad Sign:* 149.

138. Written author interview with Becnel, November 2008.

139. Ibid.

140. Author interview with Rodriguez, December 2006.

141. Ibid.

142. Mary Ann French, "For Black Authors, the Same Old Story? A Round-table Look at Literary Roadblocks Facing African Americans," *Washington Post*, 13 June 1994: C1. Nathan McCall, *Makes Me Wanna Holler: A Young Black Man in America* (New York: Random House, 1994).

142. Geoffrey Canada, *Fist Stick Gun Knife* (Boston: Beacon, 1996); Mona Ruiz with Geoff Boucher, *Two Badges: The Lives of Mona Ruiz* (Houston: Arte Publico, 1997); Snoop Dogg with Davin Seay, *Tha Doggfather: The Times, Trials and Hardcore Truths of Snoop Dogg* (New York: William Morrow, 1999); Bill Lee, *Chinese Playground: A Memoir* (San Francisco: Rhapsody, 1999); Reymundo Sanchez, *My Bloody Life: The Making of a Latin King* and *Once a King, Always a King: The Unmaking of a Latin King* (Chicago: Chicago Review Press, 2000 & 2003); Colton Simpson with Ann Pearlman, *Inside the Crips: Life Inside LA's Most Notorious Gang* (New York: St. Martin's, 2005); Terrell Wright, *Home of the Body Bags* (Venice, CA: Senegal, 2005); DaShaun "Jiwe"

Morris, *War of the Bloods in my Veins: A Street Soldier's March Toward Redemption* (New York: Scribner, 2008).

144. Brumble kindly provided me a copy of his bibliography for what he terms "Tribal Warrior Autobiographies."

145. In fact, Brumble's bibliography dates back to 1930, when he believes the first street-gang autobiography was published (according to his classification in terms of texts that demonstrate elements of tribal warrior cultures). See also Brumble's "Stanley 'Tookie' Williams, Gangbanger Autobiography, and Warrior Tribes," *Journal of American Studies* 44, no. 1 (February 2010): 155–70 (160).

146. BET's *American Gangster*, season 3, episode 2, "Monster Kody Scott: The Pen and The Gun." In author correspondence with Shakur in 2008–9, he explained that he had optioned *Monster* for film five times and was still in negotiations. In further correspondence in 2011, Shakur confirmed "I have a deal-in-hand with director, Billy Wright."

147. Sanyika Shakur, *T.H.U.G. L.I.F.E.* (New York: Grove/Atlantic, 2008).

148. In written author correspondence with Rodriguez in July 2011, he explained that he had previously been offered $3.5 million for the film rights to *Always Running* but that this offer was withdrawn when the stock market crashed in October 2008 (the writer's strike of that time had also caused problems for potential film projects). Rodriguez currently has a director interested in a possible movie, and a friend working on a potential cable series of the story for television, though neither is definite.

149. *Crips and Bloods: Made in America* (Stacy Peralta, 2009).

150. For example, Eminem's *Relapse* (Aftermath, Interscope & Shady, 2009), slickly produced by Dr. Dre, shot straight to the top of the *Billboard* album chart upon its release.

Chapter Two

1. The title of this chapter takes inspiration from Sanford Pinsker's book review of the same name. See Pinsker, "Home Boys Between Hard Covers," *Virginia Quarterly Review* 70, no. 4 (August 1994): 758–73.

2. James Procter, *Stuart Hall* (London: Routledge, 2004): 38, 40.

3. For example, see Eithne Quinn's *Nuthin' But a "G" Thang: The Culture and Commerce of Gangsta Rap* (New York: Columbia University Press, 2005): 17–18.

4. Paul John Eakin (ed.), *The Ethics of Life Writing* (Ithaca: Cornell University Press, 2004): 3–4.

5. See www.tookie.com. Clothing company Benetton controversially used photographs of death row inmates, together with interviews with the prisoners and excerpts of their writings, in an advertising campaign in 2000. See Auli Ek, *Race and Masculinity in Contemporary American Prison Narratives* (New York: Routledge, 2005): 55.

6. Timothy Dow Adams, *Telling Lies in Modern American Autobiography* (Chapel Hill: University of North Carolina Press, 1990): ix.

7. Ibid.: 14.

8. Eakin (ed.), *The Ethics of Life Writing*: 3.

9. Laura Marcus, *Auto/biographical Discourses: Theory, Criticism, Practice* (Manchester, UK: Manchester University Press, 1994): 7.

10. For instance, see the critical work on Audre Lorde's memoir *Zami* (London: Persephone, 1982), which detailed her life as a black lesbian, including Barbara DiBernard, "Zami: A Portrait of an Artist as a Black Lesbian," *Kenyon Review* 13, no. 4 (Fall 1991): 195–213; Erin Carlston, "*Zami* and the Politics of Plural Identity," in Susan Wolfe and Julia Penelope (eds.), *Sexual Practice/Textual Theory: Lesbian Cultural Criticism* (Cambridge, MA: Blackwell, 1993): 226–36.

11. Edward Saïd, *Culture and Imperialism* (London: Chatto & Windus, 1993); Gayatri Spivak, *In Other Worlds: Essays in Cultural Politics* (London: Methuen, 1987).

12. Andrew Milner and Jeff Browitt, *Contemporary Cultural Theory*, 3rd ed. (London: Routledge, 2002): 144.

13. Life writing scholars have noted that "transformation undergirds the American experience." See Gail Jardine, "To be Black, Male, and Conscious: Race, Rage, and Manhood in America," *American Quarterly* 48, no. 2 (1996): 385–93 (386).

14. Eakin (ed.), *The Ethics of Life Writing*: 5.

15. Marcus, *Auto/biographical Discourses*: 195.

16. Eldridge Cleaver, *Soul On Ice* (London: Jonathan Cape, 1969); James Carr, *Bad: The Autobiography of James Carr* (London: Pelagian, 1975).

17. Brian Jarvis, *Cruel and Unusual: Punishment and US Culture* (London: Pluto, 2004): 107.

18. Robin Kelley, *Race Rebels: Culture, Politics and the Black Working Class* (New York: Free Press, 1994): 163.

19. Henry Louis Gates Jr., *Loose Cannons: Notes on the Culture Wars* (Oxford, UK: Oxford University Press, 1992): 62–63.

20. Quinn, *Nuthin' But a "G" Thang*: 25; Kelley, *Yo' Mama's Disfunktional!: Fighting the Culture Wars in Urban America* (Boston: Beacon Press, 1998): 37.

21. Quinn, *Nuthin' But a "G" Thang*: 25.

22. Genaro Padilla, *My History, Not Yours: The Formation of Mexican American Autobiography* (Madison: University of Wisconsin Press, 1993): 8–9.

23. Ibid.: 10.

24. For example, see two renowned contemporary Chicano memoirs: Oscar Zeta Acosta's *The Autobiography of a Brown Buffalo* (San Francisco: Straight Arrow, 1972) and Richard Rodriguez's *Hunger of Memory: The Education of Richard Rodriguez* (New York: Bantam, 1983).

25. Marcus, *Auto/biographical Discourses*: 7.

26. David Brumble, "The Gangbanger Autobiography of Monster and Warrior Literature" in *American Literary History* 12, nos. 1 and 2 (Spring/Summer 2000): 158–86; and "Stanley 'Tookie' Williams, Gangbanger Autobiography, and Warrior Tribes," *Journal of American Studies* 44, no. 1 (February 2010): 155–70.

27. Herbert Leibowitz, *Fabricating Lives: Explorations in American Autobiography* (New York: Alfred A. Knopf, 1989): 3.

28. For example, Kelley is concerned with the music's "linguistic inventiveness" or "serious slang" with its puns, metaphors, and similes. See Kelley, *Yo' Mama's Disfunktional!*: 37.

29. Though there were exceptions, including the group Public Enemy.

30. Quinn, *Nuthin' But a "G" Thang*: 25.

31. Jon Pareles, "Gangster Rap: Life and Music in the Combat Zone," *New York Times*, 7 October 1990: section 2.29.

32. There are further reasons that prompt more concern over music than film, including the styles of consumption. The solitary possibilities of listening to music (in a youth's bedroom, on a personal stereo, or in a car) were out of reach of parental control. By comparison, watching films has traditionally been a more communal experience (using the family video player or in a cinema) with more regulatory controls, such as checking for age upon purchase of tickets.

33. Pareles, "Gangster Rap."

34. William Andrews (ed.), *African American Autobiography: A Collection of Critical Essays* (Englewood Cliffs, NJ: Prentice Hall, 1993): 2.

35. Jeffrey Ogbar, *Black Power: Radical Politics and African American Identity* (Baltimore: John Hopkins University Press, 2005). Carlos Munoz Jr., *Youth, Identity, Power: The Chicano Movement* (London: Verso, 1989).

36. Munoz Jr., *Youth, Identity, Power*: 8.

37. Milner and Browitt, *Contemporary Cultural Theory*: 128.

38. Ogbar, *Black Power*: 4.

39. Kenneth Mostern, *Autobiography and Black Identity Politics: Racialization in Twentieth Century America* (Cambridge, UK: Cambridge University Press, 1999): 9.

40. H. Bruce Franklin, *Prison Literature in America: The Victim as Criminal and Artist* (Oxford, UK: Oxford University Press, 1989): 236.

41. Bell Gale Chevigny (ed.), *Doing Time: Twenty Five Years of Prison Writing* (New York: Arcade, 1999); Joy James (ed.), *The Angela Y. Davis Reader* (Oxford, UK: Blackwell, 1998); Auli Ek, *Race and Masculinity*; Peter Caster, *Prisons, Race and Masculinity in Twentieth Century US Literature and Film* (Columbus: Ohio State University Press, 2008); Jarvis, *Cruel and Unusual*.

42. Caster justifies how his work departs from that of Ek, claiming she is not concerned with past practices and historical contexts to the extent that Caster believes is required. Caster, *Prisons, Race and Masculinity*: 19.

43. For further detail on this point see Ek, *Race and Masculinity*: 2.

44. See chapter 3 of Franklin's *Prison Literature*, "Plantation to Penitentiary": 73–123.

45. H. Bruce Franklin (ed.), *Prison Writing in Twentieth Century America* (New York: Penguin, 1998): 11–13.

46. Franklin, *Prison Literature*: 241.

47. Ogbar, *Black Power*: 96.

48. Mostern, *Autobiography and Black Identity Politics*: 145.

49. Ibid.: 160.

50. Ek, *Race and Masculinity*: 55.

51. Gates, *Loose Cannons*: 65.

52. Jean Genet's introduction to Jackson's, *Soledad Brother*: 18.

53. Jarvis, *Cruel and Unusual*: 113; Franklin, *Prison Literature*: 234.

54. Francis Mulhern, "The Politics of Cultural Studies," *Monthly Review* 47, no. 3 (July–August 1995): 31–40.

55. Franklin is referenced in Ek, *Race and Masculinity*: 2–3.

56. Author interview with Angela Davis, December 2006.

57. Kelley, *Race Rebels*: 183.

58. Ek, *Race and Masculinity*: 2.

59. Ek voices concern that in public discourses on crime, race has been highlighted while poverty has been overlooked. Ibid.: 10.

60. Quinn, *Nuthin' But a "G" Thang*: 30.

61. Kali Tal, "From Panther to Monster: Black Popular Culture Representations of Resistance from the Black Panther Movement of the 1960s to *Boyz N The Hood*," in Elaine Richardson and Ronald Jackson (eds.), *African American Rhetoric(s): Interdisciplinary Perspectives* (Carbondale: Southern Illinois University Press, 2004): 37–58 (40).

62. Todd Boyd, *Am I Black Enough for You? Popular Culture from the 'hood and Beyond* (Bloomington: Indiana University Press, 1997): 102. Similarly, publisher of gang memoirs Alex Alonso contends that Rodriguez, Williams, and Shakur are "bandwagoners" to earlier prison authors from the 1960s such as George Jackson and Malcolm X, whose texts carry weighty revolutionary and political meanings. Author interview with Alonso, December 2006.

63. Graeme Turner, *British Cultural Studies* (New York: Routledge, 1992): 76.

64. Ibid.: 94.

65. Stuart Hall, "New Ethnicities," in Linda Alcoff and Eduardo Mendieta (eds.), *Identities: Race, Class, Gender, and Nationalities* (Oxford, UK: Wiley-Blackwell Press, 2002): 90–95 (91).

66. Quinn, *Nuthin' But a "G" Thang*: 17.

67. Procter, *Stuart Hall*: 126.

68. Hall (ed.), *Representation: Cultural Representations and Signifying Practices*, 5th ed. (Milton Keynes, UK: Open University Press, 2001).

69. Hall, "What is this 'Black' in Black Popular Culture?" in Gina Dent (ed.), *Black Popular Culture* (Seattle: Bay Press, 1992): 21–33.

70. Ibid.: 26.

71. Hall, "The Spectacle of the Other," in Hall (ed.), *Representation*: 223–83 (235).

72. Martin Jankowski, *Islands in the Street: Gangs and American Urban Society* (Berkeley: University of California Press, 1992): 284–309; Malcolm Klein, *The American Street Gang: Its Nature, Prevalence, and Control* (Oxford, UK: Oxford University Press, 1995): 40. See also Quinn, *Nuthin' But a "G" Thang*: 19.

73. Hall, "The Spectacle of the Other," in Hall (ed.), *Representation*: 277.

74. Boyd, *Am I Black Enough for You?*: 132–33.

75. bell hooks, *We Real Cool: Outlaw Culture* (New York: Routledge, 2004) and *Black Looks: Race and Representation* (Boston, MA: South End, 1992). For further criticism on black representations, see Patricia Hill Collins, *Black Sexual Politics: African Americans, Gender and the New Racism* (New York: Routledge, 2004).

76. Arthur Pettit, *Images of the Mexican American in Literature and Film* (College Station: Texas A&M University Press, 1980). See also Charles Tatum, *Chicano Popular Culture and Chicano Literature* (Tucson: University of Arizona Press, 2001).

77. Coramae Richey Mann, *Unequal Justice: A Question of Color* (Bloomington: Indiana University Press, 1988): 144.

78. Kobena Mercer, *Welcome to the Jungle: New Positions in Black Cultural Studies* (New York: Routledge, 1994).

79. Hall, "The Spectacle of the Other," in Hall (ed.), *Representation*: 230.

80. Boyd, *Am I Black Enough for You?*; Ek, *Race and Masculinity*; Brumble, "The Gangbanger Autobiography of Monster."

81. Tal, "From Panther to Monster," in Richardson and Jackson (eds.), *African American Rhetoric(s)*: 37–58.

82. Janet Staiger, *Media Reception Studies* (New York: New York University Press, 2005): 2.

83. As detailed in the Introduction to this book, culture scholars such as Tricia Rose have argued for the need to consider text and context simultaneously and with equal importance. See Rose, "Black Texts/Black Contexts," in Gina Dent (ed.), *Black Popular Culture* (Seattle: Bay Press, 1992): 223–27 (223). See also Turner, *British Cultural Studies*: 131.

84. Simon During (ed.), *Cultural Studies Reader* (London: Routledge, 1993): 4.

85. Turner, *British Cultural Studies*: 131.

86. Ibid.: 130.

87. See Charlotte Brunsdon and David Morley, *The Nationwide Television Studies* (New York: Routledge, 1999). This edition includes Morley's classic study as well as Charlotte Brunsdon's *Everyday Television: Nationwide*.

88. Turner, *British Cultural Studies*: 135. See also Mark Jancovich, "David Morley, the *Nationwide* Studies," in Martin Barker and Anne Beezer (eds.), *Reading into Cultural Studies* (London: Routledge, 1992): 134–48.

89. Morley, *Family Television* (London: Routledge, 1986).

90. Janice Radway, *Reading the Romance: Women, Patriarchy and Popular Literature* (Chapel Hill: University of North Carolina Press, 1991).

91. Radway, "Reading *Reading the Romance*," in John Storey (ed.), *Cultural Theory and Popular Culture* (London: Prentice Hall, 1994): 292–309.

92. Ibid.

93. Greg Dimitriadis, *Friendships, Cliques and Gangs: Young Black Men Coming of Age in Urban America* (New York: Teachers College, 2003) and *Performing Identity, Performing Culture: Hip Hop as Text, Pedagogy and Lived Practice* (New York: Peter Lang, 2001); Robin Means Coleman (ed.), *Say It Loud! African American Audience, Media and Identity* (New York: Routledge, 2002).

94. Herman Gray, "Foreword," in Coleman (ed.), *Say It Loud!*: viii.

95. Coleman, "The *Menace II Society* Copycat Murder Case and Thug Life: A Reception Study with a Convicted Criminal," in Coleman (ed.), *Say It Loud*: 249–84 (251).

96. Dimitriadis, *Performing Identity, Performing Culture*: 3.

Chapter Three

1. Examples include: S. Craig Watkins, *Representing: Hip Hop Culture and the Production of Black Cinema* (Chicago: University of Chicago Press, 1998); Eithne Quinn,

Nuthin' But a "G" Thang: The Culture and Commerce of Gangsta Rap (New York: Columbia University Press, 2005).

2. NWA, "Fuck Tha Police" (Priority/Ruthless Records, 1988).

3. *Menace II Society* (Hughes Brothers, 1993). See the discussion of *Menace* in Watkins, *Representing*: 196.

4. Ice-T, "Colors," *Colors: Soundtrack* (Warner Bros. Records, 1988).

5. Luis J. Rodriguez, *Always Running—La Vida Loca: Gang Days in LA* (New York: Touchstone, 1994). All page citations will be parenthesized within the text preceded with *AR*. Stanley "Tookie" Williams, *Redemption: From Original Gangster to Nobel Prize Nominee* (Preston, UK: Milo Books, 2004). All page citations will be parenthesized within the text preceded with *R*. Sanyika Shakur, *Monster: The Autobiography of an LA Gang Member* (New York: Penguin, 1994). All page citations will be parenthesized within the text preceded with *M*.

6. Michael Walzer, *Just and Unjust Wars: A Moral Argument with Historical Illustrations*, 4th ed. (New York: Basic, 2006): 52.

7. Author interview with Rodriguez, January 2008.

8. In the 1960s and 1970s it was "a great time to be a street criminal" because the likelihood of punishment was low. See Stephen Levitt and Stephen Dubner, *Freakonomics* (London: Penguin, 2006): 101.

9. Clayborne Carson, "Rethinking African American Political Thought in the Post-Revolutionary Era," in Brian Ward and Tony Badger (eds.), *The Making of Martin Luther King and the Civil Rights Movement* (London: Macmillan, 1996): 115–27 (125).

10. Ronald Reagan's speech delivered at the Conservative Political Action Conference in Washington, D.C., on 11 February 1988. See www.conservative.org/pressroom/reagan/reagan1988.asp.

11. For further discussion on the death penalty as a form of violence, see James Gilligan, *Violence: Reflections on Our Deadliest Epidemic* (New York: Vintage, 1997): 184.

12. Peter Caster, *Prisons, Race and Masculinity in Twentieth Century US Literature and Film* (Columbus: Ohio State University Press, 2008): 14–17.

13. Kobena Mercer, *Welcome to the Jungle: New Positions in Black Cultural Studies* (New York: Routledge, 1994): 137.

14. Malcolm Klein, *The American Street Gang: Its Nature, Prevalence, and Control* (Oxford, UK: Oxford University Press, 1995): 112–19.

15. Mike Davis, *City of Quartz* (London: Verso, 1990): 267.

16. The "rules" of gangbanging dictate that you never report to the police. Justice (or revenge) is to be enacted by gangs, not by the authorities.

17. Richard Libman Rubenstein, "Group Violence in America, its Structures and Limitations," in Ted Robert Gurr and Hugh Davis Graham (eds.), *Violence in America: Historical and Comparative Perspectives* (Beverly Hills: Sage, 1979): 437–54 (442).

18. Foucault is cited in Caster, *Prisons, Race and Masculinity*: 124.

19. Quinn, *Nuthin' But a "G" Thang*: 108.

20. David Brumble, "The Gangbanger Autobiography of Monster and Warrior Literature," in *American Literary History* 12, nos. 1 and 2 (Spring/Summer 2000): 158–86 (159).

21. Author interview with Klein, December 2006.

22. Brumble, "Stanley 'Tookie' Williams, Gangbanger Autobiography, and Warrior Tribes," *Journal of American Studies* 44, no. 1 (February 2010): 155–70.

23. Ibid.: 155.

24. Ibid.: 166.

25. Ibid.

26. See John Hagedorn, "Gang Violence in the Post-industrial Era," in Michael Tonry and Mark Moore (eds.), *Youth Violence* (Chicago: University of Chicago Press, 1998): 365–420 (396).

27. Geoffrey Canada, *Fist Stick Gun Knife* (Boston: Beacon, 1996): x.

28. Nathan McCall, *Makes Me Wanna Holler: A Young Black Man in America* (New York: Random House, 1994): 115.

29. Ibid.

30. Female rappers include Sister Souljah and Boss. Memoirs include Mona Ruiz's *Two Badges: The Lives of Mona Ruiz* (Houston: Arte Publico, 1997) and Gini Sykes's biographical collection *8 Ball Chicks: A Year in the Violent World of Girl Gangsters* (New York: Doubleday, 1997). Klein contends that the proportion of all gang members who are female is often found to be 15 percent or more. See Klein's *Chasing After Street Gangs: A Forty Year Journey* (Upper Saddle River, NJ: Pearson Prentice Hall, 2007): 33.

31. In a collection of essays exploring Mexican masculinities (which includes a piece by Rodriguez), editor Ray Gonzalez notes the irony that all the men he selected for his project were writers. See Gonzalez (ed.), *Muy Macho: Latino Men Confront Their Manhood* (New York: Anchor, 1996): xv.

32. Dinesh D'Souza, *The End of Racism* (New York: Free Press, 1995): 515.

33. This prompts comparisons with those gangsta rappers who, despite their misogynistic and sexually objectifying lyrics, hold their female managers, mentors, and record executives in high esteem. See Quinn's *Nuthin' But a "G" Thang*: 135.

34. bell hooks, *Black Looks: Race and Representation* (Boston, MA: South End, 1992): 90, 94.

35. hooks, *We Real Cool: Black Men and Masculinity* (New York: Routledge, 2004): 67.

36. Gilligan, *Violence*: 237.

37. D'Souza, *The End of Racism*: 273. In D'Souza's discussion about the stereotyping of black males, he cites Taylor Cox's *Cultural Diversity in Organizations*. Cox's list includes "Athletes, good dancers, expressive in communication, poor, too concerned about what they wear, uneducated, oversexed, on welfare, funny."

38. Susan Faludi, *Stiffed: The Betrayal of the American Man* (London: Chatto & Windus, 1999): 482.

39. hooks, *Black Looks*: 94.

40. Mercer, *Welcome to the Jungle*: 149.

41. Faludi, *Stiffed*: 482.

42. Mark Horowitz, "In Search of Monster," *Atlantic*, no. 272 (December 1993): 28–37.

43. Though a machine gun is obviously not a handgun, Canada used the term "handgun generation" in reference to those youth for whom owning and using a gun is a regular part of urban life. See *Fist Stick*: x.

44. Stephen Vaughn, *Freedom and Entertainment: Rating the Movies in an Age of New Media* (Cambridge, UK: Cambridge University Press, 2006): 1.

45. Jack Nachbar and Kevin Lause (eds.), *Popular Culture* (Madison: University of Wisconsin Press, 1992): 7.

46. Michael Lynch and Lenny Krzycki, "Popular Culture as an Ideological Mask: Mass-Produced Popular Culture and the Remaking of Criminal Justice-Related Imagery," *Journal of Criminal Justice* 26, no. 4 (1998): 321–36 (325).

47. See various charts detailing crime rates in Albert Reiss and Jeffrey Roth (eds.), *Understanding and Preventing Violence* (Washington D.C.: National Academy, 1993): 81.

48. Nachbar and Lause (eds.), *Popular Culture*: 7.

49. Yvonne Tasker, *Spectacular Bodies: Gender, Genre and the Action Cinema* (New York: Routledge, 2002): 73–90.

50. In an author interview with Twilight Bey (a former gang member during Williams's heyday) in December 2006, he praised gang members for dedicating themselves to weightlifting as it requires "extreme dedication and discipline." Tasker deems this a "sort of armour against the world" in *Spectacular Bodies*: 123.

51. Stuart Hall has called this "a racialized regime of representation." See Hall, "The Spectacle of the Other," in Hall (ed.), *Representation: Cultural Representations and Signifying Practices*, 5th ed. (Milton Keynes, UK: Open University Press, 2001): 223–83 (269).

52. Auli Ek, *Race and Masculinity in Contemporary American Prison Narratives* (New York: Routledge, 2005): 104.

53. Ibid.: 53.

54. Ibid.: 100–101.

55. For further discussions of Mexican masculinities, see Gonzalez (ed.), *Muy Macho*; Robert McKee Irwin, *Mexican Masculinities* (Minneapolis: University of Minnesota Press, 2003); Alfredo Mirande, *Hombres Y Machos: Masculinity and Latino Culture* (Boulder, CO: Westview, 1997).

56. Reification involves removing something from its original context and placing it in a separate situation so that it then lacks its initial connections and powers. See Timothy Bewes, *Reification or the Anxiety of Late Capitalism* (London: Verso, 2002).

57. There are ironies here surrounding the narrator's love of a classic American comedy show, for as a young black youth in 1980s America he is in many ways an outsider to mainstream American society.

58. For example, Jonathan Munby notes that, as blaxploitation films thrived in the 1970s, there arose an anthropological fascination with African American works that celebrated the badman as a culture hero. He suggests that the films of Rudy Ray Moore elaborate on the badman of black folklore. See Munby's "Signifyin' Cinema: Rudy Ray Moore and the Quality of Badness," *Journal for Cultural Research* 11, no. 3 (July 2007): 203–19. Quinn examines how the nihilistic gangbanger and enterprising hustler depicted in rap lyrics have developed out of the badman and trickster figures in black expressive culture. She also argues that different variations of the bad nigger can be witnessed throughout Tupac's career. See Quinn, *Nuthin' But a "G" Thang*: 92–93, 175. For general information on this topic, see John Roberts, *From Trickster to Badman:*

The Black Folk Hero in Slavery and Freedom (Philadelphia: University of Pennsylvania Press, 1989).

59. William Van Deburg, "Villains, Demons, and Social Bandits," in Ward (ed.), *Media, Culture, and the Modern African American Freedom Struggle* (Gainesville: University Press of Florida, 2001): 197–210.

60. Ibid.: 199. See also Van Deburg, *Hoodlums: Black Villains and Social Bandits in American Life* (Chicago: University of Chicago Press, 2004).

61. Gilligan believes shame is the ultimate cause of violence, instigated by downward social mobility, unemployment, and race discrimination. He argues: "when violence is defined as criminal, many people see it and care about it. When it is simply a by-product of our social and economic structure, many don't see it and it is hard to care about something you cannot see." See Gilligan, *Violence*: 67, 194–95, 236.

62. Todd Boyd, *Am I Black Enough for You? Popular Culture from the 'hood and Beyond* (Bloomington: Indiana University Press, 1997): 5.

63. Linda Steiner, "The Uses of Autobiography," in Catherine Warren and Mary Douglas Vavrus (eds.), *American Cultural Studies* (Chicago: University of Illinois Press, 2002): 115–33 (123).

64. The popular urban youth novel *Monster* by Walter Dean Myers was named because the protagonist is called a "monster" by the prosecuting lawyer in court (New York: Amistad, 2001).

65. Journalist Celeste Fremon notes that "Gang member as monster" is "a bad diagnosis that is guaranteed not to bring us closer to a cure." See Fremon, *Father Greg Boyle and the Gangs of East LA* (Albuquerque: University of New Mexico Press, 1995): 9.

66. Kali Tal, "From Panther to Monster: Black Popular Culture Representations of Resistance from the Black Panther Movement of the 1960s to *Boyz N The Hood*," in Elaine Richardson and Ronald Jackson (eds.), *African American Rhetoric(s): Interdisciplinary Perspectives* (Carbondale: Southern Illinois University Press, 2004): 37–58 (42).

67. It is worth noting that Shakur, in a publicity interview, explained that he never watched blaxploitation films during his youth. See Faludi, *Stiffed*: 476. Monster details being fascinated by *Mission: Impossible* and *Rat Patrol*, which do not carry Afrocentric or nationalist and political messages. See Shakur, *Monster*: 41.

68. Bakari Kitwana, *The Hip Hop Generation: Young Blacks and the Crisis in African American Culture* (New York: Basic, 2002): xiii.

69. Ibid.: xiv.

70. hooks, *Black Looks*: 27.

71. Mercer, *Welcome to the Jungle*: 145.

72. For similar discussions of such incompatibility, see Boyd, *Am I Black Enough for You?*: 104, 97.

73. *Menace II Society* (Hughes Brothers, 1993); *Boyz N The Hood* (John Singleton, 1991).

74. Cliff Blodget, a partner at record company Rap-A-Lot, claims his market research demonstrated a demand for harsher lyrics, and he urged artists like the Geto Boys to write them. See Jon Pareles, "Gangster Rap: Life and Music in the Combat Zone," *New York Times*, 7 October 1990: section 2.29.

75. Prison scholar Peter Caster claims 1968 marks the shift "from revolutionary possibility to a nation exhausted by perceived threats of cultural change, race, crime, and plural identity." See Caster, *Prisons, Race and Masculinity*: 60–61.

76. Ronald Reagan as cited in Caster, *Prisons, Race and Masculinity*: 77–78.

Chapter Four

1. Jonathan Munby, *Under a Bad Sign: Criminal Self-Representation in African American Popular Culture* (Chicago: University of Chicago Press, 2011).

2. Melvin Oliver, James Johnson, and Walter Farrell, "Anatomy of a Rebellion: a Political-Economic Analysis," in Robert Gooding-Williams (ed.), *Reading Rodney King: Reading Urban Uprising* (New York: Routledge, 1993): 117–41 (127).

3. Mike Davis, *City of Quartz* (London: Verso, 1990): 307.

4. Gary Clabaugh, "The Educational Legacy of Ronald Reagan," *Horizons* (Summer 2004): 256–59 (257).

5. Davis, *City of Quartz*: 307.

6. Oliver, Johnson, and Farrell, "Anatomy of a Rebellion" in Gooding-Williams (ed.), *Reading Rodney King*: 127.

7. Ibid.

8. Bakari Kitwana, *The Hip Hop Generation: Young Blacks and the Crisis in African American Culture* (New York: Basic, 2002): 28; Watson Swail, Alberto Cabrerra, and Chul Lee, *Latino Youth and the Pathway to College* (Washington D.C.: Educational Policy Institute, 2004).

9. In an author interview with Rodriguez in December 2006, he spoke further about his literary intentions: "I wanted to have a very literary manner of doing this book—use a lot of literary devices."

10. Tim Libretti, "Is there a Working Class in US Literature? Race, Ethnicity and the Proletarian Literary Tradition," *Radical Teacher (Working Class Studies)*, no. 46 (Spring 1995): 22–26 (23); Vincent Perez, "'Running' and Resistance: Nihilism and Cultural Memory in Chicano Urban Narratives," *MELUS* 25, no. 2 (Summer 2000): 133–46.

11. Thomas's referencing of Rodriguez's "singular voice" again raises questions of representativeness.

12. David Anderson, "Curriculum, Culture, and Community: the Challenge of School Violence" in Mark Moore and Michael Tonry (eds.), *Youth Violence* (Chicago: University of Chicago Press, 1998): 317–63 (317).

13. Eithne Quinn, *Nuthin' But a "G" Thang: The Culture and Commerce of Gangsta Rap* (New York: Columbia University Press, 2005): 145.

14. Oliver, Johnson, and Farrell, "Anatomy of a Rebellion" in Gooding-Williams (ed.), *Reading Rodney King*: 117–41. While the schools in South Central were predominantly African American in the early 1980s, even at schools in inner-city Mexican American neighborhoods at that time the dropout rate was approximately 50 percent. See James Diego Vigil, "Community Dynamics and the Rise of Street Gangs," in Marcelo Suarez-Orozco and Mariela Paez (eds.), *Latinos: Remaking America* (Berkeley: University of California Press, 2002): 97–109 (104).

15. David Brumble, "The Gangbanger Autobiography of Monster and Warrior Literature" in *American Literary History* 12, nos. 1 and 2 (Spring/Summer 2000): 158–86 (162).

16. Vigil, "Community Dynamics," in Suarez-Orozco and Paez (eds.), *Latinos*: 104.

17. Author interview with Sergeant Wes McBride, December 2006. In further written correspondence with McBride in 2011, he clarified: "Reading and writing alone does not guarantee gang free life. It is one of the spokes needed to make the wheel to roll away from the gang."

18. Todd Boyd, *Am I Black Enough for You? Popular Culture from the 'hood and Beyond* (Bloomington: Indiana University Press, 1997): 10.

19. Quinn, *Nuthin' But a "G" Thang*: 24, 35, 202; Boyd, *Am I Black Enough for You?*: 11; Robin Kelley, *Race Rebels: Culture, Politics and the Black Working Class* (New York: Free Press, 1994): 209–10.

20. Boyd, *Am I Black Enough for You?*: 10.

21. Bakhtin as quoted in Henry Louis Gates Jr., *Loose Canons: Notes on the Culture Wars* (Oxford, UK: Oxford University Press, 1992): 43.

22. Ibid.

23. For example, see William Shaw, *Westsiders: Stories of Boys in the Hood* (London: Bloomsbury, 2000): 41.

24. Williams with Barbara Becnel, *Tookie Speaks Out Series* (New York: Rosen, 1996). The quotation here is taken from *Gangs and Your Friends*: 18.

25. Brian Cross, *It's Not About a Salary: Rap, Race and Resistance in LA* (New York: Verso, 1993): 68. This forms part of a process identified by gang scholar James Diego Vigil as "choloization," whereby linguistic and cultural confusion arose between English and Spanish: "the term is derived from *Cholo*—a self-descriptive label that street youths use on a regular basis. It reflects their cultural marginality and tendency to create their own language and style, sometimes called Spanglish." See Vigil, "Community Dynamics," in Suarez-Orozco and Paez (eds.), *Latinos*: 103.

26. Kelley, *Race Rebels*: 163.

27. Brumble, "The Gangbanger Autobiography of Monster."

28. Malcolm Little with Alex Haley, *The Autobiography of Malcolm X* (London: Penguin, 1965): 19; Eldridge Cleaver, *Soul on Ice* (London: Jonathan Cape, 1969): 26, 155.

29. Such an act is highly significant in light of the way in which slaves were denied permission to speak their native African languages. See Henry Louis Gates Jr. (ed.), *Bearing Witness: Selections from African American Autobiography in the Twentieth Century* (New York: Pantheon, 1991): 6. In a written author interview in November 2008, Becnel (Williams's friend and co-author) confirmed that Williams was fluent in Swahili.

30. Rodriguez, "Writing Off Our Youth," *Prison Life* (October 1994): 8–9.

31. Brian Jarvis, *Cruel and Unusual: Punishment and US Culture* (London: Pluto, 2004): 112.

32. Little with Haley, *The Autobiography of Malcolm X*: 9.

33. Cleaver, *Soul On Ice*: 26.

34. Williams, *Life in Prison* (New York: Morrow, 1998).

35. Arnold Schwarzenegger, "Statement of Decision," *City News Service*, 12 December 2005.

36. For example, in the memoir's glossary, barrio terms such as "Vatito," "Vato Loco," and "Chota" are mixed with revolutionary expressions such as "La Raza," "Regeneracíon," and "Teatro." See Luis J. Rodriguez, *Always Running: La Vida Loca—Gang Days in LA* (New York: Touchstone, 1994): 253–60.

37. Williams and Becnel, *Tookie Speaks Out Series*. There are six books in the series. The sample glossary words here are taken from *Gangs and Violence*: 23.

38. Author correspondence with Shakur in 2008–9.

39. Kenneth Mostern, *Autobiography and Black Identity Politics: Racialization in Twentieth Century America* (Cambridge, UK: Cambridge University Press, 1999): 162–63.

40. Laura Marcus, *Auto/biographical Discourses* (Manchester, UK: Manchester University Press, 1994): 168.

41. Ibid.

42. Nicolas Kanellos, "Orality and Hispanic Literature of the US," in Lavonne Brown Ruoff and Jerry Ward (eds.), *Redefining American Literary History* (New York: Modern Language Association of America, 1990): 117.

43. Oral expression has a long history among other ethnic and subjugated groups, for example Native American chants. Verbal folktales and performative poems formed part of an expressive tradition for African Americans who were denied the right to inscribe culture. Moreover, poetry holds significance for recent Mexican history: the 1960s Chicano Renaissance sparked a wave of social protest poetry from artists who were culturally frustrated and struggling to find a literary position in mainstream America. See Kanellos, "Orality and Hispanic Literature," in Brown Ruoff and Ward (eds.), *Redefining American Literary History*: 117; Joseph Sommers, "Critical Approaches to Chicano Literature" in Sommers and Tomas Ybarra-Frausto (eds.), *Modern Chicano Writers: A Collection of Critical Essays* (Englewood Cliffs, NJ: Prentice Hall, 1979): 38.

44. Author interview with Alonso, December 2006.

45. Gates (ed.), *Bearing Witness*: 6.

46. Ibid.

47. Prison scholars have regularly drawn comparisons between the institution of slavery and modern-day prisons. For example, see Jarvis, *Cruel and Unusual*: 79–92.

48. Heather Andrea Williams, *Self-Taught: African American Education in Slavery and Freedom* (Chapel Hill: University of North Carolina Press, 2005). See also Kim Warren, "Language and Liberation," *Reviews in American History* 33, no. 4 (2005): 510–17.

49. In a collection of essays by prisoner Mumia Abu-Jamal, who features in *Blue Rage*'s acknowledgments, he regularly cites complicated court documents to prove points. See Jamal, *Live from Death Row* (Reading, MA: Addison-Wesley, 1995).

50. Heather Williams, *Self-Taught*.

51. Other parallels can be drawn between the situation of slaves and modern-day prisoners. For example, slaves frequently escaped without their possessions, then became victims of low wages, failed crops, and fraud. They often pursued an education without being able to afford study aids such as pencils and paper. See Warren, "Language and Liberation": 510–17. Prison narrators, in particular death row authors, similarly often wrote under extreme conditions. Abu-Jamal, for example, was denied use of a typewriter because it was deemed a dangerous weapon. See Jarvis, *Cruel and Unusual*: 124.

Chapter Five

1. Janet Staiger, "Taboos and Totems: Cultural Meanings of *The Silence of the Lambs*," in Jim Collins and Hilary Radner (eds.), *Film Theory Goes To The Movies* (New York: Routledge, 1993): 142–54.

2. Ibid.:143. The word "spectorial" is taken from the Latin *spect* meaning "to watch, to see, to look."

3. Using LexisNexis, I sampled a broad range of newspapers, magazines, as well as a few television transcripts where the memoirs had been reviewed for news programs and documentaries. This chapter will employ approximately thirty-five of those articles for each memoir. I acknowledge that LexisNexis tends not to involve centrist and populist publications and excludes radical presses, though I believe I have a sufficiently broad sample to appease this deficiency. The names of authors and page numbers were not always supplied.

4. It was also the *Los Angeles Times* in which Williams chose to release a full-page advertisement/essay in the days prior to his death, to explain "What I Would Do with the Rest of My Life." See *Los Angeles Times*, 7 December 2005.

5. Author interview with a former journalist from the *Los Angeles Times* who wishes to remain anonymous, December 2006.

6. Martin Jankowski, *Islands in the Street: Gangs and American Urban Society* (Berkeley: University of California Press, 1992): 284–309.

7. Ibid.: 286.

8. Malcolm Klein, *The American Street Gang: Its Nature, Prevalence, and Control* (Oxford, UK: Oxford University Press, 1995): 5.

9. Jankowski, *Islands in the Street*: 285.

10. Ibid.: 286.

11. For example, see Mike Davis, "War in the Streets," *New Statesman*, 11 November 1988: 28.

12. Written author interview with Katz, December 2006. Also author interviews with another former *Los Angeles Times* journalist (anonymity requested) in December 2006, who made reference to Katz's positive coverage and spoke very highly of his work. In an author interview in January 2008, Klein said the media has progressed greatly since his early days of gang research. Klein claims we can now identify a few "very good and very genuine crime writers," citing Katz as an example.

13. Craig Reinarman and Harry Levine, "The Crack Attack: America's Latest Drug Scare, 1986–1992," in Joel Best (ed.), *Images of Issues—Typifying Contemporary Social Problems* (New York: Aldine de Gruyter, 1995): 147–79.

14. Klein, *American Street Gang*: 40.

15. See chapter 3, "Media and Moral Panics," in Yvonne Jewkes, *Media and Crime* (London: Sage, 2004): 63–83; Best (ed.), *Images of Issues*.

16. For more information see William Van Deburg, *Hoodlums: Black Villains and Social Bandits in American Life* (Chicago: University of Chicago Press, 2004): 216–18.

17. Graeme Turner, *British Cultural Studies* (New York: Routledge, 1992): 76.

18. Stuart Hall, "The Spectacle of the Other," in Hall (ed.), *Representation: Cultural Representations and Signifying Practices*, 5th ed. (Milton Keynes, UK: Open University Press, 2001): 223–83 (277).

19. bell hooks, "Sexism and Misogyny: Who Takes the Rap? Misogyny, Gangsta Rap and the Piano," *Z Magazine*, September 1994: 13.

20. Reuben Sosa Villegas, "In a Word, Gangster's Book is Unacceptable," *Rocky Mountain News*, 9 January 1994.

21. Ibid.

22. Reinarman and Levine, "Crack Attack," in Best (ed.), *Images of Issues*: 153. Roger Fowler also examines such scare language in *Language in the News: Discourse and Ideology in the Press* (London: Routledge, 1991): 165–66.

23. Villegas, "In a Word."

24. Michiko Kakutani, "Illuminating Gang Life in LA: It's Raw," *New York Times*, 23 July 1993: C27; "I Blasted Him Thrice in the Chest," *Press Enterprise*, 26 December 1993.

25. Patricia Holt, "On the Road to—and From—Gang Life in LA," *San Francisco Chronicle*, 8 April 1993.

26. "Always Running," *Kirkus Reviews*, 1 December 1992; Jonathan Kozol, "Review," www.amazon.com/Always-Running-Vida-Loca-L/dp/0671882317. The website contains a shortened version of Kozol's review that was originally written as marketing quotations for the back of the book, as confirmed in an author interview with Rodriguez in January 2008.

27. "Always Running," *Progressive* 57, no. 9 (September 1993): 43.

28. Holt, "On the Road."

29. Ilan Stavans, "Always Running," *Nation* 256, no. 14 (12 April 1993): 494.

30. Villegas, "In a Word."

31. These include "Always Running," *Kirkus Reviews*; Holt, "On the Road"; Molly Okeon, "Gang Member-Turned Writer to Speak at College," *Inland Valley Daily Bulletin* (Ontario), 13 January 2005; Ginger Rutland, "The Rap on Gangsters," *Sacramento Bee*, 25 September 2006; Sandy Cohen, "Gangs of LA—Former Member Says His Controversial Book Is Still Relevant Ten Years Later," *Copley News Service*, 27 October 2005.

32. Villegas, "In a Word"; Lou Gelfand, "If You Ran the Newspaper," *Star Tribune* (Minneapolis), 14 November 1993: 35A.

33. Examples include "Always Running," *Kirkus Reviews*; Paul Ruffins, "West Coast Stories," *Washington Post*, 7 February 1993; Dolores and Roger Flaherty, "A Life of Sex, Drugs and Violence," *Chicago Sun Times*, 13 February 1994: 13.

34. Holt, "On the Road."

35. Stavans, "Always Running": 494.

36. Holt, "On the Road."

37. Kozol, "Review."

38. Ruffins, "West Coast Stories"; Jonathan Kozol, "Review."

39. Stavans, "Always Running": 494; John Rogers, "Always Running Author Settles into Literary Celebrity," Associated Press's *Entertainment News*, 31 October 2005.

40. Michael Gougis, "Cultural Café Fills a Need in Sylmar," *Daily News of Los Angeles*, 30 December 2002.

41. Laurel Graeber, "New and Noteworthy Paperbacks," *New York Times*, 24 April 1994: section 7.25; "Books For Vacation Reading," *New York Times*, 6 June 1993: section 7.34.

42. Holt, "On the Road"; Carol Anshaw, "A Poet Tells of Life with LA Gangs," *Chicago Sun Times*, 14 February 1993; Gregg Barrios, "Author's Novel Recycles Without Pizzazz," *San Antonio Express News*, 28 August 2005; Stavans, "Always Running": 494; Piri Thomas, "Review," www.amazon.com/Always-Running-Vida-Loca-L/dp/0671882317. As with Kozol, Thomas's review was written for marketing purposes, to appear as promotional "blurb" on the back of the memoir itself.

43. Ruffins, "West Coast Stories"; "Morning Drive Time," Video Monitoring Services of America, 29 March 2005; "Parent Wants Gang Memoir Pulled from San Diego School Libraries," Associated Press, 28 January 1999; "Latino Readings," *Washington*

Post, 14 May 1995; "Writers Honored Saturday," *Chicago Sun Times*, 15 May 1994; "Eight Latinos Named Local Heroes of the Year," *City News Service*, 5 September 2003.

44. H. Bruce Franklin (ed.), *Prison Writing in Twentieth Century America* (New York: Penguin, 1998): 13.

45. Anshaw, "A Poet Tells of Life with LA Gangs"; Rudy Arispe, "Gang Survivor Spins Experience into Literary Gold," *Connexion*, 18 August 2005.

46. *Mid Morning Edition*, CLTV-TV (Chicago), 7 October 1998.

47. Barrios, "Author's Novel Recycles."

48. Released by Touchstone, this edition celebrated ten years since the release of the paperback version.

49. Michael Coffey and Lisa Kendall, "In Aftermath of LA Riots, a Lively Diversity of Voices," *Publishers Weekly* 239, no. 55 (28 December 1992): 24.

50. "Always Running," *Kirkus Reviews*; Ruffins, "West Coast Stories"; "Latino Readings," *Washington Post*.

51. Sean Coughlan, "Needle Matches," *Times*, 27 April 1996; Ruffins, "West Coast Stories."

52. Kakutani, "Illuminating Gang Life": C27.

53. Mark Horowitz, "In Search of Monster," *Atlantic*, no. 272 (December 1993): 28–37.

54. John Mitchell and Cheo Hodari Coker, "A Monster on the Run: Street Gang Member's Conversion Goes Awry," *Los Angeles Times*, 27 May 1996. For financial references, see also Christopher Reed, "Monster Turns Up on LA Porch," *Guardian*, 30 May 1996; Susan Faludi, "Ghetto Star," *Los Angeles Weekly*, 6 October 1999; Deborah Hastings, "Celebrity Author Promotes Autobiography," *Sarasota Herald-Tribune* (Florida), 28 June 1993; "Glamour in the 'Hood," *Newsweek*, 13 September 1999; "Monsta," CBS News Transcripts, 7 November 1993.

55. Those that reference the film rights include Faludi, "Ghetto Star"; Hastings, "Fondness for Fans Foils Fugitive," *The Free Lance-Star* (Fredericksburg, Virginia), 30 May 1996; Mitchell and Coker, "A Monster on the Run." Shakur's house is referenced by Hastings, "Fondness for Fans," and, "Kody Monster Scott Arrested After Another Run-in with Police," Associated Press, 17 July 2004.

56. Eithne Quinn details the "individualist, get-rich-quick, entrepreneurial ethos" of this era. See Quinn, *Nuthin' But a "G" Thang: The Culture and Commerce of Gangsta Rap* (New York: Columbia University Press, 2005): 45.

57. Ibid.: 42. See also chapter 2 of Robin Kelley, *Yo' Mama's Disfunktional! Fighting the Culture Wars in Urban America* (Boston: Beacon, 1998): 43-77, aptly titled "Looking to Get Paid: How Some Black Youth Put Culture to Work."

58. S. Craig Watkins, *Representing: Hip Hop Culture and the Production of Black Cinema* (Chicago: University of Chicago Press, 1998): 184.

59. "Monsta," *60 Minutes*, CBS, 31 July 1994.

60. The details of the dispute in *Buzz* are explained in Horowitz, "In Search of Monster": 28–37. See also Leonce Gaiter, "He's Your Monster, Not Mine," *Buzz*, June/July 1993: 25–26.

61. Horowitz, "In Search of Monster": 28–37.

62. Ibid.

63. Other examples include: Brent Staples, "When Only Monsters Are Real," *New York Times*, 21 November 1993: section 4.16; Jonetta Rose Barras, "Literary Lock-up;

the Self-Imposed Bondage of Black Writers," *City Paper* (Washington, D.C.), 28 October–3 November 1994; Mary Ann French, "For Black Authors, the Same Old Story? A Round-table Look at Literary Roadblocks Facing African Americans," *Washington Post*, 13 June 1994.

64. Horowitz, "In Search of Monster": 28–37.

65. Ibid.

66. hooks, "Sexism and Misogyny," *Z Magazine*: 13. hooks also explores similar concerns over white patriarchal exploitation of black culture in *Black Looks: Race and Representation* (Boston, MA: South End, 1992) and *We Real Cool: Black Men and Masculinity* (New York: Routledge, 2004).

67. Gelfand, "If You Ran the Newspaper": 35A.

68. Ibid.

69. Eleanor Cowell Aloha, "Inmate Author Made Out As Hero," *Oregonian*, 7 July 1993.

70. Ibid.

71. Gelfand, "If You Ran the Newspaper": 35A.

72. Ibid. Gelfand was very well-respected; he held the position of reader's representative for twenty-three years.

73. Quinn, *Nuthin' But a "G" Thang*: 8.

74. Todd Boyd, *Am I Black Enough for You? Popular Culture from the 'hood and Beyond* (Bloomington: Indiana University Press, 1997): 132–33.

75. Ibid.: 133.

76. Stuart Hall, "What Is This 'Black' in Black Popular Culture?" in Gina Dent (ed.), *Black Popular Culture* (Seattle: Bay Press, 1992): 21–33 (26); Hall, "The Spectacle of the Other," in Hall (ed.), *Representation*: 235.

77. Horowitz, "In Search of Monster": 28–37.

78. These include Kakutani, "Illuminating Gang Life": C27; Horowitz, "In Search of Monster": 28–37; Mitchell and Coker, "A Monster on the Run."

79. Horowitz, "In Search of Monster": 28–37.

80. Kakutani, "Illuminating Gang Life": C27. I acknowledge that this is also the house style of the *New York Times*. Fowler illustrates that there are deliberately different ways of saying the same thing in newspaper coverage encouraging different responses, citing "Gorby" and "Mr. Gorbachev" as an example. See Fowler, *Language in the News*: 4.

81. Kakutani, "Illuminating Gang Life": C27.

82. *Publishers Weekly* confirmed that they have approximately the same number of male and female reviewers, except for children's books, which involves mainly female reviewers.

83. Franklin, *Prison Literature in America: The Victim as Criminal and Artist* (Oxford, UK: Oxford University Press, 1989): 126.

84. Ibid.

85. Amy Wallace, "The Monster Deal," *Sunday Age* (Melbourne), 25 April 1993: 6.

86. "Monsta," CBS News Transcripts.

87. Kakutani, "Illuminating Gang Life": C27; "Monsta," CBS News Transcripts.

88. Those who interviewed him in prison include Faludi, "Ghetto Star"; Aloha, "Inmate Author Made Out As Hero"; Alexander Cockburn, "Beat the Devil," *Nation* 254 (1 June 1992); "Monsta," CBS News Transcripts.

89. Hastings, "Celebrity Author"; Aloha, "Inmate Author Made Out As Hero."

90. There is also other evidence in the narrative that the author has not fully converted. For example, the cover photograph flaunts the author as a fully-fledged gangbanger under the title, and in the acknowledgments he admits he has not fully renounced gangsterism by thanking his wife "who waits patiently for my change." See Shakur, *Monster*: v.

91. Kakutani, "Illuminating Gang Life": C27.

92. Examples include Faludi, "Ghetto Star"; Jacquie Paul, "Author Faces Parole Problem," *Press Enterprise*, 10 March 1996; "Monster Sought by Authorities," *Press Enterprise*, 12 March 1996.

93. Patrick McGreevy, "Monster Goes from Bestseller List to Most Wanted List," *Los Angeles Times*, 15 February 2007.

94. Ryan Oliver, "Former Member of Crips Jailed," *Daily News of Los Angeles*, 17 July 2004; Paul, "Author faces parole problem."

95. "Glamour in the 'Hood," *Newsweek*; McGreevy, "Throwing the Book at Monster." See also Ashley Powers, "A Case Against Him in His Own Words," *Los Angeles Times*, 12 April 2006.

96. Faludi, "Ghetto Star."

97. Hastings, "Fondness for Fans."

98. For example, see "California's Prisons Bar Interviews with Inmates," *Houston Chronicle*, 29 December 1995; "California Cuts Off Face-to-Face Interviews with Prisoners," Associated Press, 28 December 1995.

99. Staiger, "Taboos and Totems," in Collins and Radner (eds.), *Film Theory*: 144.

100. Jankowski, *Islands in the Street*: 305–6.

101. Faludi, "Ghetto Star."

102. Examples include Wallace, "The Monster Deal": 6; Robert Lusetich, "Monster with Attitude," *Weekend Australian*, 1 June 1996; Reed, "Monster Turns Up on LA porch"; Mitchell and Coker, "A Monster on the Run"; Horowitz, "In Search of Monster": 28–37; McGreevy, "Monster Goes from Bestseller List to Most Wanted List."

103. Celeste Fremon, *G-Dog and the Homeboys: Father Greg Boyle and the Gangs of East LA* (Albuquerque: University of New Mexico Press, 1995): 9.

104. Examples include: Lusetich, "Monster with Attitude"; Paul, "Author Faces Parole Problem"; Mitchell and Coker, "A Monster on the Run."

105. Hugo Martin, "In South LA, a Clash over Nobel Nominee," *Los Angeles Times*, 7 December 2000: B1; Rita Cosby, "Interview with Stanley Williams & Vernon Crittendon," *The Big Story* (weekend edition), Fox News, 20 November 2004.

106. Chris Greer, "Delivering Death: Capital Punishment, Botched Executions, and the American News Media," in Paul Mason (ed.), *Captured by the Media: Prison Discourse in Popular Culture* (Devon, UK: Willan, 2006): 84–102 (85). For example, an article in *People* provides the ages of the victims and quotes from a victim's relative. See Bob Meadows, Howard Breur, and Andrea Orr, "Does Tookie Deserve to Die?" *People* 64, no. 24 (12 December 2005): 99.

107. George Curry, "Tookie Williams Executed but Debate over His Life Continues," *Buckeye Review*, 13 December 2005. This article was balanced, additionally presenting information from Williams's perspective. I merely cite this paragraph as an example of the style of coverage written from the victim's perspective.

108. David Schmid, "Idols of Destruction: Celebrity and the Serial Killer," in Su Holmes and Sean Redmond (eds.), *Framing Celebrity: New Directions in Celebrity Culture* (London: Routledge, 2006): 291, 306.

109. Lewis Yablonsky, "Nobel Nominee Doesn't Belong in Death Chamber; The Former LA Gangster Could Be a Force For Good," *Los Angeles Times*, 19 September 2002; Fremon, "Behind the Crips Mythos," *Los Angeles Times*, 20 November 2007.

110. Elizabeth Mehren, "Do Not Follow in My Footsteps: Gangbanging Brought Tookie Williams to Death Row. Can a Series of Children's Books That Decry Violence Bring Him to Redemption?" *Los Angeles Times*, 11 September 1996; John Simerman, "California Redeemer: Stanley Williams, Founder of an Infamous LA Street Gang, Writes Children's Books While on Death Row. Is it Enough to Win Him Clemency?" *Montreal Gazette*, 22 November 2005.

111. See www.amazon.com/review/product/. Though they are not "official" book reviews, it is interesting to browse some of the reader reviews listed on amazon.com and barnesandnoble.com.

112. Simerman, "California Redeemer."

113. Ruffins, "West Coast Stories."

114. Villegas, "In a Word."

115. "Black California Death Row Inmate Is Nominated for the Nobel Peace Prize," *Jet*, 25 December 2000–1 January 2001; Martin, "In South LA": B1; Simerman, "California Redeemer"; Phil Gasper, "California Murders Tookie Williams," *Counterpunch*, 13 December 2005, www.counterpunch.org.

116. Author interview with Lieutenant Paul Vernon, a spokesperson for the Media Relations Unit at the LAPD, December 2006.

117. The letter was cited in Martin, "In South LA." It is a classic newspaper persuasive strategy to use persons of high prestige, stressed by quoting their name and official title in full as detailed in Fowler, *Language in the News*: 118.

118. Holmes and Redmond, "Introduction," in Holmes and Redmond (eds.), *Framing Celebrity*: 290.

119. Leon Bing, *Do or Die: For the First Time, Members of America's Most Notorious Gangs—The Crips and The Bloods—Speak for Themselves* (New York: Harper Collins, 1991).

120. Hastings, "Celebrity Author"; "Glamour in the 'Hood," *Newsweek*.

121. Paula Chin and Nancy Matsumoto, "Making of a Monster," *People* 41, no. 10 (21 March 1994). Published in partnership with CNN, the magazine claims to be concerned with stories of human interest, but its reputation is based on its preoccupation with celebrity culture.

122. Faludi, "Ghetto Star."

123. Richard Dyer, as quoted in Holmes and Redmond, "Introduction," in Holmes and Redmond (eds.), *Framing Celebrity*: 121.

124. "Glamour in the 'Hood," *Newsweek*.

125. For example, *People* looks at Jamie Foxx's relationship with Williams. See Meadows, Breur, and Orr, "Does Tookie Deserve to Die?": 99.

126. James Rainey, "Glitz and Gore of Williams Case Draws Foreign Media," *Los Angeles Times*, 11 December 2005: B1.

127. The editor of *Horn Books Magazine* was cited in Mehren's "Do Not Follow in My Footsteps."

128. "Milo Calls for Support Against Execution Threat," *Bookseller*, 11 November 2005.

129. Milo would release a posthumous edition with a prologue by Becnel detailing the execution itself. This text carried a slightly different title: *Redemption: The Last Testament of Stanley "Tookie" Williams-Gang Leader turned Nobel Prize Nominee.*

130. Staiger, *Media Reception Studies* (New York: New York University Press, 2005): 2.

131. "Autobiography of the Former Gang Leader and Prison Activist, Executed in 2005," *Kirkus Reviews*, 1 October 2007; Fremon, "Behind the Crips Mythos."

132. "Autobiography of the Former Gang Leader," *Kirkus Reviews*.

133. Fremon, "Behind the Crips Mythos." This demonstrates what media scholars term "diachronic study," whereby different paradigms change the reception of both book and author. See Fowler, *Language in the News*: 226.

134. Caitlin Kelly, "Drama Sells His Books," *New York Daily News*, 9 December 2005.

135. Ibid.

136. Heidi Benson, "The Execution of Stanley Tookie Williams; Books: Execution Brought Interest in Williams' Anti-gang Writings, a Surge in Sales," *San Francisco Chronicle*, 14 December 2005: A12.

137. Villegas, "In a Word."

138. Staiger, "Taboos and Totems," in Collins and Radner (eds.), *Film Theory*: 142–54.

Chapter Six

1. Christine Gledhill, "Pleasurable Negotiations," in John Storey (ed.), *Cultural Theory and Popular Culture: A Reader*, 2nd ed. (London: Prentice Hall, 1994): 236–49 (244).

2. The term "interpretive communities" was coined by the literary theorist Stanley Fish in 1976 and has been influential in reader-response criticism. Fish did not believe that text and author were separate entities. Instead he argued it is the reader who "makes" a text. In this chapter, the schoolchildren are an interpretive community. For more information, see Janice Radway, "Interpretive Communities and Variable Literacies: The Functions of Romance Reading," *Daedalus* 113, no. 3 (Summer 1984): 49–73.

3. Some of the schools requested anonymity in this study, so I have kept them all nameless.

4. Joke Hermes, *Re-reading Popular Culture* (Oxford, UK: Blackwell, 2005): 92–93.

5. Ibid.

6. Three of these young men requested anonymity, so I have kept them all nameless.

7. For example, I am aware that the sample of schoolchildren might be considered too small to be representative of all schools in East LA and South LA, or that I should have considered whether the responses differed according to age.

8. The music demonstrated an emotional attachment to the decaying ghetto, simultaneously turning these descriptions of an impoverished locale into marketable images. See Eithne Quinn, *Nuthin' But a "G" Thang: The Culture and Commerce of Gangsta Rap* (New York: Columbia University Press, 2005): 76–78.

9. Greg Dimitriadis, *Performing Identity, Performing Culture: Hip Hop as Text, Pedagogy and Lived Practice* (New York: Peter Lang, 2001): 114.

10. According to the questionnaires, at least half of the respondents regularly read a newspaper or watch a news program.

11. Allen Carey-Webb, "Youth Violence and the Language Arts: A Topic for the Classroom," *English Journal* 84, no. 5 (September 1995): 29–37 (32).

12. Author interview with Klein, December 2006. When interviewed, probation officer Mary Ridgway and former gang officer Sergeant Wes McBride also believed such memoirs had the ability to lure youths into gangs.

13. Robin Means Coleman, "The *Menace II Society* Copycat Murder Case and Thug Life: A Reception Study with a Convicted Criminal," in Coleman (ed.), *Say it Loud: African American Audiences, Media and Identity* (New York: Routledge, 2002): 249–84 (251).

14. Several schools confirmed they used ghetto action films in the classroom because, as the teacher at school C explained, "it builds connections with kids' everyday lives. The more connections we can build with these kids, it makes it more relevant for them, so they are more likely to come to school."

15. Coleman, "*Menace II Society*," in Coleman (ed.), *Say It Loud*: 262–63.

16. Carl Husemoller Nightingale, *On the Edge: A History of Poor Black Children and Their American Dreams* (New York: Basic Books, 1993): 178, 180.

17. Author interview with Rodriguez, December 2006.

18. Author correspondence with Shakur in 2008–9.

19. Their opposing sets of arguments represented what other students at other schools had also said of the children's series.

20. See the website of the American Library Association: www.ala.org/ala/oif/bannedbooksweek/bbwlinks/100mostfrequently.htm. *Always Running* generated significant press coverage around these school challenges, particularly in California newspapers. For example, see Elizabeth Johnson, "Trustees Vote 4–3 for Book," *Modesto Bee*, 16 December 2003: B1.

21. For further discussion on this point, see Stephen Vaughn, *Freedom and Entertainment: Rating the Movies in an Age of New Media* (Cambridge, UK: Cambridge University Press, 2006): 70.

22. Quinn, *Nuthin' But a "G" Thang*: 87.

23. Vaughn, *Freedom and Entertainment*: 53.

24. *Monster* and *Blue Rage* have never appeared on the American Library Association's annual list of the most challenged books, though Leon Bing's *Do or Die* (in which Shakur originally found fame) was challenged by several school boards for encouraging gang affiliation.

25. Quinn, *Nuthin' But a "G" Thang*: 136.

26. Dimitriadis, *Performing Identity, Performing Culture*: 29.

27. Ibid.: 70, 91.

28. In an author interview in December 2006, Angela Davis demonstrated strong views on the need for flexible and alternative educational curricula, arguing that "texts

such as these can play a major role in creating radical historical memory. It's important to create historical memory."

29. I acknowledge that, as already highlighted in chapter 6, hardcore gang members are unlikely to attend school.

30. Rodriguez, too, believed that Tupac's work could engage students' minds with the shape and form of poetry, a literary style that they might have previously loathed. He suggested that Tupac's poetry be used as a means of introducing students to Shakespeare. Angela Davis feels it is imperative that children use texts at school that are "relevant to their lives," because education is often "boring" with "no attempt to tap into the creativity of young people." Author interviews, December 2006.

31. Educational scholar Henry Giroux has explored the use of popular culture to benefit schooling (he deems cinema a "teaching machine"), arguing for the need to replace a boring curriculum that has no relevance for students' lives in modern-day America. See Giroux's *Fugitive Cultures: Race, Violence and Youth* (New York: Routledge, 1996): 13, 83.

32. See www.schoollibraryjournal.com; www.ala.org; www.voya.com.

33. See Gilles Deleuze and Félix Guattari, *Anti-Oedipus: Capitalism and Schizophrenia*, translated by R. Hurley et al. (Minneapolis: University of Minnesota Press, 1983).

34. Carey-Webb, "Youth Violence and the Language Arts": 29.

35. Greg Dimitriadis, *Friendships, Cliques and Gangs: Young Black Men Coming of Age in Urban America* (New York: Teachers College, 2003): 4.

36. Hermes, *Re-reading Popular Culture*: 80.

Conclusions

1. Susan Faludi, *Stiffed: The Betrayal of the American Man* (London: Chatto & Windus, 1999): 495.

2. See Michael Kammen, "The Problem of American Exceptionalism: A Reconsideration," *American Quarterly* 45, no. 1 (March 1993): 1–43.

3. Shelley Fisher Fishkin, "Crossroads of Cultures: The Transnational Turn in American Studies," *American Quarterly* 57, no. 1 (2005): 15–57.

4. Richard Slotkin, *Regeneration through Violence: The Mythology of the American Frontier 1600–1860* (Middletown, CT: Wesleyan University Press, 1973).

5. Author correspondence with Shakur, 2008–9.

6. Author interview with Rodriguez, December 2006. Rodriguez explained that this comment meant that the 1980s was "the start of the most violent period of gang history in U.S. history."

7. Similar to George Lipsitz contending that we must let the actual music and musicians define the way we write or think about music. See "Listening to Learn and Learning to Listen," *American Quarterly* 42, no. 4 (December 1990): 615–36.

8. Kevin Starr, *Coast of Dreams: A History of Contemporary America* (London: Allen Lane, 2005): 87.

9. Michael Coffey and Lisa Kendall, "In Aftermath of LA Riots, a Lively Diversity of Voices," *Publishers Weekly* 239, no.55 (28 December 1992): 24.

10. In author correspondence with Shakur in 2008–9, he confirmed he had not previously read *Always Running*, but did so when supplied with a copy and had much positive praise for the memoir. He felt he could relate to many of Rodriguez's experiences.

11. Sonia Rodriguez with Reymundo Sanchez, *Lady Q: The Rise and Fall of a Latin Queen* (Chicago: Chicago Review Press, 2010); Ice-T with Douglas Century, *Ice: A Memoir of Gangster Life and Redemption* (New York: One World, 2011). Wright informed scholar David Brumble by personal communication that he is at work on a second volume of autobiography; see Brumble's "Stanley 'Tookie' Williams, Gangbanger Autobiography, and Warrior Tribes," *Journal of American Studies* 44, no. 1 (February 2010): 155–70 (160).

12. Rodriguez's new memoir was again released by Touchstone.

13. Further author correspondence with Shakur in 2011 indicated he has no publishing contract, but is currently penning further memoirs. He explained that he would like to seek a publisher and "do the rounds" upon his release from prison in August 2012.

14. Written author interview with Becnel, November 2008.

15. John Pomfret, "Chronicler of Life as a Crip Is on Trial," *Washington Post*, 2 March 2006.

16. Margaret B. Jones, *Love and Consequences: A Memoir of Hope and Survival* (New York: Riverhead, 2008).

17. Though some reviewers did deem *Love and Consequences* to be survival or misery literature, for the most part these readers suggested the narrative could be aligned with other contemporary street gang memoirs.

18. "Opinion: Margaret Seltzer's Fake Memoir," *Los Angeles Times*, 6 March 2008.

19. For example, see Motoko Rich, "Gang Memoir, Turning Page, Is Pure Fiction," *New York Times*, 4 March 2008; Scott Timberg and Josh Getlin, "Bogus Memoir Sparks Criticism of Publishing Industry," *Los Angeles Times*, 5 March 2008.

20. For discussion of Triple Crown, see chapter 2, "Cash Rules Everything Around Me," in James Annesley, *Fictions of Globalization: Consumption, the Market and the Contemporary American Novel* (London: Continuum, 2006): 13–26.

21. See www.triplecrownpublications.com for a full list of its titles; seventy-eight novels have been released since its inception in 2001.

22. James Vicini, "Number of US Prisoners Has Biggest Rise in 6 Years," *Reuters*, 27 June 2007; Adam Liptak, "1 in 100 US Adults Behind Bars," *New York Times*, 28 February 2008.

23. California Department of Corrections and Rehabilitation, "Fourth Quarter 2008 Facts & Figures" on official website: www.cdcr.ca.gov.

24. Ibid.; Manning Marable, "Incarceration vs. Education: Reproducing Racism and Poverty in America," *Race, Poverty and Environment; A Journal for Social and Environmental Justice* 15, no. 1 (Fall 2008): 59–61.

25. Paul Rogers & Leigh Poitinger, "California Budget Mess; Where Did Our Money Go?" *Mercury News* (San Jose), 8 February 2009.

26. The EPE Research Center report (2009) included analysis of data from the National Center for Education Statistics, U.S. Department of Education. See Ed Kopko, "Does Spending More on Education Work? State Rankings of Education Spending" taken from blog.bestandworststates.com.

27. Marc Lifsher and Alana Semuels, "California Unemployment Rises to Record 11.5% in May," *Los Angeles Times*, 20 June 2009.

28. Kevin Johnson, "FBI: Burgeoning Gangs Behind Up To 80% of US Crime," *USA Today*, 29 January 2009. Though archived gang statistics from the LAPD were used in chapter 1, the LAPD stopped offering total gang membership figures in 2006.

29. Barack Obama, *Dreams from My Father: A Story of Race and Inheritance* (New York: Three Rivers, 1995).

30. Obama, *The Audacity of Hope* (New York: Crown, 2006): 29.

31. Ibid.: 133.

32. Marshall Fine, "The Music Mogul," *Cigar Aficionado*, 23 June 2009.

BIBLIOGRAPHY

Note on the sources: where articles were accessed via LexisNexis, page numbers, and names of authors were not always supplied.

Abdul-Alim, Jamaal, "Telling Truth About Gangs Is the Best Education For Kids at Risk," *Milwaukee Journal Sentinel* (Wisconsin), 18 December 2005: 3.

Abu-Jamal, Mumia, *Live from Death Row* (Reading, MA: Addison-Wesley, 1995).

Acosta, Oscar Zeta, *The Autobiography of a Brown Buffalo* (San Francisco: Straight Arrow, 1972).

Acuna, Rodolof F. (ed.), *Anything but Mexican: Chicanos in Contemporary Los Angeles* (London: Verso, 1996).

Allen, Carl, "Searching For a Way Out of South Central Los Angeles," *Buffalo News*, 12 September 1993.

Allen, John, "Literature, Lives and Teachers," *Pedagogy: Critical Approaches to Teaching Literature, Language, Composition and Culture* 3, no. 2 (2003): 304–11.

"Always Running," *Kirkus Reviews*, 1 December 1992.

"Always Running," *Progressive* 57, no. 9 (September 1993): 43.

"Always Running," *Publishers Weekly* 240, no. 5 (1 February 1993): 86.

Andrews, William L. (ed.), *African American Autobiography: A Collection of Critical Essays* (Englewood Cliffs, NJ: Prentice Hall, 1993).

Andrews, William L., Frances Smith Foster, and Trudier Harris (eds.), *The Concise Oxford Companion to African American Literature* (Oxford, UK: Oxford University Press, 2001).

Angelou, Maya, *I Know Why the Caged Bird Sings* (New York: Bantam, 1983).

Annesley, James, *Fictions of Globalization: Consumption, the Market and the Contemporary American Novel* (London: Continuum, 2006).

Ansen, David, and Spike Lee, "The Battle for Malcolm X," *Newsweek*, 26 August 1991.

Anshaw, Carol, "A Poet Tells of Life with LA Gangs," *Chicago Sun Times*, 14 February 1993.

Arispe, Rudy, "Gang Survivor Spins Experience into Literary Gold," *Connexion*, 18 August 2005.

Asim, Jabari, "Holding on to Memories," *St. Louis Post-Dispatch*, 15 May 1994.

Athens, Lonnie, "Dominance, Ghettos and Violent Crime," *Sociological Quarterly* 39, no. 4 (Autumn 1998): 673–91.

——, "Violent Encounters: Violent Engagements, Skirmishes, and Tiffs," *Journal of Contemporary Ethnography* 34, no. 6 (December 2005): 631–78.

"Autobiography of the Former Gang Leader and Prison Activist, Executed in 2005," *Kirkus Reviews*, 1 October 2007.

Bakeer, Donald, *Crips: The Story of the South Central LA Street Gang from 1971–1985* (Los Angeles: Precocious, 1987).

Bal, Mieke, *Narratology: Introduction to the Theory of the Narrative* (Toronto: University of Toronto Press, 1985).

Barker, Martin, and Anne Beezer (eds.), *Reading into Cultural Studies* (London: Routledge, 1992).

Barras, Jonetta Rose, "Literary Lockup: The Self-Imposed Bondage of Black Writers," *Washington City Paper*, 28 October–3 November 1994.

Barrios, Gregg, "Author's Novel Recycles Without Pizzazz," *San Antonio Express News*, 28 August 2005.

Baxter, Vern, and A. V. Margavio, "Honor, Status, and Aggression in Economic Exchange," *Sociological Theory* 18, no. 3 (November 2000): 399–416.

Becnel, Barbara, "The Crips Co-founder Now Realizes Violence Does Not Solve Anything," *Los Angeles Times*, 22 August 1993: 3.

Benson, Heidi, "The Execution of Stanley Tookie Williams: Execution Brought Interest in Williams' Anti-Gang Writings, a Surge in Sales," *San Francisco Chronicle*, 14 December 2005: A12.

Best, Joel (ed.), *Images of Issues: Typifying Contemporary Social Problems*, 2nd ed. (New York: Aldine de Gruyter, 1995).

Bewes, Timothy, *Reification, or the Anxiety of Late Capitalism* (London: Verso, 2002).

Bing, Leon, *Do or Die: For the First Time, Members of America's Most Notorious Gangs—The Crips and The Bloods—Speak for Themselves* (New York: Harper Collins, 1991).

——, "In the Brutal World of LA's Toughest Gangs," *Time* 139, no. 11 (16 March 1992): 12–16.

——, "Reflections of a Gangbanger," *Harper's*, no. 61 (August 1988): 26–28.

——, "The Talk of the Town," *New Yorker*, no. 18 (19 July 1993): 25–26.

——, "When You're a Crip (or a Blood)," *Harper's*, no. 58 (March 1989): 51–59.

"Black California Death Row Inmate Is Nominated for the Nobel Peace Prize," *Jet*, 25 December 2000–1 January 2001.

"Blue Rage, Black Redemption," *Kirkus Reviews*, 1 October 2007.

Bonczar, Thomas, and Allen J. Beck, "Lifetime Likelihood of going to State or Federal Prison," Bureau of Justice Statistics Special Report (March 1997), http://bjs.ojp.usdoj.gov/content/pub/pdf/Llgsfp.pdf

Boyd, Todd, *Am I Black Enough for You? Popular Culture from the 'hood and Beyond* (Bloomington: Indiana University Press, 1997).

Brown, Claude, *Manchild in the Promised Land* (New York: Signet, 1965).

Brown, Cupcake, *A Piece of Cake: A Memoir* (London: Bantam, 2006).

Brown, Monica, *Gang Nation: Delinquent Citizens in Puerto Rican, Chicano and Chicana Narratives* (Minneapolis: University of Minnesota Press, 2002).

Brumble, David A., "The Gangbanger Autobiography of Monster and Warrior Literature," *American Literary History* 12, nos. 1 and 2 (Spring/Summer 2000): 158–86.

——, "Stanley 'Tookie' Williams, Gangbanger Autobiography, and Warrior Tribes," *Journal of American Studies* 44, no. 1 (February 2010): 155–70.

Brunsdon, Charlotte, and David Morley, *The Nationwide Television Studies* (New York: Routledge, 1999).

"California Cuts Off Face-to-Face Interviews With Prisoners," *Associated Press*, 28 December 1995.

"California's Prisons Bar Interviews with Inmates," *Houston Chronicle*, 29 December 1995.

Canada, Geoffrey, *Fist Stick Gun Knife* (Boston: Beacon, 1996).

Carey-Webb, Allen, *Literature and Lives: a Response-Based, Cultural Studies Approach to Teaching English* (Urbana, IL: National Council of Teachers of English, 2001).

——, "Youth Violence and the Language Arts: A Topic for the Classroom," *English Journal* 84, no. 5 (September 1995): 29–37.

Carlston, Erin, "*Zami* and the Politics of Plural Identity," in Susan Wolfe and Julia Penelope (eds.), *Sexual Practice/Textual Theory: Lesbian Cultural Criticism* (Cambridge, MA: Blackwell, 1993): 226–36.

Carr, James, *Bad: The Autobiography of James Carr* (London: Pelagian, 1975).

Cartwright, Garth, *More Miles Than Money: Journeys Through American Music* (London: Serpent's Tail, 2009).

Caster, Peter, *Prisons, Race and Masculinity in Twentieth Century US Literature and Film* (Columbus: Ohio State University Press, 2008).

Chevigny, Bell Gale, *Doing Time: Twenty Five Years of Prison Writing* (New York: Arcade, 1999).

Chin, Paula, and Nancy Matsumoto, "Making of a Monster," *People* 41, no. 10 (21 March 1994).

Clabaugh, Gary, "The Cutting Edge: The Educational Legacy of Ronald Reagan," *Horizons* (Summer 2004): 256–59.

Cleaver, Eldridge, *Soul on Ice* (London: Jonathan Cape, 1969).

Cockburn, Alexander, "Beat the Devil," *Nation* 254 (1 June 1992), available on www.streetgangs.com.

Coffey, Michael, and Lisa See Kendall, "In Aftermath of LA Riots, a Lively Diversity of Voices," *Publishers Weekly* 239, no. 55 (28 December 1992): 24.

Cohen, Sandy, "Gangs of LA—Former Member Says His Controversial Book Is Still Relevant Ten Years Later," *Copley News Service*, 27 October 2005.

Cosby, Rita, "Interview with Stanley Williams and Vernon Crittendon," *Big Story* (weekend edition), Fox News, 20 November 2004.

Coughlan, Sean, "Needle Matches," *Times* (London), 27 April 1996.

Cowell Aloha, Eleanor, "Inmate Author Made Out As Hero," *Oregonian*, 7 July 1993.

Cross, Brian, *It's Not About a Salary: Rap, Race and Resistance in LA* (London: Verso, 1993).

Curry, George E., "Tookie Williams Executed But Debate Over His Life Continues," *Buckeye Review*, 13 December 2005.

Darder, Antonia, "Latino Youth: Pedagogy, Praxis, and Policy," *Latino Studies* 4, no. 3 (2006): 302–4.

Davis, Angela, *Are Prisons Obsolete?* (New York: Seven Stories, 2003).

———, *An Autobiography* (New York: Random House, 1974).

Davis, Mike, *City of Quartz* (London: Verso, 1990).

———, "War in the Streets," *New Statesman*, 11 November 1988: 27–30.

De Witte, Paul, "A Chilling Portrayal of Gang Life in Los Angeles," *Toronto Star*, 9 October 1993.

Deacon, David, *Researching Communications: A Practical Guide to Methods in Media and Cultural Analysis* (London: Hodder Arnold, 1999).

D'Souza, Dinesh, *The End of Racism* (New York: Free Press, 1995).

Deleuze, Giles, and Félix Guattari, *Anti-Oedipus: Capitalism and Schizophrenia*, translated R. Hurley et al. (Minneapolis: University of Minnesota Press, 1983).

Dent, Gina (ed.), *Black Popular Culture* (Seattle: Bay Press, 1992).

DiBernard, Barbara, "Zami: A Portrait of an Artist as a Black Lesbian," *Kenyon Review* 13, no. 4 (Fall 1991): 195–213.

Dimitriadis, Greg, *Friendships, Cliques and Gangs: Young Black Men Coming of Age in Urban America* (New York: Teachers College Press, 2003).

———, *Performing Identity, Performing Culture: Hip Hop as Text, Pedagogy and Lived Practice* (New York: Peter Lang, 2001).

Dogg, Snoop, and Davin Seay, *Tha Doggfather: The Times, Trials and Hardcore Truths of Snoop Dogg* (New York: William Morrow, 1999).

Dow Adams, Timothy, *Telling Lies in Modern American Autobiography* (Chapel Hill: University of North Carolina Press, 1990).

During, Simon (ed.), *Cultural Studies Reader* (London: Routledge, 1993).

Eakin, Paul John (ed.), *The Ethics of Life Writing* (Ithaca: Cornell University Press, 2004).

"Eight Latinos Named Local Heroes of the Year," City News Service, 5 September 2003.

Ek, Auli, *Race and Masculinity in Contemporary American Prison Narratives* (New York: Routledge, 2005).

Faludi, Susan, "Ghetto Star," *Los Angeles Weekly*, 6 October 1999.

———, *Stiffed: The Betrayal of the American Man* (London: Chatto & Windus, 1999).

Farr, Jory, "True Gangster Stories," *Press Enterprise*, 11 June 1993.

Fine, Marshall, "The Music Mogul," *Cigar Aficionado*, 23 June 2009.

Fisher Fishkin, Shelley, "Crossroads of Cultures: The Transnational Turn in American Studies," *American Quarterly* 57, no. 1 (2005): 15–57.

Flaherty, Dolores, and Roger Flaherty, "A Life of Sex, Drugs and Violence," *Chicago Sun Times*, 13 February 1994: 13.

Fowler, Roger, *Language in the News: Discourse and Ideology in the Press* (London: Routledge, 1991).

Franklin, H. Bruce (ed.), *Prison Literature in America: The Victim as Criminal and Artist* (Oxford, UK: Oxford University Press, 1989).

———, *Prison Writing in Twentieth Century America* (New York: Penguin, 1998).

Freire, Paulo, *Pedagogy of the Oppressed* (London: Penguin, 1996).

Fremon, Celeste, "Behind the Crips Mythos: Blue Rage, Black Redemption by Stanley Tookie Williams," *Los Angeles Times*, 20 November 2007.

———, *G-Dog and the Homeboys: Father Greg Boyle and the Gangs of East Los Angeles*, 2nd ed. (Albuquerque: University of New Mexico Press, 2004).

French, Mary Ann, "For Black Authors, the Same Old Story? A Round-table Look at Literary Roadblocks Facing African Americans," *Washington Post*, 13 June 1994.

Gaiter, Leonce, "He's Your Monster, Not Mine," *Buzz*, June/July 1993: 25–26.

Gasper, Phil, "California Murders Tookie Williams," *CounterPunch*, 13 December 2005, www.counterpunch.org.

———, "Tookie Williams and the Politics of the Death Penalty," *MRZine* (*Monthly Review* Foundation online), 11 November 2005, www.mrzine.monthlyreview.org.

Gates Jr., Henry Louis, *Bearing Witness: Selections from African American Autobiography in the Twentieth Century* (New York: Pantheon, 1991).

———, *Figures in Black: Words, Signs and the Racial Self* (Oxford, UK: Oxford University Press, 1989).

——— (ed.), *Loose Canons: Notes on the Culture Wars* (Oxford, UK: Oxford University Press, 1992).

Gelder, Ken, and Sarah Thornton (eds.), *The Subcultures Reader* (London: Routledge, 1997).

Gelfand, Lou, "If You Ran the Newspaper," *Minneapolis Star Tribune*, 14 November 1993: 35A.

Gilligan, James, *Violence: Reflections on our Deadliest Epidemic* (New York: Vintage, 1997).

Giroux, Henry, *Fugitive Cultures: Race, Violence and Youth* (New York: Routledge, 1996).

"Glamour in the 'Hood," *Newsweek*, 13 September 1999.

Gledhill, Christine, "Pleasurable Negotiations," in John Storey (ed.), *Cultural Theory and Popular Culture: A Reader*, 2nd ed. (London: Prentice Hall, 1994): 236–49.

Goines, Donald, *White Man's Justice, Black Man's Grief* (Los Angeles: Holloway House, 1973).

———, *Whoreson: The Story of a Ghetto Pimp* (Los Angeles: Holloway House, 1972).

Gonzalez, Ray (ed.), *Muy Macho: Latino Men Confront Their Manhood* (New York: Anchor, 1996).

Gooding-Williams, Robert (ed.), *Reading Rodney King: Reading Urban Uprising* (New York: Routledge, 1993).

Gordon, Edmund, "Cultural Politics of Black Masculinity," *Transforming Anthropology* 6, no. 1 and 2 (January 1997): 36–53.

Gougis, Michael, "Cultural Café Fills a Need in Sylmar," *Daily News of Los Angeles*, 30 December 2002.

Graeber, Laurel, "Books for Vacation Reading," *New York Times*, 6 June 1993: section 7.34.

———, "New and Noteworthy Paperbacks," *New York Times*, 24 April 1994: section 7.25.

Griffith, Beatrice, *American Me* (Boston: Houghton Mifflin, 1948).

Guevara Urbina, Martin, "Latinos/as in the Criminal and Juvenile Justice Systems," *Critical Criminology* 15, no. 1 (March 2007): 41–99.

Gurr, Ted Robert, and Hugh Davis Graham (eds.), *Violence in America: Historical and Comparative Perspectives* (Beverly Hills: Sage, 1979).

Gutierrez, Hector, "Gang Life a Crazy Life Survivor Says," *Rocky Mountain News*, 17 March 1994.

Hall, Stuart, "New Ethnicities," in Linda Alcoff and Eduardo Mendieta (eds.), *Identities: Race, Class, Gender and Nationalities* (Oxford, UK: Wiley-Blackwell, 2002): 90–95.

——— (ed.), *Representation: Cultural Representations and Signifying Practices*, 5th ed. (Milton Keynes, UK: Open University Press, 2001).

Hanson, Victor, *Mexifornia: A State of Becoming* (San Francisco: Encounter, 2004).

Hastings, Deborah, "Celebrity Author Promotes Autobiography," *Sarasota Herald-Tribune* (Florida), 28 June 1993.

———, "Fondness for Fans Foils Fugitive," *The Free Lance-Star* (Fredericksburg, Virginia), 30 May 1996.

Hebdige, Dick, *Subcultures: The Meaning of Style* (London: Routledge, 1979).

Hermes, Joke, *Re-Reading Popular Culture* (Oxford, UK: Blackwells, 2005).

Hill Collins, Patricia, *Black Sexual Politics: African Americans, Gender and the New Racism* (New York: Routledge, 2004).

Himes, Chester, *Cotton Comes to Harlem* (New York: G. P. Putnam's Sons, 1965).

———, *My Life of Absurdity* (Garden City, New York: Doubleday, 1976).

———, *The Quality of Hurt* (London: Michael Joseph, 1973).

———, *The Real Cool Killers* (New York: Avon, 1959).

"His Own Words," *Oregonian*, 29 June 1993.

Holmes, Su, and Sean Redmond (eds.), *Framing Celebrity: New Directions in Celebrity Culture* (Abingdon, UK: Routledge, 2006).

Holt, Patricia, "On the Road to—and From—Gang Life in LA," *San Francisco Chronicle*, 8 April 1993.

hooks, bell, *Black Looks: Race and Representation* (Boston, MA: South End, 1992).

———, *Outlaw Culture: Resisting Representations* (New York: Routledge, 1994).

———, "Sexism and Misogyny: Who Takes The Rap? Misogyny, Gangsta Rap and The Piano," *Z Magazine*, September 1994: 13.

———, *We Real Cool: Black Men and Masculinity* (New York: Routledge, 2004).

Horowitz, Mark, "In Search of Monster," *Atlantic*, no. 272 (December 1993): 28–37.

Hunt, Darnell M., *Screening the Los Angeles Riots: Race, Seeing, and Resistance* (Cambridge, UK: Cambridge University Press, 1997).

Husemoller Nightingale, Carl, *On the Edge: A History of Poor Black Children and Their American Dreams* (New York: Basic, 1993).

"I Blasted Him Thrice in the Chest," *Press Enterprise*, 26 December 1993.

Ibarraran Bigalondo, Amaia, "Wolves, Sheep and *Vatos Locos*: Reflections of Gang Activity in Chicano Literature," *Journal of English Studies* 4 (2003-4): 107-113.

Ice-T with Douglas Century, *Ice: A Memoir of Gangster Life and Redemption* (New York: One World, 2011).

Ice-T with Heidi Siegmund, *The Ice Opinion: Who Gives a Fuck?* (New York: St. Martin's, 1994).

Jackson, George, *Soledad Brother: The Prison Letters of George Jackson* (London: Jonathan Cape, 1970).

Jah, Yusuf, and Sister Shah'Keyah, *Uprising: Crips and Bloods Tell the Story of America's Youth in the Crossfire* (New York: Touchstone, 1997).

Jankowski, Martin, *Islands in the Street: Gangs and American Urban Society* (Berkeley: University of California Press, 1992).

Jardine, Gail, "To Be Black, Male, and Conscious: Race, Rage, and Manhood in America," *American Quarterly* 48, no. 2 (1996): 385–93.

Jarvis, Brian, *Cruel and Unusual: Punishment and US Culture* (London: Pluto, 2004).

Jewkes, Yvonne, *Media and Crime* (London: Sage, 2004).

Johnson, Claudia Durst, *Youth Gangs in Literature: Exploring Social Issues Through Literature* (Westport, CT: Greenwood, 2004).

Johnson, Elizabeth, "Trustees Vote 3–4 for Book it Shouldn't be on Reading List," *Modesto Bee*, 16 December 2003: B1.

Johnson, Kevin. "FBI: Burgeoning Gangs Behind Up to 80% of US Crime," *USA Today*, 29 January 2009.

Jones, Margaret B., *Love and Consequences: A Memoir of Hope and Survival* (New York: Riverhead, 2008).

Kakutani, Michiko, "Illuminating Gang Life in LA: It's Raw," *New York Times*, 23 July 1993: C27.

Kammen, Michael, "The Problem of American Exceptionalism: A Reconsideration," *American Quarterly* 45, no. 1 (March 1993): 1–43.

Katz, Susan Roberta, "Teaching in Tensions: Latino Immigrant Youth, Their Teachers, and the Structures of Schooling," *Teachers College Record* 100, no. 4 (Summer 1999): 809–40.

Kelley, Robin D. G., *Race Rebels: Culture, Politics and the Black Working Class* (New York: Free Press, 1994).

———, *Yo' Mama's Disfunktional! Fighting the Culture Wars in Urban America* (Boston: Beacon, 1998).

Kelly, Caitlin, "Drama Sells His Books," *New York Daily News*, 9 December 2005.

Kinnear, Karen, *Gangs: A Reference Handbook* (Santa Barbara: ABC-Clio, 1996).

Kitwana, Bakari, *The Hip Hop Generation: Young Blacks and the Crisis in African American Culture* (New York: Basic, 2002).

Klein, Malcolm, *The American Street Gang: Its Nature, Prevalence and Control* (Oxford, UK: Oxford University Press, 1995).

———, *Chasing After Street Gangs: A Forty Year Journey* (Upper Saddle River, NJ: Pearson Prentice Hall, 2007).

"Kody Monster Scott Arrested After Another Run-in With Police," Associated Press, 17 July 2004.

Kopko, Ed, "Does Spending More on Education Work? State Rankings of Education Spending," blog.bestandworststates.com.

"Latino Readings," *Washington Post*, 14 May 1995.

Lavonne Brown Ruoff, A., and Jerry W. Ward Jr., *Redefining American Literary History* (New York: Modern Language Association, 1990).

Leibowitz, Herbert, *Fabricating Lives: Explorations in American Autobiography* (New York: Alfred A. Knopf, 1989).

Lee, Bill, *Chinese Playground: A Memoir* (San Francisco: Rhapsody, 1999).

Lee, Matthew, "Concentrated Poverty, Race and Homicide," *Sociological Quarterly* 41, no. 2 (21 April 2005): 189–206.

Levitt, Stephen D., and Stephen J. Dubner, *Freakonomics* (London: Penguin, 2006).

Libretti, Tim, "Is There a Working Class in US Literature? Race, Ethnicity and the Proletarian Literary Tradition," *Radical Teacher (Working Class Studies)*, no. 46 (Spring 1995): 22–26.

"Life in Prison; Children's Review," *Publishers Weekly* 245, no. 25 (22 June 1998): 93.

Lifsher, Marc, and Alana Semuels, "California Unemployment Rises to Record 11.5% in May," *Los Angeles Times*, 20 June 2009.

Lipsitz, George, "Listening to Learn and Learning to Listen," *American Quarterly* 42, no. 4 (December 1990): 615–36.

Liptak, Adam, "1 in 100 US Adults Behind Bars," *New York Times*, 28 February 2008.

Little, Malcolm, with Alex Haley, *The Autobiography of Malcolm X* (London: Penguin, 1965).

Lorde, Audre, *Zami: A New Spelling of My Name* (London: Persephone, 1982).

Lusetich, Robert, "Monster with Attitude," *Weekend Australian*, 1 June 1996.

McCall, Nathan, *Makes Me Wanna Holler: A Young Black Man in America* (New York: Random House, 1994).

McGreevy, Patrick, "Monster Goes from Bestseller List to Most Wanted List," *Los Angeles Times*, 15 February 2007.

McKee Irwin, Robert, *Mexican Masculinities* (Minneapolis: University of Minnesota Press: 2003).

Marable, Manning, "Incarceration vs. Education: Reproducing Racism and Poverty in America," *Race, Poverty and Environment: A Journal for Social and Environmental Justice* 15, no. 1 (Fall 2008): 59–61.

Marcus, Laura, *Auto/biographical Discourses* (Manchester, UK: Manchester University Press, 1994).

Martin, Hugo, "In South LA, a Clash Over Nobel Nominee," *Los Angeles Times*, 7 December 2000: B1.

Martinez, Ruben, "The Mother's Perspective," www.zonezero.com/exposiciones/fotografos/rodriguez/rubenmtz.html.

Mason, Paul (ed.), *Captured by the Media: Prison Discourse in Popular Culture* (Devon, UK: Willan, 2005).

Meadows, Bob, with Howard Breur and Andrea Orr, "Does Tookie Deserve to Die?" *People* 64, no. 24 (12 December 2005): 99.

Means Coleman, Robin R. (ed.), *Say It Loud: African American Audiences, Media and Identity* (New York: Routledge, 2002).

Mehren, Elizabeth, "Do Not Follow In My Footsteps: Gangbanging Brought Tookie Williams to Death Row. Can a Series of Children's Books That Decry Violence Bring Him to Redemption?" *Los Angeles Times*, 11 January 2004.

Mercer, Kobena, *Welcome to the Jungle: New Positions in Black Cultural Studies* (New York: Routledge, 1994).

Mid Morning Edition, CLTV–TV (Chicago), 7 October 1998.

Milner, Andrew, and Jeff Browitt, *Contemporary Cultural Theory: An Introduction*, 3rd ed. (London: Routledge, 2002).

"Milo Calls for Support Against Execution Threat," *Bookseller*, 11 November 2005.

Mirande, Alfredo, *Hombres Y Machos: Masculinity and Latino Culture* (Boulder, CO: Westview, 1997).

Mitchell, John, and Cheo Hodari Coker, "A Monster on the Run: Street Gang Member's Conversion Goes Awry," *Los Angeles Times*, 27 May 1996.

"Monsta," CBS News Transcripts, 7 November 1993.

"Monsta," *60 Minutes*, CBS, 31 July 1994.

"Monster Sought by Authorities," *Press Enterprise*, 12 March 1996.

Moreno Areyan, Alex (ed.), *Mexican Americans in Los Angeles* (Mount Pleasant, SC: Arcadia, 2010).

Morning Drive Time, Video Monitoring Services of America, 29 March 2005.

Moore, Joan, "Bearing the Burden: How Incarceration Policies Weaken Inner-City Communities," in Vera Institute of Justice, *The Unintended Consequences of Incarceration* (conference papers, 1996): 73–75.

Moore, Mark H., and Michael Tonry, *Youth Violence* (Chicago: University of Chicago Press, 1998).

Mora, Pablo, "LA Gang Terrors Ring Chillingly True," *Denver Post*, 13 March 1994.

Morley, David, *Family Television* (London: Routledge, 1986).

Morris, DaShaun "Jiwe," *War of the Bloods in My Veins: A Street Soldier's March Toward Redemption* (New York: Scribner, 2008).

Mostern, Kenneth, *Autobiography and Black Identity Politics: Racialization in Twentieth Century America* (Cambridge, UK: Cambridge University Press, 1999).

Moya, Paula, "This Is Not Your Country! Nation and Belonging in Latina/o Literature," *American Literary History* 17, no. 1 (Spring 2005): 183–95.

Mulhern, Francis, "The Politics of Cultural Studies," *Monthly Review* 47 (July–August 1995): 31–40.

Munby, Jonathan, "From Gangsta to Gangster: The Hood Film's Criminal Allegiance with Hollywood," in James Chapman, Mark Glancy, and Sue Harper (eds.), *The New Film History* (New York: Palgrave, 2007): 166–79.

———, *Public Enemies, Public Heroes—Screening the Gangster from Little Caesar to Touch of Evil* (Chicago: University of Chicago Press, 1999).

———, "Signifyin' Cinema: Rudy Ray Moore and the Quality of Badness," *Journal for Cultural Research* 11, no. 3 (July 2007): 203–19.

———, *Under a Bad Sign: Criminal Self-Representation in African American Popular Culture* (Chicago: University of Chicago Press, 2011).

Munoz Jr., Carlos, *Youth, Identity and Power: The Chicano Movement* (London: Verso, 1989).

Myers, Walter Dean, *Monster* (New York: Amistad, 2001).

Nash, Margo, "Once Upon a Time," *New York Times*, 18 September 2005.

Obama, Barack, *The Audacity of Hope: Thoughts on Reclaiming the American Dream* (New York: Crown, 2006).

———, *Dreams from My Father: A Story of Race and Inheritance* (New York: Three Rivers, 1995).

Ogbar, Jeffrey, *Black Power: Radical Politics and African American Identity* (Baltimore: Johns Hopkins University Press, 2004).

Okeon, Molly, "Gang Member–Turned Writer to Speak at College," *Inland Valley Daily Bulletin* (Ontario, CA), 13 January 2005.

Oliver, Ryan, "Former Member of Crips Jailed," *Daily News of Los Angeles*, 17 July 2004.

Padilla, Genaro M., *My History, Not Yours: The Formation of Mexican American Auto-biography* (Madison: University of Wisconsin Press, 1993).

Palmer, Jerry, *Potboilers: Methods, Concepts and Case Studies in Popular Fiction* (London: Routledge, 1991).

Pareles, Jon, "Gangster Rap: Life and Music in the Combat Zone," *New York Times*, 7 October 1990: section 2.29.

"Parent Wants Gang Memoir Pulled From San Diego School Libraries," Associated Press, 28 January 1999.

Patton, Stacey, "The Rap on Whites Who Try to Act Black," *Washington Post*, 16 March 2008.

Paul, Jacquie, "Author Faces Parole Problem," *Press Enterprise*, 10 March 1996.

Perez, Vincent, "'Running' and Resistance: Nihilism and Cultural Memory in Chicano Urban Narratives," *MELUS* 25, no. 2 (Summer 2000): 133–46.

Pettit, Arthur G., *Images of the Mexican American in Literature and Film* (College Station: Texas A&M University Press, 1980).

Pinkney, Alphonso, *The Myth of Black Progress* (Cambridge, UK: Cambridge University Press, 1984).

Pinsker, Sanford, "Home Boys Between Hard Covers," *Virginia Quarterly Review* 70, no. 4 (August 1994): 758–73.

Pomfret, John, "Chronicler of Life as a Crip Is on Trial," *Washington Post*, 2 March 2006: A03.

Powers, Ashley, "A Case Against Him in His Own Words," *Los Angeles Times*, 12 April 2006.

"Prison Author of *Monster* on Run from Parole Board," Associated Press, 3 May 1996.

Procter, James, *Stuart Hall* (London: Routledge, 2004).

Quinn, Eithne, *Nuthin' But a "G" Thang: The Culture and Commerce of Gangsta Rap* (New York: Columbia University Press, 2005).

Radway, Janice, "Interpretive Communities and Variable Literacies: The Functions of Romance Reading," *Daedalus* 113, no. 3 (Summer 1984): 49–73.

———, "Reading *Reading the Romance*," in John Storey (ed.), *Cultural Theory and Popular Culture: A Reader*, 2nd ed. (London: Prentice Hall, 1994): 292–309.

———, *Reading the Romance: Women, Patriarchy and Popular Literature* (Chapel Hill: University of North Carolina Press, 1991).

"Rage, Redemption, Rehabilitation," *Los Angeles Sentinel*, 8–14 December 2005: A6.

Rainey, James, "Glitz and Gore of Williams Case Draws Foreign Media," *Los Angeles Times*, 11 December 2005: B1.

Reed, Christopher, "Monster Turns Up on LA Porch," *Guardian* (UK), 30 May 1996.

Reiss, Albert, and Jeffrey Roth (eds.), *Understanding and Preventing Violence* (Washington D.C.: National Academy Press, 1993).

Rich, Motoko, "Gang Memoir, Turning Page, Is Pure Fiction," *New York Times*, 4 March 2008.

Roberts, John W., *From Trickster to Badman: The Black Folk Hero in Slavery and Freedom* (Philadelphia: University of Pennsylvania Press, 1990).

Rodriguez, Luis J., *Always Running: La Vida Loca—Gang Days in LA* (New York: Curbstone, 1993). Reprinted 1994 by Touchstone in New York.

———, *East Side Stories: Gang Life in East LA* (New York: PowerHouse, 2000).

————, *It Calls You Back: An Odyssey Through Love, Addiction, Revolutions and Healing* (New York: Touchstone, 2011).

————, *It Doesn't Have to Be This Way: A Barrio Story* (San Francisco: Children's Book Press, 1999).

————, *Music of the Mill* (New York: Rayo, 2005).

————, "Writing Off Our Youth," *Prison Life* (October 1994): 8–9.

Rodriguez, Richard, *Hunger of Memory: The Education of Richard Rodriguez* (New York: Bantam, 1983).

Rodriguez, Sonia, with Reymundo Sanchez, *Lady Q: The Rise and Fall of a Latin Queen* (Chicago: Chicago Review Press, 2010).

Rogers, John, "Always Running Author Settles into Literary Celebrity," Associated Press's *Entertainment News*, 31 October 2005.

Rogers, Paul, and Leigh Poitinger, "California Budget Mess; Where Did Our Money Go?" *Mercury News* (San Jose), 8 February 2009.

Romo, Ricardo, *East LA: History of a Barrio* (Austin: University of Texas Press, 1983).

Rose, Tricia, *Black Noise: Rap Music and Black Culture in Contemporary America* (Hanover, NH: University Press of New England, 1994).

Ruffins, Paul, "West Coast Stories," *Washington Post*, 7 February 1993.

Ruiz, Mona, and Geoff Boucher, *Two Badges: The Lives of Mona Ruiz* (Houston: Arte Publico, 1997).

Rutland, Ginger, "The Rap on Gangsters," *Sacramento Bee*, 25 September 2006.

Saïd, Edward, *Culture and Imperialism* (London: Chatto & Windus, 1993).

Sanchez, Reymundo, *My Bloody Life: The Making of a Latin King* (Chicago: Chicago Review Press, 2000).

Santiago, Danny, *Famous All Over Town* (New York: Plume Printing, 1984).

Sawhney, Deepak Narang, "Palimpsest: Towards a Minor Literature in Monstrosity," in Keith Ansell-Pearson (ed.), *Deleuze and Philosophy: The Difference Engineer* (London: Routledge, 1997): 130–46.

Schatzberg, Rufus, and Robert J. Kelly, *African Americans Organized Crime: A Social History* (New Brunswick, NJ: Rutgers University Press, 1997).

Schiesel, Mark, and Mark Dose (eds.), *City of Promise: Race and Historical Change in Los Angeles* (Claremont, CA: Regina, 2006).

"School Officials Remove Book About Gang Life From Modesto Classrooms," Associated Press, 1 November 2003.

Schwarzenegger, Arnold, "Statement of Decision," *City News Service*, 12 December 2005.

Scott, Kershaun, "Monster Rap," *Los Angeles Weekly*, 6 December 2002.

Senechal de la Roche, Roberta, "Why Is Collective Violence Collective?" *Sociological Theory* 19, no. 2 (17 December 2002): 126–44.

Serjeant, Jill, "Little Glamour in LA, Gang Capital of America," *Reuters*, 8 February 2007.

Shakur, Sanyika, *Monster: The Autobiography of an LA Gang Member* (New York: Atlantic, 1993). Reprinted 1994 by Penguin in New York.

————, *T.H.U.G. L.I.F.E.* (New York: Grove/Atlantic, 2008).

Shaw, William, *Westsiders: Stories of Boys in the Hood* (London: Bloomsbury, 2000).

Simerman, John, "California Redeemer: Stanley Williams, Founder of an Infamous LA Street Gang, Writes Children's Books While on Death Row. Is it Enough to Win Him Clemency?" *Montreal Gazette*, 22 November 2005.

Simpson, Colton, and Ann Pearlman, *Inside the Crips: Life Inside LA's Most Notorious Gang* (New York: St Martin's, 2005).

Singer, J., and R. Shagoury, "Stirring Up Justice: Adolescents Reading, Writing, and Changing the World," *Journal of Adolescent and Adult Literacy* 49, no. 4 (December 2005): 318–339.

Slim, Iceberg, *Pimp: The Story of My Life* (Los Angeles: Holloway House, 1969).

Slotkin, Richard, *Regeneration through Violence: The Mythology of the American Frontier, 1600–1860* (Middletown, CT: Wesleyan University Press, 1973).

Soja, Edward, and Allen Scott (eds.), *The City: LA and Urban Theory at the End of the Twentieth Century* (Berkeley: University of California Press, 1996).

Sommers, Joseph, and Tomas Ybarra-Frausto (eds.), *Modern Chicano Writers: A Collection of Critical Essays* (Englewood Cliffs, NJ: Prentice Hall, 1979).

Spivak, Gayatri, *In Other Worlds: Essays in Cultural Politics* (London: Methuen, 1987).

Stacy, Lee (ed.), *Mexico and the US* (New York: Marshall Cavendish, 2003).

Staiger, Janet, *Media Reception Studies* (New York: New York University Press, 2005).

——, "Taboos and Totems: Cultural Meanings of *The Silence of the Lambs*," in Jim Collins and Hilary Radner (eds.), *Film Theory Goes To The Movies* (New York: Routledge, 1993): 142-154.

Staples, Brent, *Parallel Time: Growing Up in Black and White* (London: Harper Perennial, 1995).

——, "When Only Monsters Are Real," *New York Times*, 21 November 1993: section 4.16.

Starr, Kevin, *Coast of Dreams: A History of Contemporary America* (London: Allen Lane, 2005).

Statistical Service Center, *Book Industry Trends 1993 Covering the Years 1987–1997* (New York: Book Industry Study Group, 1993).

Stavans, Ilan, "Always Running," *Nation* 256, no. 14 (12 April 1993): 494.

Steiner, Linda, "The Uses of Autobiography," in Catherine Warren and Mary Douglas Vavrus (eds.), *American Cultural Studies* (Chicago: University of Illinois Press, 2002): 115–33.

Stokes, David Lewis, "Respect the Possibility of Redemption," *Providence Journal*, 20 January 2006.

Stringer, Vickie, *Let That Be the Reason* (Columbus, OH: Triple Crown, 2002).

Suarez-Orozco, Marcelo M., and Mariela M. Paez (eds.), *Latinos: Remaking America* (Berkeley: University of California Press, 2002).

Swail, Watson S., Alberto F. Cabrerra, and Chul Lee, *Latino Youth and the Pathway to College* (Washington D.C.: Educational Policy Institute, 2004), part of the American Higher Education Report Series.

Sykes, Gini, *8 Ball Chicks: A Year in the Violent World of Girl Gangsters* (New York: Doubleday, 1997).

Tal, Kali, "From Panther to Monster: Black Popular Culture Representations of Resistance from the Black Panther Movement of the 1960s to *Boyz N The Hood*," in Elaine B. Richardson and Ronald L. Jackson (eds.), *African American Rhetoric(s):*

Interdisciplinary Perspectives (Carbondale: Southern Illinois University Press, 2004): 37–58.

Tasker, Yvonne, *Spectacular Bodies: Gender, Genre and the Action Cinema* (New York: Routledge, 2002).

Tatum, Charles M., *Chicano Popular Culture and Chicano Literature* (Tucson: University of Arizona Press, 2001).

Thomas, Piri, *Down These Mean Streets* (1967; rprt. New York: Vintage, 1997).

Thompson, Tony, "Nominated Four Times for the Nobel Peace Prize . . . on Death Row," *Observer* (UK), 28 November 2004.

Thrasher, Frederic, *The Gang: A Study of 1303 Gangs in Chicago* (Chicago: University of Chicago Press, 1928).

Timberg, Scott, and Josh Getlin, "Bogus Memoir Sparks Criticism of Publishing Industry," *Los Angeles Times*, 5 March 2008.

Tindall, George, and David Shi, *America: A Narrative History* (New York: W. W. Norton, 1993).

Turner, Graeme, *British Cultural Studies* (New York: Routledge, 1992).

Valles, Victor M., and Rodolfo D. Torres, *Latino Metropolis* (Minneapolis: University of Minnesota Press, 2000).

Van Deburg, William L., *Hoodlums: Black Villains and Social Bandits in American Life* (Chicago: University of Chicago Press, 2004).

Vargas, Joao H. Costa, *Catching Hell in the City of Angels: Life and Meanings of Blackness in South Central Los Angeles* (Minneapolis: University of Minnesota Press, 2006).

Vaughn, Stephen, *Freedom and Entertainment: Rating the Movies in an Age of New Media* (Cambridge, UK: Cambridge University Press, 2006).

Vicini, James, "Number of US Prisoners Has Biggest Rise in 6 Years," Reuters, 27 June 2007.

Vigil, James Diego, *Barrio Gangs: Street Life and Identity in Southern California* (Austin: University of Texas Press, 1988).

———, *A Rainbow of Gangs: Street Cultures in the Mega-City* (Austin: University of Texas Press, 2002).

Villegas, Reuben Sosa, "In a Word, Gangster's Book Is Unacceptable," *Rocky Mountain News*, 9 January 1994.

Wallace, Amy, "The Monster Deal," *Sunday Age* (Melbourne), 25 April 1993: 6.

Ward, Brian (ed.), *Media, Culture, and the Modern African American Freedom Struggle* (Gainesville: University Press of Florida, 2001).

Warren, Kim, "Language and Liberation," *Reviews in American History* 33, no. 4 (2005): 510–17.

Watkins, S. Craig, *Representing: Hip Hop Culture and the Production of Black Cinema* (Chicago: University of Chicago Press, 1998).

Weinraub, Bernard, "Reagan, Lobbying for Bork, Calls Judge Tough on Crime," *New York Times*, 29 August 1987.

Weyr, Tom, "Marketing America's Psychos," *Publishers Weekly* 240, no. 15 (April 12 1993): 38-41. (4).

Williams, Heather Andrea, *Self-Taught: African American Education in Slavery and Freedom* (Chapel Hill: University of North Carolina Press, 2005).

Williams, Stanley "Tookie," *Blue Rage, Black Redemption: A Memoir* (Pleasant Hill, CA: Damamli, 2004). Reprinted 2004 as *Redemption: From Original Gangster to Nobel Prize Nominee* and subsequently as *Redemption: The Last Testament of Stanley "Tookie" Williams-Gang Leader Turned Nobel Prize Nominee* by Milo Books in Preston, UK; 2007 by Touchstone in New York as *Blue Rage, Black Redemption: A Memoir.*

———, *Life in Prison* (New York: Morrow, 1998). Reprinted 2001 by SeaStar Publishing in Des Moines, Washington.

———, "What I Would Do with the Rest of My Life," *Los Angeles Times*, 7 December 2005.

Williams, Stanley "Tookie," with Barbara Becnel, *Tookie Speaks Out Against Gang Violence Series* (New York: Rosen Publishing Group, 1996). Reprinted 1997 by PowerKids Press in Center City, MN, and 2008 by Damamli Publishing Company in Pleasant Hill, CA.

Wright, Terrell C., *Home of the Body Bags* (Venice, CA: Senegal, 2005).

"Writers Honored Saturday," *Chicago Sun Times*, 15 May 1994.

Wyatt, David, *Five Fires: Race, Catastrophe and the Shaping of California* (Oxford, UK: Oxford University Press, 1999).

Yablonsky, Lewis, *Gangsters: Fifty Years of Madness, Drugs and Death on the Streets of America* (New York: New York University Press, 1998).

———, "Nobel Nominee Doesn't Belong in Death Chamber; The Former LA Gangster Could be a Force For Good," *Los Angeles Times*, 19 September 2002.

Zvirin, Stephanie, "Gangs and Drugs; Children's Review," *Booklist* 93, no. 12 (15 February 1997).

INDEX

CPSIA information can be obtained at www.ICGtesting.com
Printed in the USA
BVOW040635190612

293029BV00002B/3/P